Wer

LABOUR BONDAGE IN WEST INDIA

SURAT COLLECTORATE

Surat Collectorate and Baroda Division

Scale of Miles

Reduced by Photozincography
Gov.t Photozinc. Office Poona 1888

SEA

ARABIAN SEA

BROACH COL:

to Ahmadabad

BARODA STATE.

BARODA STATE

RAJPIPLA

BARODA STATE

DANGS

NASIK COL:

SURGÁNA NASIK COL:

SURGÁNA

NASIK COL:

NASIK COLLECTORATE

DAMAN

THÁNA COL:

from Borsad

from Jáwhar

to Páne

D A M A N

SURAT

NAVSARI

BULSAR

PARDI

DHARAMPUR

BARODA STATE

CHIKHLI

GANDEVI

BANSDA

BARDOLI

MANDVI

JALALPOR

OLPAD

LABOUR BONDAGE IN WEST INDIA
From Past to Present

JAN BREMAN

To Wendy Olsen

[signature]
10.01.2007

OXFORD
UNIVERSITY PRESS

OXFORD

UNIVERSITY PRESS

YMCA Library Building, Jai Singh Road, New Delhi 110 001

Oxford University Press is a department of the University of Oxford. It furthers the
University's objective of excellence in research, scholarship, and education
by publishing worldwide in

Oxford   New York

Auckland   Cape Town   Dar es Salaam   Hong Kong   Karachi   Kuala Lumpur
Madrid   Melbourne   Mexico City   Nairobi   New Delhi   Shanghai   Taipei   Toronto

With offices in
Argentina   Austria   Brazil   Chile   Czech Republic   France   Greece   Guatemala
Hungary   Italy   Japan   Poland   Portugal   Singapore   South Korea   Switzerland
Thailand   Turkey   Ukraine   Vietnam

Oxford is a registered trademark of Oxford University Press
in the UK and in certain other countries

Published in India
by Oxford University Press, New Delhi

First published 2007

ISBN 13: 978-0-19-568521-3
ISBN 10: 0-19-568521-0

Typeset in Agaramond 10.5/12.5
by Sai Graphic Design, New Delhi 110 055
Printed at Pauls Press, New Delhi 110 020
Published by Oxford University Press
YMCA Library Building, Jai Singh Road, New Delhi 110 001

Contents

Plates

Preface

I first began studying the underclass in rural Gujarat, west India, in the early1960s. On the basis of anthropological fieldwork in two villages in the region which was then the Surat district, I outlined the changing relations between landless workers and the farmers who employed them. This transformation essentially entailed the gradual fading away of a system of attached labour in the preceding decades. No doubt, the remnants of labour bondage were still clearly visible but it was no longer the regime under which the majority of agricultural labourers lived and worked. The question to be addressed was what had replaced the *hali* system and whether emancipation from a state of subjugation had led to an improvement in economic and social conditions at the bottom of the rural order. The results of this first fieldwork were published in my book *Patronage and Exploitation: Changing Agrarian Relations in South Gujarat.*[1]

A new round of research ten years later in the same region and on the same theme focused on the declining significance of agriculture as the main source of employment. Agriculture was unable to provide enough work to keep pace with a steadily growing landless population. An extension in scale of the rural labour market seemed to provide a solution to the increasing pressure on what was already a very tight livelihood. Going out in search of work was by no means a new phenomenon, but in the 1970s and 1980s I observed a great increase in the percentage of landless households from which one or more members left the village for varying lengths of time because of insufficient demand for their labour. Noticeably few of these workers, who had become footloose, left the village for good. Many returned either at the end of the working day or, if they stayed away longer, always before the onset of the monsoon. Daily commuting and seasonal migration were thus the most common forms of labour circulation. Moreover, the exit of landless labourers from the village economy was offset by the arrival of men and women from elsewhere, usually at harvest time. Clearly, migration was not a one-way traffic.

In my next study, entitled *The Market for Non-Agrarian Labour: The Formal versus the Informal Sector*[2], I described how the workforce made redundant in the agrarian economy joined the rapidly growing reserve army in what became known as the informal sector in the cities. There is a tendency in the literature on the subject to equate urbanization with migration. Without wishing to underestimate the significance of this chain of mobility, as I continued my fieldwork I became increasingly convinced of the enormous magnitude of rural-to-rural labour movements. On the basis of my earlier observation that, in addition to the landless workers who left the village, others arrived in search of work, I concluded in my study focused on this issue that the scale, nature, and direction of labour mobility was not determined solely by supply and demand: *Of Peasants, Migrants and Paupers: Rural Labour Circulation and Capitalist Production in West India.*[3]

My local-level studies in rural south Gujarat were conducted within the context of changes that have taken place in the regional economy in the past half century. This is particularly true of the western part of the plain, which has since long been the main focus of peasant production and where population pressure on the agrarian resource base is highest. This zone is part of the north–south axis along which rapid urban-industrial development occurred from the 1960s onwards. Vapi, Valsad, Bilimora, Navsari, and Surat are growth poles of economic activity clustered along the railway line and the national highway from Mumbai via Vadodara to Ahmedabad. A wide variety of industrial workshops have also grown up along the traffic arteries that link these urban centres and they, too, attract workers from hinterlands nearby and faraway. The surplus workers driven out from the villages find employment not only in industry, but also in construction, transport, trade, and services. I have put on record the patterns of work and labour in this 'golden corridor' in successive publications. The main characteristic of the urban-industrial development that has emerged is informality. Casual rather than permanent work, low pay, and no or insufficient formal skilling are the most prominent features of this employment modality. Wages are based not on the length of the working day but on piece rate and job work. In addition to casualization and contractualization, the rotation of labour over different sectors of the economy—such as construction, transport, or services—is a major characteristic of this informal labour system. An aspect to which I devoted substantial attention is the phenomenon of neo-bondage, that is, the tying of labour to employers or their agents in a way that is substantially different from

the attachment of farm labourers to their masters in the past. My findings
from rural and urban fieldwork conducted over an extended period of
time at both the points of departure and arrival of migrant workers
have been compiled in *Footloose Labour: Working in India's Informal
Economy*.[4]

The sites of my initial fieldwork in south Gujarat have remained an
important yardstick in monitoring the changes in labour relations
throughout the second half of the twentieth century. After my first visit
in 1962–3, I returned ten years later for a brief stay in Chikhligam and
Gandevigam. Between 1986 and 1991, whilst conducting fieldwork
elsewhere in south Gujarat, I took time off to investigate whether the
trend I had observed earlier had continued. The results of this repeat
study twenty-five years on were published in *Beyond Patronage and
Exploitation: Changing Agrarian Relations in South Gujarat*.[5] I
concluded that the income from work outside the village and outside
the agricultural sector had become indispensable to the survival of
landless households. In spite of a slight improvement in the material
quality of their lives, only a few had succeeded in escaping bitter poverty.
The gap that separated this underclass from the better-off segments in
the village had grown visibly in the past decades. To try and eliminate,
or at least alleviate, the deprivation suffered by the most vulnerable
categories among the rural population, the government had launched a
plethora of schemes and programmes over the years designed to improve
their condition. Why has this policy had such a negligible impact? In
addition to lack of political will, this failure has also been attributed to
faults in implementation by public agencies. But the main reason is
seen to be the unwillingness and incapacity of the target group itself to
make effective use of measures that after all amount to positive
discrimination in their favour. I was told time and again by employers
and officials that these people had only themselves to blame for their
poverty. So many efforts had been made to assure the landless class of a
better existence, but they had little or no effect. This segment simply
did not possess the qualities required to move forward. Such explanations
stress the inadequate social awareness and the corresponding lack
of ambition which ensure that the support so generously given cannot
put an end to their misery. These defects are explained by the
natural inferiority of the landless, rather than in the quality of the
policy pursued.

From the findings of my empirical research I conclude that, despite the repeated promises of leading politicians within and outside the state of Gujarat, poverty alleviation has remained a low priority. The various programmes and schemes that were announced one after the other had one thing in common—even if they were actually implemented they did not reach the majority of those they were intended to help so liberally. This observation is prompted by my retrospective look at the dynamics of social and political development before and since Independence, and is the basis of new fieldwork in south Gujarat carried out during 2004–6. However, the process of pauperization experienced by the landless mass has a deeper cause. The model of economic development applied in the second half of the twentieth century was founded on adding value to the means of production that tended to generate a low output. Productivity could be enhanced by injecting capital in the form of credit, loans, or grants. To benefit from this strategy it was of course necessary to own at least some means of production, no matter how negligible, in the form of land, tools, or other assets. But the agricultural labourers in the villages where I conducted my research are not only landless but completely bereft of property. Many barely owned the labour power which is their only means of survival: their employers decide how and when it is used, rather than they themselves. The lack of productive assets and the dependency in which the members of these low-ranking castes continue to live means that they have neither the physical nor the social capital necessary to assert themselves and make progress. The strategy of exclusion to which this rural-agrarian underclass is subjected explains why it has been left behind in the process of economic growth that slowly gained momentum half a century ago. In a subsequent study to be published in 2007, I shall present the outcome of the new round of fieldwork I have conducted in the villages which I started to investigate nearly half a century ago. To give more depth to my recent findings on the events of today and to place them in a longer time perspective, this book focuses on the historical antecedents of the ongoing subordination of rural labour in what has come to be hailed as a booming economy.

I used an earlier draft of Chapter 4 to deliver the A.R. Desai Memorial Lecture at the Department of Sociology, University of Mumbai on 16 February 2006. A grant from Anti-Slavery International in London enabled me to produce and publish this book. The Amsterdam School for Social Science Research and the Indo-Dutch Programme on

Alternatives in Development (IDPAD) helped in funding the archival research carried out in Mumbai and Delhi.

Ahmedabad/Amsterdam, August 2006   JAN BREMAN

Notes

1. The study published under this title by the California University Press in 1974 was a translation of my PhD thesis 'Meester en Knecht' [Master and Servant] at the Universiteit van Amsterdam in 1970. An Indian edition came out in 1979, Manohar, Delhi.
2. In Baks and Pillai (eds), *Winners and Losers*, pp. 122–66. In 1971–2, on the basis of my fieldwork findings, I wrote an essay on the concept of the informal sector. The essay was published in English in three parts in *Economic and Political Weekly*, vol. 11, November–December 1976, pp. 1870–6, pp. 1905–8, pp. 1939–43. Later on these essays were included in *Wage Hunters and Gatherers* (1994).
3. See also, Breman, 'Seasonal Migration and Co-operative Capitalism', 1978–9.
4. Cambridge University Press, Cambridge, 1996. In an attempt to inform a wider public of the miserable existence of those dependent on the informal sector for their survival, I revisited the locations of my fieldwork in south Gujarat some years later with photographer Ravi Agarwal. The resulting photographs, accompanied by a text I wrote together with my friend Arvind Das, were published as *Down and Out: Labouring under Global Capitalism in India*.
5. Breman, *Beyond Patronage and Exploitation* (1993).

1

Land Rights on the Tribal Frontier before the Colonial Era

Domestication of the Dublas

The Dublas were one of the tribal categories which, in the distant past, had become subjugated to high-caste Hindu landowners as bonded servants. As elsewhere on the South Asian subcontinent, the gradual expansion of the Hindu majority put a stop to the tribal way of life of nomadic clans who made a living as shifting cultivators. The Dublas have traditionally lived in the central plain of south Gujarat. Their identity as agricultural labourers is closely interwoven with the state of servitude which held them captive under Hindu domination. It is not known when and how they were denied free access to land, but this occurred so long ago that it has disappeared from the collective memory. During my research among these landless groups, I never heard them claim that the land they were working on had once been taken away from their ancestors. The only evidence to support the suspicion that they might not have always been landless is the continued process of expropriation in the nineteenth and twentieth centuries among tribal groups in neighbouring areas, which is well documented in colonial records. During my recurrent fieldwork in south Gujarat I encountered Dublas who were petty owners of inferior plots of land that were of no interest to members of higher castes, or which had been discarded by peasant proprietors towards the end of the nineteenth century when the colonial administration had extended the tax system to include even the least fertile land. In my view, it would be incorrect to see these marginal owners as the descendants of Dublas who once possessed more agricultural property. There is no factual evidence that the large majority of them were the victims of a gradual process of agrarian regression before or during the colonial era.

The confinement of the Dublas in a state of dependency at the bottom of the Hindu order can also be traced to the way in which high-caste settlers established themselves on the plain of south Gujarat. The Anavil

Brahmans played a prominent role in the development of the agricultural economy, but there can be no certainty as to when this process started and how it moved forward. Did the Anavil Brahmans hold leading positions and dominate the peasants before the region was opened up? Or was their elevation as landlords the result of the introduction of more advanced agricultural techniques, in which the plough played a pivotal role? Lastly, it is not clear whether the Anavil Brahmans belonged to the original population of south Gujarat or migrated there from elsewhere. The latter scenario fits in with the widely accepted account of the gradual expansion of Hindu civilization through the influx of castes into regions inhabited by tribes, as recorded in the colonial era. J.A. Baines summarizes this process of colonization as a moving frontier whereby the Hindu order slowly but steadily penetrated into 'wild lands':

Wherever they have settled in large masses, as in the Gangetic Doab or Oudh, or in compact local colonies, which probably preceded their advance as a sacerdotal body, they have taken to cultivation on the same lines as the ordinary peasantry, except that they but very rarely put their hands to the plough, though they go as far as standing on the crossbar of the harrow to lend their weight to that operation. Owing to this caste-imposed restriction, probably, it may be noted that where the Brahman has settled otherwise than as a part of a larger community, he is the centre of a well-defined system of predial servitude, his land being cultivated for him by hereditary serfs of undoubtedly Dasyu descent. This is the case of the Masthan of Orissa and Gujarat [i.e., the Anavils], and with the Haiga or Halvika of Kanara, and the Nambutiri of the Malabar Coast, all of whom have settled in very fertile country (Baines 1912: 28).

The Anavil Brahmans themselves attribute their arrival in south Gujarat to divine intervention. In their origin myths, Rama, on his way back from Ceylon, decided to turn the wild country through which he travelled into a settled peasant landscape. He ordered Hanuman to fetch Brahmans from the Ganges plain to build villages and cultivate the land. The colonists were prepared to carry out this order on the condition that they would have authority over the local people, so that the latter could do the unclean physical labour, especially tilling the soil, which they as Brahmans should not have to do themselves.[1] According to an alternative account, the Anavils were not brought in from elsewhere but raised above the darker-skinned inhabitants of the region by Rama or Krishna. To emphasize their elevated social status, they purified themselves by bathing in the warm springs near Anaval, in the interior of Surat district. This baptism marked the birth of the caste and Anaval is held sacred as their place of origin.[2] The impure—or at least suspected as impure—origins of the Anavils explains why Brahman priest castes have little respect for them. They refer to them disparagingly as *pithokatho* Brahmans, a reference to their alleged predilection—and not only in the distant past—for strong liquor and non-vegetarian food.

All of these origin myths make a link between the role of the Anavil Brahmans as agrarian colonists and the servitude of the Dublas as their labourers. In the literature, this relationship is explained in terms of the inability of the subjugated tribal group to maintain themselves as owner-cultivators in Hindu society. At some indeterminate time in the past they found themselves unable to survive independently, either suddenly or as the result of a gradual process, which resulted in them losing their autonomy and becoming attached to their high-caste patrons. In his path-breaking study of the development of the pre-colonial economy, Kosambi endorsed this explanation.

Many tribal people had fallen into servitude in times of famine and one step away were the tribal castes or poorest cultivators who had at the same time incurred a debt which could not be repaid by generation after generation. This accounts for the retained castes such as Cheruman in Malabar, the Koltas of Jaunsar-Bawar in the Himalayan foothills near Almora, the Halis of Gujarat, and the like (Kosambi 1956: 353).

What these historical reconstructions generally fail to take into account is the presence of other social formations than landlords and servants, who represent only the two extremes of agrarian society in rural south Gujarat. There were, of course, many other groups living in the region than just the Anavil Brahmans and the Dublas. The Kolis, who lived on the coast and on the central plain had established themselves as small peasant owners and were much more numerous. Before the Mughal emperors had penetrated Gujarat, political power was in the hands of petty chiefs. In their collective memory, the Kolis believe that they are descendants of these local leaders. By the early colonial era they had already lost their original tribal identity. Their gradual absorption into the lower levels of the caste hierarchy ran parallel to the humble position they occupied in the emerging agrarian system. The Kanbi Patels are a peasant caste who now live mainly in north and central Gujarat but who, according to early colonial records, also used to live in the more southerly parts of the region. Their ancestors most probably moved south after sustained drought led to serious food shortages. After pioneers had built up new lives in south Gujarat, they were followed by kinsmen and other fellow caste members. This migration continued for many decades, acquiring new impetus at the end of the nineteenth century after another period of sustained drought. The Kanbi Patels developed into a strong peasant caste in south Gujarat and, although they remained economically and socially inferior to the Anavil Brahmans, they made such strides in economic progress that they emerged as a typical upwardly mobile caste, leaving the poor Koli peasants behind. The Kolis' tribal origins were so unmistakable and their economic position so fragile that they were not considered *ujliparaj*, the generic name for respectable Hindu castes. An administrative report from the middle of the nineteenth century describes them as cultivators who grew only rice and millet, wore shabby clothes, and lived in miserable huts. They lived along the coast, but also inhabited more inland areas where they were tenants of Anavils and Kanbis (Bellasis 1854: 3). The report on the first census in the principality of Baroda in 1881 describes the different development of the Kanbis and Kolis as follows:

The Kanbis are now wholly submissive to Brahmanical Institutes, and are ranged as the fourth estate of the Indian community. The Kolis, at the most, are partially submissive to Brahmanism, and in many instances they have no connections with Brahmanism (*Census of the Baroda Territories, 1881*, Bombay, 1883).[3]

These agrarian classes, all of which live on the central plain, make way to the east for tribal categories like the Chodhras, Gamits, and Dhodhias, who made a living as shifting cultivators until well into the colonial era.[4] They came to be known as *kaliparaj*, black people. This name referred more to the fact that they were considered uncivilized and inferior than to their darker skin colour. Gradually, with an increase in pace in the second half of the nineteenth century, the area they inhabited was made suitable for more regular cultivation. However, since the landscape was hilly and the soil not very fertile, the yield remained far behind that of the richer black soil of the central plain. The agrarian castes of the Hindu order therefore settled in this hinterland only in much smaller numbers, if at all. The transition from the plains to the hills was gradual, however, and it would be incorrect to draw a sharp physical or social dividing line between the two zones. As should be clear, there is also no demonstrable ethnic difference between ujliparaj and kaliparaj. There is a direct link between the advent of sedentary agriculture and the transition to Hindu customs and practices as part of their incorporation in the caste system. The detribalization of the Kanbis, and to a large extent also of the Kolis, had already been completed by the beginning of the colonial era (see Toothi 1935: 116 *et seq.*; Mukhtyar 1930: 45). It is not certain whether the Anavils underwent a similar transformation in the more remote past but it is a distinct possibility. The agronomic-ecological development of south Gujarat has occurred in phases and admission to the Hindu social hierarchy, as well as the status acquired within it, must be seen as part of this evolution.

The Dublas have their own place within this configuration. Although they have lived on the plain since time immemorial, the gradual transition to new agrarian technology—with irrigation the major factor in making more continuous and intensive use of the land possible—led to them being cut off from their former independent way of life based on the extensive use of the primary means of existence. The opening up of the region to more advanced agriculture and a new mode of production meant that they were relegated to landless status. Their labour power was needed to cultivate more land and increase its yield. As the Dublas found themselves degraded to the status of agricultural labourers, the colonists experienced an increase in their economic and social status. Interdependent on each other, as dominant landowners and bonded servants, the Anavil Brahmans and Dublas represented the polar ends of the spectrum in the agrarian system that emerged in south Gujarat. In my reconstruction, the Brahmanization of the former was made possible by the servitude of the latter. Their economic subjugation also obstructed the transition of the Dublas from animism to Hinduism. To this day, they are classified along with the tribal peoples who live further inland. It was recognized at an early stage that, as a consequence of their contact with higher castes, especially the Anavils, the Dublas had gradually adopted all kinds of religious and other practices associated with what were called the civilized segments in society. However, the abject poverty in which they were accustomed to live from generation to generation hampered their acceptance as a caste. I could give many examples to support this statement. In respectable castes it was expected that marriages be performed by a Brahman priest but, as a late colonial source reports, these landless tribals were unable to afford such ceremonies.[5] During my first round of fieldwork, it was still their custom to bury their dead, and as stated in the report on the 1931 census, they did this not because of tradition, but because they did not have enough money to pay for the cremation ritual (*Census of India 1931*, vol. xix, 1932: 463). In the first census in 1881 the Dublas were registered as semi-Hindus and, by classifying them as a tribal caste I have tried to encapsulate the halfway position in which they found themselves. The late-colonial census reports started to register the Dublas as Hindus, but the official in charge of census operations wondered how they had passed into the Hindu hierarchy: 'Who converted them? Was the enumerating staff responsible? Or else was it whipped up by propaganda? Or was it the accelerated phase of a natural movement going on for years?' (*Census of India 1941*, vol. xvii, Baroda 1942: 63). The sources this official consulted pointed in the direction of the Mata or Devi movement which had become quite popular among the tribals of south Gujarat in the 1920s (see Chapter 3). The incomplete status of the Dublas as Hindus had its roots not only in their material deprivation, but also in their cultural subjugation. I will return to this in detail later but would like to mention here that their servitude made the presence of large numbers 'untouchables' superfluous. As I noted in another publication:

It is certainly no mere coincidence that where they and other similar groups from a tribal background in Gujarat also performed household services for members of high castes, the genuinely untouchable castes were poorly represented (Breman 1985: 125, fn. 2).

The Politics of Land Settlement

It is not known exactly when the wilderness was turned into cultivated agricultural land. It was, in any case, a gradual process that had begun long before the colonial era. Studies of the *ancien regime* are limited in number and extremely vague about the economic and social lives of the people, but it is reasonable to assume that there were already settlements in the river valleys on the west coast of India a thousand years ago or longer. Our knowledge of this epoch extends little further than the names of dynasties and extremely nebulous descriptions of the geographical extent of their regimes. There are no reliable records establishing the link between former centres of civilization and economic activity with the better-documented history of the last few hundred years. Historical records of relevance to our study go back no further than the era of Mughal domination over south Gujarat. In 1573, Akbar took control of the port city of Surat, close to the mouth of the Tapti river, which acquired a prominent role in the overseas trade of the Mughal empire. Extensive historical information is available on the city itself and its economic significance, notably in the records of successive Portuguese, Dutch, and British trading stations. The sources are less detailed on the situation prevalent in the surrounding rural areas, a tax domain to which twenty-eight villages belonged (Surat *athavisi*). According to a Dutch traveller, in 1772 the immediate hinterland outside the city was densely populated and there was hardly any land that was not built upon (*Surat District Gazetteer* 1962: 175, fn. 3). In 1785 another source said the same about Gandevi: 'It is well cultivated. The villages are numerous and well peopled' (Forrest 1887: 437). But a report of a journey from Surat to the south in 1784 described a landscape that was scarcely cultivated.

Although the soil is very favourable about Gaundevee, I saw but little culture: the greatest part of this district, as far as the eye could reach, is one field of high pasturage (Hove: 93–4).

These scarce reports suggest that the land around the sparse settlements was cultivated, while areas in between were still undeveloped. Communication was made more difficult by the absence of roads. Built-up areas were small and infrequent and there appears to have been no organized economic activity in the areas outside the settlements. In some regions, such as the vicinity of Bulsar, Gandevi, and Navsari, agriculture was more highly developed. The same applies to Bardoli, as we can see from this description given at the start of the nineteenth century:

It is fully cultivated and there are so many inhabitants that they cannot all find employment in Bardolee but engage themselves in cultivating ground in the neighbouring districts (Morison's Report 1812: 135).

But colonization, too, was limited. The same early colonial source tells us that, in nearby Valod, there were thick jungles populated by tigers.

The governor, who was the emperor's representative, had his seat in Surat but was also responsible for governing the agrarian hinterland. That was divided into twenty-eight *pergunnah*s, administrative districts with a small staff of officials who exercised executive and judicial authority. The primary task of collecting taxes was delegated to local notables who imposed taxes on the cultivating population and passed on the revenue to the governor's agents. The extremely thin and fragile administrative apparatus was indicative of the peripheral location of the province of Surat in the Mughal empire. The central authority could only be effective by making use of local intermediaries to collect the agricultural tax that amounted to about a third of the yield from the land. In the course of time, a group of Anavils emerged as an elite of *desai*s (literally 'lords of the land') who fulfilled the requirements for this function. They distanced themselves from the other Anavils who, as Bhathelas, had a much closer and more direct knowledge of peasant life and work. As tax collectors the desais received a previously agreed commission. They would supplement this by paying the estimated revenue in advance and then imposing a far higher tax. Mughal officials kept themselves informed of this practice by acquiring information through their own channels and setting the next tax level as close as possible to the actual levy charged by the intermediaries, who no longer assured that they would retain their profitable position, tended in turn to tax the peasants even more excessively. They were restricted in their demands only to avoid the risk of peasants fleeing to escape the heavy taxes. In an area like south Gujarat the risk of flight was even greater, since the demand for cultivators, by far, exceeded supply. A much more sensible strategy for all concerned was to increase the number of taxpayers by expanding the area of land under cultivation. This explains why the tax collectors were authorized to establish villages to encourage the still nomadic tribal groups to abandon shifting cultivation. In the mid-1920s Mukhtyar, author of the first village study in Gujarat, recorded how local people remembered the establishment of their settlement:

The founder was originally a resident of Bulsar town where his descendants still own a house and some landed property. In those palmy days of the Anavil desais of South Gujarat—when they were the practical rulers of this part, enjoying the monopoly of farming land revenue, this man is supposed to have taken a fancy to establish a new village. In his wanderings to select a suitable place he came to this part where the village is now situated to the eastern-most boundary of the Bulsar Taluka. Here he saw that there was a possibility of founding a village, with the Kaliparaj who abounded in the adjoining Dharampore territory, as the farming population. He, therefore, persuaded some of them to abandon that territory, and to come down and settle in (now) British Gujarat and form a new village. Enticed by the privilege offered to them of cultivating as much area as they liked, a group of Kaliparaj people (NB: Dhodhias) migrated to this place. Thus was laid the foundation of Atgam about two centuries ago. In course of time, Naranji Lala persuaded, by offers of pieces of land, some artisans like carpenters and servants like barbers to settle down in the village for the comfort of the cultivators. Gradually a village police force consisting of Dheds was evolved and a Bhangi family was ushered in for serving the people as sweepers and as removers of carcasses. These people were, like the artisans and personal servants, given a status in the village by being granted pieces of land (Mukhtyar 1930: 44).

The most prominent desai families, who had amassed great wealth as tax collectors, were known as *pedivalas*. They operated from small urban centres like Navsari, Chikhli, Gandevi, and Bulsar and no longer participated in the life of the peasantry. Although this elite segment had elevated themselves far above the majority of their fellow caste members, all Anavils tried to emulate their lifestyle. By leaving the cultivation of the land as much as possible to labourers, most of the Anavil Brahmans who continued to lead an agrarian lifestyle tried to claim the same nobility as their more privileged fellow caste members. It is against this background that the servitude of the Dublas in the pre-colonial economy must be seen.

Regime Change

Its location on the border of the Mughal empire made south Gujarat vulnerable to raids, some of which were instigated by displaced local chiefs who aimed at regaining their customary tribute. They belonged to Rajput dynasties from north Gujarat that had become subjugated to Muslim rulers from northern India in the early thirteenth century.[6] The petty Hindu chiefs lost their power to these rulers on the central plain but managed to establish a foothold in the less accessible hilly areas. From fortified positions in this hinterland, the heads of Rajput clans, known as *girasiya*s, made sorties into the plains. In addition to the regular taxes imposed by the Muslim rulers, the peasants in south Gujarat had to pay incidental tributes demanded by the roving Rajput bands, which were also collected by the desais (Pedder 1865: 317). Lastly, there were warlords operating from emerging power centres in western India. A Maratha army under the command of Shivaji sacked Surat in 1664 and in the years that followed, the Marathas gradually extended their reach into the city's hinterland. In 1676, they took control of Parnera, a fortress in the south, near Bulsar, and in 1719, consolidated their control by building military fortifications in Songadh. The governor of Surat managed to restore Mughal authority over the surrounding countryside for a short time but in 1759 the city fell into the hands of the British.

Throughout the eighteenth century, rival powers fought for control of south Gujarat, sometimes joining forces in short-lived coalitions. The Marathas had split into two camps, one that of the Gaekwad, the representative of the Peshwa of Pune in Gujarat, who declared his independence and took control of the Peshwa's territories. The British had launched a campaign of territorial expansion, transforming what had originally been a commercial enterprise into a colonial state, so the political and military turmoil continued. Control over the subdistrict of Bulsar, for example, passed from the Peshwa to the Gaekwad in 1716, back to the Peshwa in 1752, and then to the British in 1772. The latter were forced to relinquish it three years later, only to get it back for good in 1804. As a consequence of this power struggle, from the start of the nineteenth century first Chorasi, Chikhli, and Bulsar (between 1800 and 1804), then Olpad, Bardoli, and Pardi (in 1817) and finally, Mandvi (in 1839) fell to the British. From Baroda, which the Gaekwad had made the seat of his principality, his presence in south Gujarat remained restricted to Navsari, Gandevi, and Songhad.

The final division of south Gujarat between the British and the Gaekwad brought to an end the constantly shifting power balance that had existed in this part of west India from the second half of the seventeenth to the end of the eighteenth century. During this entire period there had been rival claims to power and authority. Successive rulers had no other option than to exploit the productive capacity of the peasantry through the system of tax farming, making it possible for the local elite to benefit from the rapid regime changes. Although their positions as tax farmers were intended to be temporary, the turmoil at higher levels of government meant that they were rarely dispossessed of their prerogatives. Many succeeded in ensuring that their lucrative position was passed on from father to son. The commission paid to the tax collectors during periods of strong governance was increased at times when the authorities were in financial difficulties by auctioning the estimated revenue to the highest bidder. He had to pay the agreed sum in advance, but would ensure that his investment was recouped several times over by selling shares in the acquired tax domain (*watan*) to family or fellow caste members. In this way, a subdistrict (pergunnah) allocated to one or more tax collectors would be divided up into a large number of shares (*khatas*). Consequently, behind the principal tax farmer (*watandar*) who had signed the contract with the government, there were a large number of shareholders (*khatedars*) who enabled him to recoup his investment in a relatively short time. The evolution of this chain of interrelated higher and lower desais resulted in a widening of the elite segment of the Anavil Brahmans. The most prominent families resided in the main town of the subdistrict in which they had shares. From there they were linked through a wide and complex network of relationships, to fellow caste members in the villages, who they had accepted as their partners. The familial ties between higher and lower shareholders were reinforced by the fact that they agreed to act as mutual guarantors for payment of the tax sum agreed in advance (Morison's report 1812: 43). According to this report, it was traditional practice in the whole region for tax to be collected in cash. Morison, who was the Collector of Surat, wrote: 'I have consulted both men and books, but cannot discover that it has ever been usual to collect the revenue in kind' (*Gazetteer of the Bombay Presidency*, vol. ii, 1877: 216).

The successive governments were badly informed about the size and economic condition of the peasantry. This ignorance strengthened the negotiating position of the tax farmers, and they took advantage of it to ensure that their privileged status helped to acquire hereditary rights, so that it could be passed on to succeeding generations. The division into higher and lower title-holders undoubtedly led to an increase in the tax burden.

The *desais* began to usurp the interior management of their villages or *khatas*, made themselves directly instead of mediately, responsible for the revenue, and reduced the *rayats* to very nearly the position of tenants-at-will. The revenue system was then briefly this: the Maratha *kamavisdar* or the farmer of the district, annually fixed the total revenue with the body of *desais*. These again divided that amount among themselves, according to their village and *khatas*, and then each *desai* got the sum for which he was responsible, and as much more as he could from his *rayats*; assessing on them nearly what rates he pleased (Pedder 1865, 1895: 316).

In contrast to the growing importance of the desais as collectors of revenue in the agrarian economy was the fact that the persistent political turmoil most probably led to flight from land by the peasants. Although they were subject to taxes, they also had a certain freedom of movement.

They would arrive with the aim of cultivating unsettled or fallow land but would leave again at the first signs of approaching danger, sometimes posed by hostilities between competing armies, but more often because of the arrival of roving bands combing the countryside for booty. Or their departure was due to the lure of another landlord, who demanded a lower tribute, the size of the tribute being a significant factor in decisions to stay or to leave. If taxpayers expressed their discontentment by departing en masse, landlords had little other choice than to set off after them and persuade them to return by promising them better conditions (Morison's reports 1812, 1819, and 1820). For a long time south Gujarat retained the character of a frontier society, where the population and the settlements in which they lived would expand and contract according to the vagaries of fortune. The peasantry continued to be highly mobile until deep into the second half of the nineteenth century, and the situation stabilized only when, with the twentieth century in sight, all land fit for agriculture had been taken up for cultivation and the colonial administration had restricted the power of the landlords.

The Dawn of the Colonial Era

How did the British set up their administration in the countryside of south Gujarat at the beginning of the nineteenth century? At first, they encountered the desais, who nominally acted as landlords on behalf of the government, but who in fact operated in their own interests. Looking back at the end of the century, Rogers was critical of the situation shortly after the transfer of power:

On the introduction of the British administration it was found that the management of the revenue was almost entirely in the hands of the Desais, cultivating Brahmins, whose original position was that of servants of the state, to whom was entrusted the collection of the revenue, in receipt of percentage allowances as remuneration for their services, had gradually changed to that of contractors for the revenue. So firmly was their influence in this character established that the members of a family were sometimes able to portion out among themselves the villages comprised in large areas of country, and, by combining together to keep the Collector in the dark as to the amount they would pay for their farms, and defraud the Government while they kept the ryots in complete subjection to themselves. They found a particular facility for this action in the lower class of cultivators in eastern and southerly parts of the country. The latter were a rude, thriftless and utterly uneducated race, whom the Desais had in many cases reduced to a condition of factual slavery, and who, it is hardly too much to say, only emerged from that condition on the advent of the Bombay and Baroda Railway and the introduction of the Revenue Survey Settlement. For many years after our acquisition of the country, accordingly, the Collector was forced to enter into annual settlements with the Desais, and make as good a bargain with them as he could. The Desais were, as a rule, punctual in their payments, and being mutually responsible for each other, security for the payment was rarely demanded from them (Rogers 1892: 170–1; see also Forrest 1887: 436–7).

At first, the colonial authorities observed the activities of the tax farmers with mistrust but lacked the means and wherewithal to redress the situation. This changed when it was decided not to recognize the landlords in the recently conquered territories of west India as *zamindars*, a title that carried more far-reaching rights than just the collection of agrarian taxes. Those bearing this title felt authorized to dispose of the agricultural land and the people living on it as they saw fit. The Permanent Settlement of 1793, which applied to eastern India (Bengal, Orissa, and Bihar), recognized the tax farmers as landlords.[7] This system was, however, not introduced in Gujarat, nor was an alternative immediately available. Having established themselves in this part of west India, the new rulers initially did not go beyond taking stock of the tax collection practices they encountered and organizing them more efficiently. They did, however, decide to do away with the system of intermediaries, which did represent a major shift in policy. In 1813, Collector Morison was instructed:

… to enter upon a more direct management of the Villages through the Agency of the Company's Servants, than would seem to prevail at present by superceding [*sic*] the undue and oppressive control exercised by the Dessoys over the cultivators which as long as it is allowed to exist must impede the progress of agricultural improvement (quoted in Rabitoy 1975: 533).

Chikhli comprised seventy-two villages, most of which were quite large, but much of the land was still uncultivated. The taxes were collected by twenty-two principal desais, with the help of an unspecified number of partners. The fifty villages in Bulsar fell under the responsibility of five principal desais, with tax collection rights divided among 140 subordinate sharers. There were often tussles for power between the families of the tax farmers, and sometimes one would submit a higher bid than a competitor. It was of course the peasants who ultimately paid the price for the rivalry that was played out over their heads (Morison's reports 1812, 1819, and 1820 referred to in the *Gazetteer of the Bombay Presidency*, vol. ii, 1877: 215, fn. 4). Gradually, an understanding of the origins and working methods of this elite class increased. As I mentioned earlier, the desais paid each other and the government in cash, traditionally in silver Broach rupees. But this circuit of monetary exchange hardly penetrated the village economy, if at all, as the cultivators paid their levies in kind as a proportion of their yield. Morison mentioned this conversion of produce into cash within and outside the local economy in a report drawn up shortly after the transfer of power, based on the verbal testimonies of informants and backed up by references to old records (Morison's reports). In 1816, the system of collecting revenue directly from the cultivators was introduced in principle but it took all of the first half of the nineteenth century to put this new regime of taxation into practice.

As described above, the desais—who had been promoted from tax collectors to tax farmers during the Mughal era—had in the subsequent period of shifting power balances used their position to further increase their authority over land and people. They did this by not only imposing much higher levies on the peasants than had previously been permitted, but also by not registering the land cultivated by the peasants in the official registers. This explains why bidders for a share (khata) in the domain of a tax farmer had to pay a much higher price than the officially permitted revenue. This commission, known as *desaigiri*, had long been fixed at 2.5 per cent of the revenue. The arrangements made were described in a colonial era report, dating from 1865, as follows:

The authorized emolument of the *desais* was cash allowance calculated at 2.5 per cent as the village revenues. This seems to have been the official remuneration of the office, and was formally confirmed by the Emperor Aurangzebe in A.D. 1669. But in Surat this limit was a merely nominal one, for all the profit which the *desais* could make from the village management were of course their own. Thus I find that shortly before the introduction of British rule, a *desai's khata* in a village in Bulsar, the *desaigiri* of 2.5 per cent on which was only Rs. 1.10, was sold for Rs. 450. The desais also appropriated a great deal of land calling it *khudkhasta, passaiter, waola,* &c. Most of this was not in their own possession, but was cultivated by the villagers, and the desais merely received the assessment upon it, instead of Government. They also occupied a good deal of Government land, cultivating it by means of their slaves, and paying low rents of assessment for it (Pedder 1865, 1895: 316).

In the years following the transfer of power, the colonial authorities were content to restrict the authority that the desais had built up over time, by reducing it in phases. These landed gentry retained their function as tax collectors but were not permitted to charge more for their services than the 2.5 per cent commission. It proved impossible, however, to reconcile this practice with the new government regulations.

For the first eight years, however, the interior management of the district differed but little from that which had prevailed under the Gaikwar's Government. The Collector indeed settled the annual *Jamabandi* (levy) of the district and the *kamavisdar* (subdistrict official) took the place of the farmer in fixing the ankda (taxable sum) of the villages, but the whole of the work of collection, &c., remained in the hands of the desais, the principal of whom, moreover, bore a most important part in the settlement of the *Jamabandi* (Pedder 1865: 54).

As the first appointed British Collector in charge of Surat district, Morison negotiated with the desais on the rate of taxation and the emolument they received for their mediation. The three-year agreements concluded by him in 1813 allowed for a progressive increase in the land revenue. He was unsuccessful, however, in forcing them to dispose of the agricultural land under their control but for which they paid the government little or insufficient taxes. In 1820, he informed his superiors of this situation:

With regard to the *desais*, these district officers used, under the native government, to make large deductions from the village collections in remuneration for their services as heads of villages, and also often pretended to claim considerable quantities of land in the same account, but actual possession of which they were seldom able to prove. Only those persons have been allowed to retain land who satisfied me that they had received the produce thereof, and the ready-money payments which they pretended to have received was reduced to what was the original custom of the country, viz. 2.5 per cent on the *jama* (Pedder 1865, 1895: 328).

After travelling through Gujarat in 1821, Governor Elphinstone stated that he was not in favour of using what were known as 'hereditary district officers' as agents between the government and the *rayats*, that is, landowning peasants. Difficult and unreliable as they were, the government could not afford to operate without their cooperation, at least not in the first few decades. The received wisdom was that the desai dislocated the old patel, but Chambers, Assistant Collector of Surat in 1833, took a different view altogether. In his opinion there had never been patels in the villages which desais claimed the property right of. It took many years to build up the line of command from the district to the local level to enforce compliance with official rules and regulations. One of the first steps was to appoint village clerks (*talatis*) who worked at the base of the agrarian economy as agents of the colonial administration. Their tasks included submitting reports on agricultural property and crop production. This system of official surveillance was, however, only a partial success. The small group of British officials in charge of the district administration continued to depend on local subordinates, most of whom came from the Anavil elite, until well in to the second half of the nineteenth century. The Anavil Brahmans ensured that the new regulations had as little adverse effect as possible on the interests of those influential members of their caste who they considered friends and relations. The colonial authorities became aware of these dubious practices when the rivalry between the desais led them to submit complaints about each other, and although the authorities were seriously concerned, they were powerless to put a stop to the fraud and collusion. Instead, they tried to secure the goodwill of the elite by turning a blind eye. In 1825, for example, two Anavil villages were exempted from tax in the hope that the members of the elite caste would show their loyalty by helping to collect the remainder of the revenue (Rogers 1892, vol. I: 179). Yet even these concessions were a failure, as the Revenue Commissioner noted despondently a few decades later:

Every sort of fraud has been perpetrated, chiefly through the agency of the Civil Courts, the subordinates of which and of the Collector's Establishment have been in league, and have, of course, profited accordingly. The whole of these proceedings afford a most remarkable instance of mismanagement and misapplication of Public Revenue (*Papers relating to a summary settlement of alienated revenues in the Bombay Presidency*, 1858: 2–3).

Despite their attempts at obstruction and sabotage, the desais gradually lost the authority they had enjoyed in previous generations. This was the result of far-reaching decisions taken by the colonial administration at the start of the nineteenth century. As mentioned above, the elite in south Gujarat were not granted the same status as that attributed to the zamindars in Bengal at the end of the eighteenth century. These Bengali counterparts of the desais had been legally designated the ultimate title-holders of the land, with the authority to impose taxes on those who actually cultivated it, unlike the desais in south Gujarat who were also landlords but did not receive this same recognition. The passage below, from Pedder's report in 1865, clearly indicates this striking difference:

The Surat *desais*, at the introduction of British rule, were thus, as nearly as possible, in the same position as the *zamindars* of Bengal before the permanent settlement. They called themselves, indeed, and are often called in early reports, *zamindars*, and had the Athavisi come under British rule a few years earlier, a permanent settlement would, in all probability, have been made with them. But opinion as to the merits of the permanent settlement had changed in the 20 years subsequent to 1789, and fortunately, the Collector of Surat from about 1807 to 1821 was Mr Morison, a man of remarkable energy and ability, and a strong adherent of the *Rayatwari* system[8]. He completely put an end to the peculiar position of the *desais* by the simple expedient of no longer fixing his assessments with them, but directly with *rayats*, and in lieu of all their emoluments, he proposed to give them the original 2.5 per cent on the revenue, employing such of them as the Collector might select as District Officers in the capacity of Amins. In the *watans* now comprising Bulsar, Chikhli, Chorasi and part of Supa, Mr Morison's arrangements, as far as the emoluments were concerned, were introduced about 1810 to 1814. The amount of *desaigiri*, however, seems to have fluctuated with the revenue for a few years, and to have been finally fixed at its present amount about 1820 (Pedder 1865, 1895: 316).

The persistent refusal of the desais to play by the colonial rules rather than evade them surreptitiously eventually led to them losing their former prerogatives and being excluded from any involvement in administrative affairs. This was made possible shortly after the middle of the nineteenth century when land registers were created in all subdistricts, recording the area of agricultural land in all villages and what it was used for. Each owner of arable land was subject to tax and had to pay it in cash directly to the authorities. This meant that the *ryotwari* system, which the government had decided to introduce in principle in 1812, was now in place. An earlier attempt by Morison to register all farmland had failed owing both to a lack of technical staff to perform the measurements and to the resistance of the local elite, who had seen it as intolerable interference in their prerogatives. In the years that followed, the colonial administration grew in strength and the administrative expertise necessary to enforce measures was greater than in the early days of its rule over south Gujarat. The Survey and Settlement Reports drawn up for the various subdistricts in turn were a rich source of information on much more than just the identity of peasants and the crops they cultivated. For the first time, there were accurate statistics on the number, nature, and location of the villages, the number of inhabitants according to gender, age, and other demographic features, and social structure in terms of caste, religious practices, and economic activities, including a classification of the working population. By compiling all source data into a *District Gazetteer*, the authorities produced a significant body of reference material. The subsequent review of the tax assessment, laid down in the *Revised Survey and Settlement Reports*, enabled them to chart developments at the base of the economy and society and use this information to monitor and expand the reach of taxation.

The above argument, substantiated by the remarks of colonial officials in the early nineteenth century, could create the impression that the ryotwari system was introduced in response to what the Bombay Presidency saw as an abuse of power by the elite in Surat district. This conclusion is, however, only partly correct. The desais in Gujarat had, after all, not acted in any way different to the zamindars in Bengal before the announcement of the Permanent Settlement. The divergence in the economic and political status of the two groups—the zamindars moving up and the desais down—was a consequence of the different tax regimes imposed in east and west India. In Bengal, the authorities in Calcutta had recognized the zamindars as landowners and given them more extensive powers than they already possessed. In 1812, however, the Court of Directors in Bombay decided to adopt the model Thomas Munro had drafted for the Madras Presidency. Consequently, the cultivating peasants in south Gujarat were designated owners of their land immediately after the transfer of power and the tax farmers were relieved of their duties. Both policies were founded on a myth that was required to legitimate the measures taken by the colonial authorities.[9] In Bengal, the official justification for recognizing the zamindars' property rights was that, in the distant past, they had been large-scale agricultural entrepreneurs. In west India, on the other hand, the system of tax farming that was in place when the colonial administration took over was seen to have emerged—also in the pre-colonial era—as a result of the erosion and eventual disappearance of the original village communities. The official explanation for this historical speculation was that the introduction of the ryotwari system essentially reinstated a peasant order with little internal differentiation. Official reports referred to remnants of the traditional village rule. The patels who functioned as village heads and maintained contacts with supra-local sources of power were allegedly squeezed out deceitfully at a later stage by the desais, whose dominance was seen as a consequence of the failure of the Mughal rulers to install an administrative apparatus on the margins of the empire which was able to skim off the cream of the agricultural surplus without eroding the autonomy of the peasant community. Elphinstone expressed himself in these terms in a memorandum reporting his impressions during his journey through Gujarat in 1821:

Every *desai* managed the village of his own *Bhag (watan)* as he pleased, and in general they displaced the old *Patels*, and carried on even the interior management of each village by means of his own agents, who were called *talukdars*. The *desai* was thus the perfect master of the people without anyone to check him (Forrest 1884: 449–50).

Malcolm Peyt confirmed this picture in 1830:

The power and influence of *Dessyes* or native District Officers is described as having destroyed all authority in the *Patels* and to have obstructed the benefit expected from the *Tallatees* who were nominated by Government to keep the village accounts (Bombay Presidency, Miscellaneous Official Publications, 15 October 1830).

But critical voices were soon heard. No amount of investigation could produce evidence to support the claim that the advent of the desais as tax farmers had occurred at the expense of a much older system, in the form of a village republic ruled by the peasants themselves. The village heads appointed by the British were government agents and bore no resemblance to their alleged predecessors, for whose existence no evidence had been forthcoming. At the end of the nineteenth century, Rogers gave a different historical reconstruction of the village community than had been made at the beginning of it:

It seems doubtful whether in the villages of which the *desais* settled for the revenue, there were ever any *Patels* (headmen) distinct from them. If such ever existed they had been so completely ousted from their position and influence that the Collector had no option in the matter of the settlements as long as the system of the responsibility of the cultivators directly to the officers of Government was not introduced. The reports of the period abound in proof that every endeavour to lessen the influence of the *desais*, and to induce the *ryots* to place confidence in the new system of administration by bringing them into personal communication with European officers, was made in pursuance of orders from Bombay as well as from the Court of Directors of the East India Company; but so great seems to have been the hold the *desais* had obtained in the management of the revenue that it was not till AD 1818 that positive orders were given to supersede them, and not till two years after this event that the order was carried into effect. It is probable, however, that after 1817–18 when the system of levying revenue directly from the *ryots* by means of village accounts was brought into force, the *desais* had not been so much contractors for revenue, as officers of the state paid by a percentage on the revenue; but so thorough was the influence they originally obtained that up to the present day there are few villages in the southern districts of the Collectorate in which the stipendiary (there are no hereditary Patelships recognized there) *Patels* are not descendants of the old *desais* (Rogers 1892: 171–2).

Introduction of the Ryotwari System

The land revenue system set up in the early nineteenth century in south Gujarat grew out of practice and owed more to expediency than to a careful assessment of the merits and demerits of alternative models. Rabitoy described it as follows:

Bombay officials were not committed to any system during this period; their commitment was to a steadily increasing revenue and a politically stable population, plus promotion. The result was a commitment to a policy of administrative expediency. It was almost incidental, that the product was an administration which appeared to be *ryotwari* in structure (Rabitoy 1975: 530).

The introduction of the ryotwari system immediately restricted the power of the desais but, as explained above, their services remained indispensable in creaming off the agricultural surplus well into the second half of the nineteenth century. Only when the colonial administration had set up its own apparatus could the annual taxes be collected from the peasantry without making use of these middlemen any longer. They were formally relieved of their status in 1867 on the basis of the recommendations of an official commission. Under this regulation, all watandars received henceforth an annual emolument of three *annas* for each *rupee* they collected. In exchange, they had to agree to surrender their right to provide the services they used to render. The compensation was not only for the principal tax farmers, but also included those who had a share in the revenue. This amounted to recognition by the government of the custom of dividing the assessment into a large number of shares and, thereby, at no extra cost since the lump sum remained the same, acknowledging a large number of title-holders. It was a concession to the elite, who were resisting—in vain—relinquishing their power over the peasant population. The desais were only too aware that official recognition of their former authority would enable them to continue to claim higher social status. It was important that this right was acknowledged by the government, not so much because of the negligible financial benefits that accrued to it, but much more as proof that they belonged to a family that had once held a position of power. They insisted on being registered in the public watan book which the government promised to keep up to date, without mention of the differences in rank that had existed between them. According to the report by the chairman of the commission, the implication that they were all equal had its origins in a strong sense of rivalry among the members of the elite, in the past and the present.

...among the *desais* of the Surat Athavisi there seems to have long existed, as there still exists, a jealousy of each other which would not permit any individual to assume the position of principals or representatives of the family in watan duties; all sharers were considered equal and, as the watan families increased, the members of them divided among themselves the desais' rights in different villages of their *Purgana*, and indeed the *desaigiri* of the same village was often divided into the *khatas* of two or more *desais*, brothers or cousins (Pedder 1865: 316).

The extent to which the principal title was divided up is illustrated by practice in Bulsar. When the new regulations were introduced, this subdistrict had four main desais from seventeen families, with a total of 350 members holding a share. The annual desaigiri was paid to the heirs of the original shareholders until several years after Independence. Its symbolic value was far higher than its monetary worth. As it was divided up among more and more descendants, collecting the minuscule payment was no longer worth the effort, but the families concerned turned it into a festive ritual. During my first fieldwork study, several informants told me how the annual trip by their fathers or grandfathers to the government office was an important day in the life of the family: always accompanied by much public pomp and circumstance.

The desais also resisted the non-service settlement imposed on them by the government by denying that it was compensation for the commission paid to them for collecting the land tax. In response to official enquiries, the native authorities confirmed that the desais' claim for compensation was indeed based on their role as managers of agricultural colonization and as founders of villages.

...in the Athavisi the *desais* do '*abadi lavni*' work (i.e. are responsible for their districts being peopled and properly cultivated) and any other work which may be assigned them... (Pedder 1865: 319).

One high-ranking official in the principality of Baroda stated that this task of cultivating and populating the land was of greater value than the land itself. Unlike peasant manpower it was, after all, available in abundance. Although it did not lead to a change in the amount of the desaigiri, the desais did see this statement as recognition of their past as founders of the agrarian system in south Gujarat.

While the British administration dismantled the system of tax farming, the desais in the parts of south Gujarat that belonged to the principality of Baroda initially retained their positions. But once the heavy taxes imposed on the peasants and the high-handed manner in which they were treated came to light, the desais in these areas also lost their power. In 1872–3, a third of all arable land in Navsari was left uncultivated out of protest and a procession of peasants went to the court in Baroda to inform the Gaekwad himself of the fraud and abuse to which they had been subjected. The delegation would have been much bigger if the tax farmers had not prevented a large number of protestors from taking part. Those who did succeed in doing so were punished severely on their return. They lost their cattle and land, were no longer permitted to use the wells, or had to surrender their homes to the Dheds. Robbed of all their possessions, they had no other choice than to move to villages under British control (Baroda Enquiry Commission 1873–5: 198, 285). The elite had gangs of supporters whom they could mobilize to break the resistance of the peasants with violence, if necessary. The tax farmers were not only servants of higher authorities but also enjoyed police and judicial authority so that they could sanction those who failed in their duties. They were authorized to use violence and the punishment they meted out was not seen as exceeding their mandate. Reports of investigations into complaints make it clear that the desais treated their fellow Anavil caste members more lightly than recalcitrant peasants who did not belong to the rural elite. One case described to the investigation commission by Anavils from the village of Veshma is typical.

We, Brahmins, declining to pay, were kept in custody in the *chowri* (stockade) for one or two days, our cattle were tied up, &c. The Kanbis suffered more. They were made to stand touching their toes with stones on their backs, and so forth, and in this way the tax was levied from us (ibid.: 400).

A short time later, taking advantage of the swelling protest among the peasants against what had become an ineffective tax regime, and undoubtedly encouraged behind the scenes by British officials, the Baroda authorities also adopted the ryotwari system. The change once again met with fierce resistance from the desais who, along with the loss of their right to collect taxes, lost the power that some of their predecessors had acquired long before the arrival of the Gaekwad in south Gujarat.

The introduction of the ryotwari system in west India drove the desais back into the ranks of the peasantry. In contrast to the zamindars in Bengal who, with the introduction of the Permanent Settlement, acquired rights as landlords which they had never before enjoyed, the former tax farmers in south Gujarat lost the power that accrued to them because of their privileged status under the *ancien regime*. In areas where the zamindari system was introduced, a hierarchy emerged in the agrarian society which was different to the structure that preceded it. But to assume from this that the introduction of the ryotwari system in other parts of South Asia led to a more egalitarian agrarian order would be incorrect. Before looking at this assumption in the specific context of the area of my fieldwork, I will give a brief sketch of the economic life in rural south Gujarat in the early colonial era.

The Village Economy

What was the nature of the village economy at the time of the British takeover? Early reports provide no more than summary information on the state of agriculture, describing only the large number of different crops that were cultivated. Food grains (rice and millet, but also coarser varieties), vegetables, and pulses accounted for the lion's share. This diversity served primarily to satisfy basic daily needs, and resulted in a production cycle that extended almost throughout the whole year. Gandevi, for example, had the following calendar in the middle of the nineteenth century.

Table 1.1 shows the situation in an area traditionally renowned for its very fertile soil and abundance of wells for irrigation. It would be inaccurate to apply this image of continuous and intensive production of such a wide variety of crops to the whole of south Gujarat. For example, the description of agricultural activities in Chikhli *taluka* in the first cadastral survey in 1865 was much less extensive. The high *jarayat* land was not suitable for intensive agriculture and was left untilled for much of the year, while the most important crops—rice and sugarcane—were only grown on the lower and irrigated ground.

The fact that the peasants were producing crops for their own consumption did not mean that each peasant household formed a self-

Table 1.1: Scheme of Cultivation in the Wet-land Area of Gandevi Around the Middle of the 19th Century

Crop	Sowing	Harvest
bajra	July	November
jowar	July	January
kodra	July	December
kapas	June	February
urad	July	May
chola	July	May
til	September	March
tuvar	July	December
gram	November	March
wheat	October	March
rice	June	November
methi	November	March
diveli	November	March
sugarcane	November (after 13 months)	December
onions	November	May
chillies	August	January
brinjal	October	February
ginger	June	December
saffron	June	December
garlic	November	December
plantains	June	March
sweet potatoes	October	April
yams	June	January
sweet yam	June	January

Source: Beyts (1868: 5).

contained and autarkic unit. Economic activity within the community was in fact more like a network in which agricultural producers and non-agrarian workers were bound together. Goods and services were not exchanged through a horizontal, egalitarian network, but on the basis of a hierarchical order with the households of the large landowners at the centre. The history of land cultivation in south Gujarat was decisive for the emergence of this stratified social setting. It is a variant of the myth of the village community that lives on in the memory of the rural elite.

Each village was originally founded by a family or association of families of the cultivating castes—Rajputs, Kunbees, Vohoras or Bhathelas, all apparently belonging to kindred tribes. These people, with their servants and 'Halis', fixed the village site, dug the well and tank, planted the groves, built the village temple, and thus exercised the right of possession. They then induced artisans to settle in their village, who were the servants of the community, and to whom they gave houses, bits of land rent-free, grain cesses, &c. Other cultivators, mostly of inferior castes, were in process of time attracted to the village, and the proprietary body permitted them to cultivate such land as they did not want themselves, but gave them no proprietary rights (Robertson 1865: 29).

This outline not only offers an insight into the development of agriculture in south Gujarat, but also suggests a pattern of interaction between the different castes in what can be recognized as the structure of the *jajmani* system described in many regions' in South Asia. I have written extensively about this network of localized exchange relations in the historical introduction to the study resulting from my first fieldwork study in south Gujarat (1974a: chapter 2). In that study, I referred to the key role of the Anavil Brahmans as members of the dominant caste in the jajmani system. They regulated access to agriculture, owned most of the cultivated land and, since they also disposed of most of the basic means of existence, controlled the labour power, products, and services of the landless and non-agrarian castes. As patrons it was their task to divide the grain, on a day-to-day basis to the agricultural labourers in their permanent employ and, after the harvest, to the members of the other castes. This was an exchange based not on equality, but on a relationship of superiority and inferiority.

As well as being asymmetrical, the relations between the various castes had a dimension that extended beyond their material value. The interaction between them also reflected the servitude of client to master. When a village was founded on the central plain of south Gujarat, the division of labour between the agrarian and non-agrarian castes was also hierarchical in nature. The *Baroda Gazetteer* provides an interesting retrospective description of the obligations imposed on the dependent castes in the past.

The word *veth* comes from *vahitu*, unprofitable labour. It is applied to the service to which the landlord has a claim in consideration for his allowing those who render it to live on his land, or giving them a certain yearly supply of grain. The persons who receive this grain and perform the labour are termed *vasayas* from the word *vasavu*, to inhabit, that is they represent the classes whose presence is essential in populating a village. They are the *kumbhar* or potter, the *valand* or barber, the *suthar* or carpenter, the *luhar* or blacksmith, the *darji* or tailor, the *mochi* or leatherworker, the *dhed* or sweeper and the *bhangi* or scavenger. In return for the grain given, or the license to build a hut on the land of the chief, the following services have to be performed without further remuneration. The potter supplies him with earthen pots; the barber makes the beds in the chief's house, lights the lamps, shampoos the legs of the members of the landlord's family, fetches supplies from the grocer, and at night acts as a torch bearer. If there are several families of potters or of barbers the grain is divided among them and they take the duty by turns. Dheds fetch fuel and fodder for the landlord and his officials and carry letters. Bhangis act as guides, and sleep in the grainyard during the harvest time to watch the grain. The other vasayas are bound to work for the landlord whenever called upon. Cultivators are bound to carry the landlord's share of grain to the grain store or to the residence of the person to whom the landlord may have sold the grain. During the journey they receive fodder for their cattle and food for the cartmen. Husbandmen, and sometimes tradesmen, are also obliged to lend bedding or pagean including cots, mattresses and quilted covers, for the use of the landlord's guests. Vagharis have to provide datan, toothsticks, for the landlord's guests and receive a day's food in return. Shepherds of the Rabari and Bharvad castes must provide milk for the landlord and his guests by turns (*Gazetteer of the Baroda State*, vol. i, 1923: 352–3).

Producing agricultural or craft products for the market was not the primary motive for economic activity in this mode of production. Generating surplus was secondary to the articulation of domination and subordination. Harvest surpluses were sold on small markets throughout the district, but more often traders went from village to village to buy what the peasants could afford to do without. In the Bombay Presidency, according to a report from 1830, Surat district was notable for its inaccessibility (Choksey 1968: 238). In the middle of the nineteenth century there were still no all-weather roads. Cart tracks were in a bad state of repair and between June and September, goods and people could only be transported by horse, ox, or buffalo (Bellasis 1854: 18). The same source mentions *atwaras*, weekly markets where traders from the nearby towns would trade consumption goods for agricultural commodities.

Banians from Bulsar, Gundevee, Chicklee, Balda Pardi, and Damaun, regularly frequent these fairs, with a variety of piece goods, cloths, cutlery, cooking utensils, beads, bangles, native ornaments, pepper, ginger, tobacco, and such articles of general consumption and luxury. The neighbouring villages attend, bringing with them garden produce, wood, salt, and grain. The mode of transacting business is generally by barter, and little money is used (Bellasis 1854: 6).

There were almost no monetary transactions within the village economy. The castes paid each other in kind for their goods and services. As we shall see, this was also the case for the 'debts' owed by the landless to their masters. Although all the advances, allowances, and other payments were measured in rupees, no money changed hands. The only important exception to this rule was that taxes had to be paid to the government in cash. In the Mughal era, the currency was the silver Broach rupee and the criteria for taxation was ownership of arable land. This did not change under colonial rule, but it applied only to the final payment to the government. Peasants paid their levy in kind, by surrendering part of their harvest to the desais. In effect, monetary transactions were only of any significance outside the local economy, and rarely concerned villagers who did not belong to the local elite. This begs the question as to where the money required to pay the land tax came from. The elite found the cash to meet this unavoidable financial commitment by selling raw materials and agricultural produce—primarily wood, rice, and *gur* made from sugarcane—sometimes on faraway markets. These goods were transported to Saurashtra and other places in the north and more especially to Bombay in the south, not over land but by water. On the mouths of rivers, there were small harbours like Bilimora, Gandevi, and Bulsar where vessels could moor at high tide to load and unload cargo (Choksey 1968: 208). This long-distance commercial trade appeared to benefit only the members of the higher and wealthier castes. The wood came from the dense forests to the east of Chikhli—felling the trees and transporting them by cart to the coast was done by the Bhathelas, Kanbis, and Bohras in the hot summer months. The impressive houses they built in the villages bore witness to their lucrative activities (Bellasis 1854: 5; Beyts 1870: 48). The same report mentions sugarcane as an important source of income, but an older source, from 1823, provides further information on the significance of this crop:

There is no part of Guzerat in which the sugarcane is cultivated to the same extent and perfection as in our own and the Gaikwar districts in the *attaveesy*. In a few villages of the Gaikwars the assessment is I believe as high as Rupees 100 a *beega* on sugarcane, and there are some Coonbees in our villages who consume all the other produce of their farms themselves, and pay their entire Revenue from Jagree (the end-product made from sugarcane) and who are as rich people in their way as any I have met with. Indeed they may be called Planters as they have 30 or 40 bond servants and cattle in proportion under them (Lumsden, Collector of Surat, 9 April 1823).

Small owners did not have the capacity to grow sugarcane. Kolis for example restricted themselves to rice and millet (Bellasis 1854: 3). If members of the lower peasant castes did grow sugarcane, it was not at their own risk and expense but as sharecroppers for the large landowners. Dhodhias in Chikhli, for instance, grew cane for the Anavils (*Gazetteer of the Bombay Presidency*, vol. ii, 1877: 62).

My conclusion contradicts the assumption that the village economy was a closed circuit that functioned solely to meet the needs of the inhabitants. No matter how important this was, monetary transactions played an important role in contacts with the outside world. But participation in these commercial activities was limited to the members of castes constituting the rural elite. They spent the income on a comfortable lifestyle that set them apart from the simpler or downright poverty-stricken existence suffered by the majority of villagers. I will look at this in more detail when I examine the relationship between landlords and labourers. First, however, I will briefly outline the settlement policy with which the colonial authorities put an end to the frontier character that had left its mark on the agricultural development of south Gujarat for so long.

Closure of the Frontier and Tribal Sedentarization

Towards the middle of the nineteenth century, it became clear that the foreign rulers intended not only to stay but to involve themselves much more directly with affairs at village level. This policy included a local administration that extended from the district headquarters right down to the base of society. Village heads and police patels were the government's agents and the appointment of talatis laid the basis for local records containing information on land ownership, crop patterns, different kinds of soil, and population movements. Small towns which functioned as service centres for the surrounding countryside were strengthened by building the first schools and health clinics. The construction of roads and of bridges across the larger rivers put an end to local isolation. Yet these large-scale infrastructural projects did not start until the second half of the century.

The primary policy for increasing agricultural production was to extend the area of cultivated land. This would not only make people better off, but was also in line with the colonial administration's objective to increase tax revenues. In their urge to raise revenue, the British initially imposed an excessively high levy. To make matters worse, they stuck steadfastly to this policy even in years when the harvest was bad. The peasants responded to this by land flight. Fields were left lying fallow in Soopa and Chikhli talukas, for example, in the early 1830s when the authorities refused to cancel or even reduce the land tax after a fall in the price of the most important crops (Choksey 1968: 80). Land flight, a classic weapon in the arsenal of peasants' resistance, remained a possibility because there was still plenty of waste land available for newcomers in the neighbouring principality of Baroda.

Before 1856, the agricultural population of the State was comparatively small and the land available for cultivation was abundant (*Baroda Economic Development Committee Report* 1920: 56).

The situation of open resources and generally low land prices applied to the whole of the central plain. It was not until the end of the nineteenth century that the supply of labour in agriculture started to outstrip demand. This shift in the primary factors of production in the more developed western part of south Gujarat was the result of a combination of demographic (gradually increasing population pressure) and economic forces (the advance of market production).

In the less fertile and less developed eastern part of the region stronger measures were required to stimulate agricultural activity. At the mercy of economic forces against which they could do little because they did not understand how to respond to them, the kaliparaj tried to preserve their autonomy by retreating and keeping a low profile in areas where the colonial state and the drive towards economic growth had as yet hardly made an impact. Just before the British takeover of Bulsar, several tribal groups left the area only shortly after having settled there, in protest at the—for them—unprecedented obligation to pay tax for land they themselves had cultivated. In 1828, they returned, only to leave again five years later to escape from moneylenders. The recurrence of nomadism was also driven by other than economic motives: an epidemic, conflicts with neighbours, or 'any trifling circumstance', as the colonial sources noted with clear irritation (*Gazetteer of the Bombay Presidency*, vol. ii, 1877: 195–6). In Chikhli, the Dhodhias continued to move around restlessly until well into the second half of the nineteenth century, but as the supply of agricultural land in the hinterland of Surat district became steadily more restricted, escape from a sedentary way of life became increasingly difficult for the new generation.

Sedentarization of the shifting cultivators in the forested hinterland of Surat district was strongly encouraged. Yet the tribal nomads stubbornly resisted the change and it took until the end of the century before they could be persuaded to settle permanently. What finally brought them to give up their nomadic way of life was rice cultivation, with which they had little experience, and the land policy of the colonial administration. In contrast to the coarse millets (*nagli* and *kodra*) that the kaliparaj had been growing for staple until then, growing rice required their constant presence from the time it was sown to the harvest several months later. Moreover, from 1872, the government no longer recognized the custom of using fallow land as commons. The demarcation of property rights and the levying of land taxes meant that the tribal peoples could only cultivate land registered in their names. The government took account of their low productive capacity by reinstating the traditional custom of setting their land tax at 25 per cent lower than that of the high-caste owners for the same type of land. Nevertheless, many of them were still unable to consolidate their holdings when the colonial officials came to the hinterland to claim their share of the harvest. Because of the low yield of the land, which the tribal peasants worked with simple tools, what was left of the harvest after the taxes had been deducted was insufficient for them to meet their basic needs, especially in bad years. The Bania gave them grain for food during the slack season and seed just before the start of the monsoon. These advances were then repaid after the harvest, and amounted to 150 per cent of the food rations supplied and double the quantity of seed. This meant that the peasants had even less left over than in the previous year, generating a spiral of debt from which escape was extremely difficult (Hardiman 1987: chapter 6). One other thing that prevented the kaliparaj from making ends meet was their drinking habits. They had always enjoyed alcoholic drinks, but now they had to pay for it. The colonial administration had issued an order banning the tribals from distilling their own liquor, toddy from the fermented sap of palm trees (especially *khajuri*) or *daru*, made from the flowers of the *mahuwa* tree. The monopoly on the sale of alcohol was almost solely in the hands of

Parsis and they of course made sure that they recouped the investment required to buy their licences through auction by charging their customers higher prices and the tribals found themselves deeper in debt as they continued a custom they had always enjoyed free of charge (Hardiman 1987: chapter 7). The subjection of the tribal peasants to the colonial tax regime meant that they lost control of their meagre means of existence. Their creditors became large landowners, but retained their debtors as tenants and sharecroppers. The real benefit for the Baniyas and Parsis lay not so much in the fact that they were the registered legal owners of land that had a relatively low value, but that they appropriated a large part of the tribal labour power. Often the ownership rights to land were transferred on the initiative of the local tax official rather than the creditor. Especially after years of famine, such as at the end of the nineteenth and the beginning of the twentieth centuries, much land changed hands. Reports by officials responsible for cadastral registration make reference to the way tribals were dispossessed of their rights of independent cultivation.

I am informed that local Revenue officers realized arrears of revenue from *Sahukars* and entered the lands concerned in the Sahukars' name (*Settlement Report of the Vyara taluka*, Baroda 1907: 9).

The settlements founded by the kaliparaj were different to the villages on the western plain. The tribal locations lacked the caste structure and the segregation into high and low that the hierarchy implied. This greater homogeneity was of course due to the lack of differentiation in occupations and of rules insisting on the social and physical distance between members of different castes. The kaliparaj had not been incorporated into the Hindu system and lived solely from agriculture, using no other means of production than their labour power. Until the start of the twentieth century, the majority continued to practise their own religious customs, which were primarily animistic, and outsiders feared the tribals' knowledge of magic. Their long-held rejection of Hinduism was grounded in resistance to a hierarchical form of social organization (Hardiman 1987: 81–2). Their settlements consisted of a collection of neighbourhoods, known as *falias*, which were located at some distance from each other and were inhabited by members of the same family and lineage. The basis of their social organization was the clan and the various tribes into which they were divided each had their own territory: the Chodhras and Gamits lived in the north of Surat district, the Kuknas and Dhodhias in the south.

These regions beyond the central plain were known as *jangli*. The term applied both to the landscape and to the people it accommodated. Their transformation from 'the position of wild unsettled squatters to that of fixed and steady cultivators' was seen as progress but the expected material improvements did not occur—the tribals did not only lose their land to moneylenders but also to distillers of strong drink. At the end of the nineteenth century, as a result of increasing pressure on the agrarian means of existence on the central plain, ujliparaj colonists penetrated the eastern hinterland of Surat district. The colonial administration was pleased at the arrival of these high-caste settlers because they proved better cultivators. They attributed this to the uneconomic behaviour of the kaliparaj, who were seen to lack certain character traits—such as regularity, sobriety, a work ethic, and a propensity to save—without which it is not possible to develop a comfortable and sophisticated way of life. In a note addressed to the Commission charged with the resurvey of the Mandvi taluka in the early twentieth century, the Collector of the Surat district did not mince words. He gave as his considered opinion that 'the majority of the Kaliparaj are idle, drunken and debased, and in fact little higher than animals' (Cole 1904). Irritated by the drinking habits of the tribals and the consequential loss of their land, one official said despairingly that the only way to develop this hinterland was to allow the tribals to die out and replace them with colonists from elsewhere (*Revised Survey and Settlement Report, Mahuva taluka* 1916:19). Later studies show that the tribals themselves, designated as adivasis after Independence, attributed their lack of development to the economic processes to which they were subjected during the colonial era.

The Adivasis knew the non-Adivasis through the exploiters only, viz. the moneylenders, the police and other government officers, and the liquor shop owners. They therefore distrusted all non-Adivasis. They did not want any 'outsider' to be present at their meetings and made a rule that if any 'outsider' came to the meeting the proceedings should stop. The 'outsider' was actually the exploiter primarily. The 'Ujaliak' (a collective name for caste Hindus) was disliked because he was an exploiter first, non-Adivasi next (I.P. Desai 1977: 52; see further Hardiman 1987).

The collective identity of the kaliparaj in the hinterland of south Gujarat was a consequence of the way in which they were incorporated into mainstream society during the twentieth century. They continued to constitute the largest population segment in their region, shared a relatively homogenous agrarian lifestyle, and in sociocultural terms were relatively far removed from the religious practices that belonged to Hinduism. Their subjugation manifested itself in a way that strengthened rather than weakened their feelings of tribal solidarity. By contrast, the Dublas of the central plain lacked the economic, political, social, and cultural space in which their communality could thrive. This contrast is the starting point for the next chapter, which considers the relations between landlords and farm labourers in the western part of south Gujarat in the first half of the nineteenth century.

Notes

1. Similar myths on the origin of agrestic slavery were narrated in other parts of India as well, for example, on the Malabar coast in 1828. 'When the God Parasharam divided the land amongst the Brahmans, they represented to him that if they were left to themselves, the lands would remain uncultivated. Accordingly, Parasharam went in search of the wild people, who at that time inhabited the jungles, collected them and presented them to the Brahmans', (Banaji 1933: 40).

2. 'Rama collected 18,000 men of the hill tribes and created the Brahmins. Sacrifice was performed on the banks of the river Ambika. For the sake of these Brahmins, Rama shot an arrow in the ground and a spring of hot Ganges gushed out. This is the Ukai spring in Bansda territory' (Khanapurkar, vol. i, 1944, pp. 7–8, see also the Report on the *Census of the Baroda Territories, 1881*, p. 146; *Gazetteer of the Bombay Presidency*, vol. ix, 1901, pp. 4–5; *Census of India, 1901*, vol. xviii, Baroda, part I, pp. 449, 477; *Census of India, 1931*, vol. xix, Baroda, part I, pp. 428, 431).

3. The Kanbis purified their behaviour so that they would be acceptable as intermediate-caste Hindus. Yet, they still held on to certain practices from their previous way of life. In this regard, Enthoven noted that the Kanbis or Patidars of Gujarat ... have much faith in sorcery, witchcraft, and the influence of the evil eye. In sickness or in difficulty they consult a sorcerer.... They believe in omens and signs (Enthoven 1920-2, vol. II: 141).

4. Bellasis said of them in 1854: 'They rudely till the soil but are very migratory and unsettled cultivators. Their use of the bow and arrow was indicative of a way of life in which hunting and gathering still played a major role. They cultivated only rough species of millet (kodra and nagli), used no tools and departed after sowing to return three or four months later for the harvest' *Gazetteer of the Bombay Presidency*, vol. ii, Gujarat: Surat and Broach, 1877: 62–3; see also S. Mehta 1934: 316.

5. S. Mehta, 'Marriage and Family Life in Gujarat', pp. 95–6.

6. See Misra, *The Rise of Muslim Power in Gujarat.*

7. For the significance and origins of this regulation see Guha, *A Rule of Property for Bengal.*

8. We get an altogether different portrait of Morison from sources quoted by Rabitoy in his essay on the introduction of land revenue administration in south Gujarat. According to the official correspondence referred to, Morison was a mediocre administrator who returned from the College of Fort William with a sentence of disapprobation and without knowledge of any Indian language. Hardly the most industrious of men, he relied completely on his head clerk Sukaram, a man against whom many patels and desais in Surat had filed complaints in a number of petitions sent to Bombay (Rabitoy 1975: 539 and 540–1).

9. I have written an essay on the origins of this myth, entitled 'The Shattered Image' (1988).

2

The System of Bonded Labour Revisited

Bondage and Patronage

The study presenting the results of my first fieldwork study in south Gujarat was entitled *Patronage and Exploitation*. I used these terms to try and indicate the essence of the relationship between landlords and landless labourers in the past. Since the Dublas lacked the means to provide for their own livelihood, they were attached to landowning households in a form of servitude which lasted for their whole lives and often continued into the next generation. The relationship was usually entered into when a high-caste landowner agreed to help a young Dubla man, often already working for him as a *govalio,* to get married, and because the young man did not have the resources to bear the cost involved, his future master would provide him with what he needed for this rite of passage. At the start of the nineteenth century, the necessary advance would be worth between ten and fifty rupees. It was not paid in cash but in the form of a quantity of grain—enough for the wedding meal and a few gifts, such as copper ornaments and articles of clothing— for the bride. By accepting the advance, the Dubla became a hali, committing himself to work for the master. He cultivated the fields throughout the year and did anything else his master requested. He had no set working hours and had to be ready to carry out orders day and night. The contract also included the hali's family members. His wife would work a few hours each day as a maid, washing clothes and the dishes, grinding the grain, fetching water from the well, cleaning out the cattle stalls, keeping the master's house clean and, if necessary, would also work in the fields. Her daughters would help her in these tasks and her sons looked after the cattle and often slept in the shed. In the morning and in the middle of the day, the hali would be given a meal, and at the end of the day he would receive his wages: enough grain (mostly millet) to meet the needs of himself and his family. He was permitted—or even instructed—to build his hut on the master's land and was given the materials needed to do so, mostly straw for the roof. The hut provided meagre shelter:

Their dwelling is a small hut, consisting of a single room; the walls made of cane plastered with mud, and the roof of thatch, some pieces of matting to sleep on and a few earthen-ware vessels, are all the furniture these huts contain (*Gazetteer of the Bombay Presidency* 1877, vol. ii: 199).

The hali would often also be granted permission to work a piece of land that belonged to his master *(vavla)* but could keep the yield for himself. In addition to his daily wage, the labourer would receive various perquisites paid in kind: clothing once a year, a blanket at the start of the winter, a pair of shoes to wear only on special occasions, and now and again—if the master was in a good mood—a little tobacco and a few annas to buy a drink or two. The master was obliged to ensure that the labourer could meet his basic needs. That meant that if there was little or no work, or if the hali was sick, he would still receive the customary grain allowance, but as an advance rather than as wages. As a consequence, the debt with which the relationship started increased as time passed because after all, the hali's low wage was barely enough to live on. By allowing the hali to supplement his income, for example, with the yield from the vavla, the master tried to ensure that he did not become even more indebted but, in reality, it was impossible to pay off the debt. Because the hali's low income did not extend to celebrations in the household, like births and marriages, or setbacks, such as illness or death, the debt grew larger rather than smaller. This cumulative shortfall in income forced the labourer to remain attached to the master, and because it was impossible to end the relationship—which had been entered into voluntarily—the contract took on the characteristics of servitude.[1] After a lifetime's work, the hali was just as poor as when he entered his master's service. Then it would be the turn of his son to seek support in getting married. He would approach his father's master before offering his services to another landowner. After all, he had grown up thanks to the generosity shown to his father.

I have characterized the social reproduction of the underclass at this extremely low level as exploitation. The Dublas were confined in an agrarian system which had relegated them to a state of landlessness and in which they could survive only by selling their labour to landowners whose predecessors had colonized the region. The report on the first cadastral survey in Chikhli taluka summarizes the situation as follows:

The Desais ... had the privilege of paying the lower rates of assessment allowed for the Kali Paraj, and have managed through the influence in the revenue administration of the parganna they have retained from the time of our predecessors in the country an influence so great, as to lead to the adoption of special measures, on the first introduction of British rule, to lessen it, and by pandering to the passion of these degraded creatures for drink, treating them at the same time with a rude sort of kindness, to get possession of the richest lands and cultivate them at the minimum of expense through their Halis (Prescott 1865: 62–3).

The 'rude sort of kindness' referred to above gives me the opportunity to explain the term 'patronage' in the title of my book. As I already said, the labourer did not bond himself to his master under duress. It was impossible to end the relationship because what the hali received by way of payment did not allow him to meet the basic needs of himself and his household. On top of the initial advance came even more new 'loans' which the labourer simply could not afford to repay with what he earned with his labour power and the balance never became a surplus. Bondage could therefore be seen as the essence of the *halipratha* system. This interpretation, however, suggests incorrectly that the main motivation for the Dubla's behaviour was to bring the relationship to an end. The fact is that neither he nor his master sought for the advance to be paid off. Although the latter tried to ensure that the outstanding 'debt' stayed within the bounds of reason, the hali was convinced that the services he rendered would never generate enough to meet his minimal needs. What his master was prepared to grant him in addition to his basic wage was in fact an indispensable supplement to make up the shortfall. The economic security the relationship offered because of this explains why the Dublas preferred to bond themselves to a master in this way. Reports that the halis were better off than Dublas who had to make a living as unattached workers must be viewed in this light. This perspective that bonded labourers must be envied rather than pitied is reflected in their name for the master: *dhaniamo, he who bestows wealth.*

These comments force us to modify the interpretation of halipratha as a form of labour bondage, although in this standard view the economic dimension of the relationship between master and labourer remains of pivotal importance. A different perspective sees landlords as taking labourers into their service not only, or not even primarily, because they needed them to farm their land. They were driven more by their desire to sustain the leisurely lifestyle they, as patrons, were accustomed to lead. The members of this elite surrounded themselves with an entourage as an expression of their political power and social eminence. For example, the man authorized to collect the taxes in Navsari treated the peasants as his subjects, as if he himself were the Gaekwad, the prince of Baroda. When, after persistent complaints, this tax farmer was finally removed from his position, he was awarded not only a one-off compensation payment of 200,000 rupees, but a separate annual allowance to enable him to keep a carriage and a sedan chair. The desai of Bulsar was bought off in the same generous manner (Wallace 1863: 468). The most prominent tax farmers acted like *rajah*s and their status afforded them political and judicial authority that made their positions virtually unassailable.

Apart from the monetary and village grants some *desais* had their own insignia: a cannon, a *phalki*, a canopy and a *chamar*, and had their own torch-bearers and attendants. Moreover they had the rights of being gifted in kind or cash by various other communities under customary law (Naik 1957: 178).

The decision by the colonial administration to no longer make use of their services meant that the desais were cut off from their most important source of income and lost the power and privileges that went with their position. The introduction of the ryotwari system institutionalized an administrative apparatus that extended from the Collector in the district headquarters to the village officials. Since this restructuring took several decades, the dislocation of the desais was also a gradual process. Behind the scenes, many of them continued to be influential, not infrequently holding positions in the colonial bureaucracy; nevertheless, the Anavil Brahmans lost their prominence in south Gujarat. The transition was not easy. The former tax farmers persisted with the lifestyle to which they were accustomed but now lacked the resources and the public exposure to do so. Administrative reports were critical of their extravagance and saw it as evidence of a superiority they no longer possessed. Yet within their own caste, respect for the Desai[2] families was unabated. They could, after all, boast a past that placed them above the other Anavils, the Bhathelas, who firmly belonged to the peasantry. It was because of the hypergamous relationship between the two groups that the latter considered it an honour to wed their daughters to the sons of the Anavils, and were prepared to pay a large dowry to ensure that these brides from a lower social category were accepted. The financial rewards of such arranged marriages were so great, often embracing not only the dowry but a continuous flow of gifts that the bride's family were obliged to give to her husband in the years following the wedding, that some Desais were tempted to marry more than one Bhathela woman. This practice sometimes meant that the first wife was neglected, and could result in her committing suicide (Naik 1957: 7).

The loss of status of the tax farmers by no means meant that they were plunged into poverty. They lost their official status but were allowed to keep the land they owned. In carrying out their previous functions, they had been able to acquire a disproportionate share of all agricultural property. As an additional benefit, they were also able to claim a lower tax rate for their land on the basis of the argument that it was worked by the kaliparaj, their Dubla labourers. As landowners, the Desais remained part of the rural elite, but they lacked the will to actually go back to a peasant way of life. It was beneath their dignity to till the land they owned and soon their idleness became legendary.

The Bhathella Desais, owing to their influence and cunning, have succeeded hitherto in keeping the Government demand to a disproportionately low figure, which enables them to take less personal interest in the cultivation of the land. Hence all the fine masonry wells in Eroo are out of order, and the Dab, a weed which may be aptly called the Nemesis of improvident tillage, holds up its head to reprove the Desai, who thinks it beneath him to be a farmer in the sense the Kaira Desai is. His pride takes another form, the pride of caste and privilege to marry 3 and 4 wives from the cultivating Bhathella class, who give him from 2000 to 4000 Rs to effect a settlement for their daughters in his home (Beyts 1868: 11).

In contrast to the Desais their fellow caste members, the Bhathelas, were thriving as never before. British officials praised them as good farmers but difficult subjects who would provide no reliable information on how much land they owned or anything else for that matter, and always tried to evade the taxes imposed on them. Some were in debt, but that was because they had entered into social commitments that went beyond what they could afford. They had better houses and more agrarian capital (land, cattle, and farm equipment) than other peasant castes. When giving details of their possessions they never forgot to mention how many servants they had. The Bhathelas attributed their economic success to the low wages they imposed on their halis.

Bhatella Brahmins are, if anything, superior to Koonbees because, in addition to better status, they have the privilege of free labour from their Hallees or bondsmen who are as a body devoted to their master's interest and reside on the farm, a circumstance which accounts for the Bhatella holdings being more generally attended to, and worked to the best of their advantage (ibid.: 8).

They modelled their behaviour on that of the Desais and acted like petty rajahs. By avoiding agricultural work as much as possible, especially ploughing the land, they showed that they ranked far above the common peasants. The halis fitted in with this lifestyle, as clients who enjoyed their protection and support. The number of servants a patron had under his protection was an indication of his status. The main criterion was not how many halis he needed, but how many he could afford. This attitude made it clear that social and political considerations were of great importance in placing the master–servant relationship in the right context. As halis the Dublas were not only farm labourers but also clients who, by displaying deference and obedience to their dhaniamo, emphasized his status and power. With their servile behaviour, the servants added lustre to parties and receptions in the house of the master. Until the middle of the twentieth century, it was customary for farmhands and housemaids to sing the praises of their employer and his grandeur:

...on the next day of *Holi,* the Dubla women in every village go to the house of their *dhaniamas,* dance and sing songs in their praise, describing the stately mansion of their master, with a lamp in every niche and with diamonds and rubies in plenty, with a house full of women folk, daughters-in-law and servants (P.G. Shah 1958: 144).

The seigneurial style of the patron meant that he had to treat his underlings with generosity and affection. The first survey and settlement report for the subdistrict of Chikhli called the Dublas 'the most degraded in their circumstances and character of all agricultural classes'. Most of them were halis, whom the reporter classified as slaves of the Desais and Bhathelas, but he qualified this opinion with the following remark:

From close enquiries I have made, I can say with certainty that these poor people are treated with kindness and consideration, and are looked upon as humble dependents who have great claims on their masters and their families (Prescott 1865: 51).

The life of a petty rajah required the presence of clients to command the respect that became such a patron. As prominent citizens, the Anavils had shared interests which they defended against outsiders, but they were also each other's competitors for status and power. The hali was expected to support his master, while he tried to bring his rivals into disrepute by trying to persuade their servants to be disloyal. If a hali let his master down in some way, it was always possible that they had been moved to do so by a third party. The members of the dominant caste were always assertive with each other, full of suspicion and envy, and were not afraid of expressing these feelings in their dealings with the colonial administration.

I would have passed over any allusion to the character of the Bhatellas, were they not a power in the community, exercising great influence over the minds of the people who are numerically stronger than themselves. Captain Newport thus photographs them in 1822: My intercourse with the Bhatella Brahmins has been extensive and intimate, and as individuals I found them obsequious and servile when they expected benefit; would seldom or never answer a question direct until its object had been guessed at, and then, guided by interested motives, would either evade it by pretended ignorance or by direct falsehood. Indeed experience has proved to Government that some of the most respectable are not trustworthy (Beyts 1868: 9).

In the above report, servants are identified as Dublas and masters as Anavil Brahmans but this was not always the case. First of all, although the majority of Dublas were halis, not all of them were labourers. The sources do not specify how those members of this tribal caste who remained unbonded made a living or what their economic situation was. To assume that this minority chose to live and work in freedom is less plausible than that, for a variety of reasons, they had not succeeded in finding a master who was prepared to provide them with a livelihood. The fact that the status of a bonded labourer was not seen as inferior suggests that the latter reason was more likely.

No social degradation attaches to the position of a Hali. Men of this class intermarry with the independent members of their own tribe (*Gazetteer of the Bombay Presidency*, vol. ii, 1877: 198).

In addition, there appear to have been varying degrees of labour bondage. The *bhandela* halis were always available to attend to their master's wishes and were entirely dependent on him for all their own needs, while the *chhuta* halis worked only on days that they were needed and did not receive an annual bonus in the form of clothing, etc. They could, however, obtain an advance if they asked for it. If the master had no work for them they could offer their services to other landowners and keep whatever they earned. Since this information comes from a source dating from the early twentieth century, it is possible that the gradation in degrees of bondage among halis only emerged in the late nineteenth century (*Revision Settlement Report of the Palsana taluka* 1911: 5).

Secondly, although the majority of halis were Dublas, they could also come from other kaliparaj groups. The 1877 *Gazetteer* listed their different social identities:

They are to be found throughout the district, and belong to different branches of the aboriginal population. In Mandvi they are Chodhras; in Pardi, Naikas; in Bulsar Dhondhias; and Dublas in all parts of the District. Kolis, though reckoned to the fair races, contain among their number, families who have sunk into the position of serfs (vol. II: 197–8).

What labourers from different backgrounds had in common was that they invariably belonged to poor and low-ranking categories that sought the protection of a master because they were unable to provide for their own basic needs. The masters, too, came from different groups. The records do not make it clear whether all Anavil Brahmans kept halis. Many Bhathelas and their wives still worked the land themselves and it was beyond the means of many of these small-scale landowners to keep bonded labourers. Nor were all dhaniamos Anavil Brahmans—Kanbis and Bohras with a larger than average plot of land kept halis, and Parsis and Baniyas, who were only involved in agriculture at a distance, had halis as house servants. Interestingly, in the late colonial era, a number of tribal landowners also employed bonded labourers. A survey of the Chodhras in the north of Surat district, conducted around 1930, showed that a process of economic differentiation had been set in motion. Members of this tribal community who had become landless were faced with no other choice than to bond themselves to the households of large landowners. They were known as halis but, according to the author of the study, their living conditions were incomparably better than those of the halis employed by members of the higher castes on the central plain.

There is a marked contrast in the treatment and status of a hali in an Ujliparaj family, and a hali of an aboriginal peasant-proprietor. In a Raniparaj family, the hali remains a member of the family and enjoys all rights and privileges enjoyed by a member of the family. He takes the same food as his master and often dines with him, he dresses almost like him, and sleeps in the same room near him. He is hardly ever scolded and never penalized (B.H. Mehta 1933: 542).

This shows that the master–servant relationship was more a matter of lifestyle than social identity. The Bohras, for example, were Muslims while the Parsis practised their own religion, but both engaged halis. Yet, despite all these variations, many studies continued to associate bonded labourers with the Dublas and most of the masters with the Anavil landowners (Choksey 1968: 55).

The Colonial View

How did the colonial administration view the institution of halipratha? The officials responsible for setting up the agricultural system in newly acquired districts mentioned in their reports the large number of slaves kept by the landowners. In 1815, the first Collector of Surat wrote:

The Dessaees Buttela Brahmuns in Parchole Soopa, and some other Pergunnahs, possess as large a portion of slaves as may be found perhaps in any part of India. Those who are frequently attached to the soil, as well as bond-servants who voluntarily engage to labour in payment of loans made to them for their marriages, or the like occasions, at times run away from their master, and such cases are brought before the Magistrate. Sometimes the master is to blame and sometimes the servant, and no particular inferences arise on the cases of this I am acquainted with as to the treatment of slaves. The slaves are all of the Coolee Dooblas, and other poor classes of the Hindoos, who are in this zillah much addicted to drinking toddy, and a very debauched, improvident and inferior race. I believe the slaves to be more comfortable than the free portion of their respective castes (Lumsden, 8 August 1815).[3]

This memorandum was in reply to a circular letter in which the authorities asked for information and advice on how to prevent slavery in the possessions of the East India Company, a circular that was part of an extensive colonial survey conducted in preparation for a parliamentary debate on slavery in Britain. Reporting on the status of slavery was so protracted because the issue was on the political agenda for very a long period.[4] Memoranda from 1835–6 were apparently intended to reconsider the use of the term 'slavery', pointing out that the halis in Surat district were so called because they ploughed the land (*hal* = plough).

They are persons, or their offspring, who have sold their labour for an advance of money, and who are bound to serve the lender and its heir, until they are able to repay the sum. They almost entirely consist of Dooblas and other low castes of Hindoos. The master is bound to feed and clothe them, give them a piece of land and to defray their marriage expenses, the sum laid out on the latter however being added to the original amount, for which their services became his (Grant, quoted in Banaji 1933).

In the same document, this official noted that halis could not be transferred to another master against their will. He considered it impossible to establish the legal rights of both parties, but was of the opinion that, according to the customs of the country, the property rights of the master should be recognized. The Collector of Surat described the halis as 'hereditary bondsmen'. They were obliged to work for their master, because, after all, he had paid for their upbringing and marriage, and they could only become free again by paying off their debts.

The authorities modified their opinion of the halipratha, describing it as a form of voluntary servitude. It was, in this revised assessment, entered into voluntarily and maintained by the bonded debt of the hali. Refuting the earlier idea that it was a relationship based on coercion, official statements now suggested that the halis were usually treated well and, when questioned, indicated that they did not seem to mind their lack of freedom.

The reason why he sticks to the Dhaniama is that he helps him on all occasions of death, marriage, etc. In a way the Dhaniama is his Sahukar [moneylender]. I called a few Hallees of each kind and questioned them closely and to my great surprise found that they were quite contented with their lot (*Revision Settlement Report of the Palsana taluka* 1911: 5).

Collector Lumsden had already observed in 1825 that, in his opinion, the halis were better off than the Dublas who had no master. Half a century later, this had become the authorized view : '...*halis* are still, as a rule, better off than those of their clan who are free labourers' (*Gazetteer of the Bombay Presidency*, vol. ii, 1877: 200–1). I would like to note, however, that such statements should not be taken at face value. Even if they were based on face-to-face communication, the information given was probably hearsay, gathered from conversations at which masters were present and could have acted as translators between the reporter and the halis. High-ranking colonial administrators would only rarely, if at all, come into direct contact with the agrarian underclass.

Notwithstanding this possible distortion in the colonial sources as a result of biased information, the 'free' choice of landless labourers to enter into servitude was quite understandable given the lack of alternative means of survival. In bondage they knew that, throughout the year, they were guaranteed either work or an allowance that would ensure that they could fulfil their basic needs. In contrast to opinions insisting that the bondage practised was not so bad, there were other voices which spoke out strongly against the ongoing practice of agrestic slavery, considered to be much worse in India than in the Caribbean:

I have been in two English slave-colonies and one French, and in none of them have I seen anything to be compared with the utterly abject and wretched state and inhuman appearance of the Cherumars on the Malabar Coast. Witness Colonel Welsh narrated his own experience from 1817–9 in the region which is now Kerala. 'The general condition of the agrestic slaves was everywhere bad. They enjoyed little comfort, had coarse, precarious and scanty food, insufficient clothing and frequently none at all; and there was no provision to protect them in their old age and sickness (*Report of the Select Committee of the House of Commons*, 1832, Appendix paras 3 and 5, p. 449).

On the other hand, several officials maintained that slavery in India was not of such a distressing nature as to call for the government's intervention. According to them, these slaves were well treated and had no reason to complain of their lack of freedom. Out of indifference and apathy, they showed themselves to be not interested at all in their emancipation (Banaji 1933: 20). Other arguments were also voiced against prohibiting what had always been sanctioned. Thus the warning of William Chaplin, the Commissioner of the Deccan in Bombay Presidency in 1823:

... all at once to stop the purchase or sale would be equipollant to the destruction of what always has been deemed a marketable commodity, and it would be at variance with the spirit of rule which is to follow the usages of the country (Chaplin 1824).

The authorities held different opinions on how often halis ran away, but they agreed that in legal disputes, when intervention became unavoidable, they should place the interests of the masters first. In 1837, the Political Commissioner for Gujarat warned that any other strategy would contravene the landowners' sense of justice and could lead to discontentment:

Claims for the restoration of fugitive slaves are by no means infrequent; and in such a rude state of society as exists in this province, non-compliance would not only be regarded as great injustice, but be apt to lead to acts of violence and retaliation. I would, therefore, suggest that, except when decided ill-treatment appears to have taken place, I should be authorised to interfere to cause the restoration of run-away slaves, or compensation and satisfaction to their owners from the parties obtaining them (Sutherland, in Banaji 1933: 318).

The picture that emerges largely confirms the interpretation by Gyan Prakash of the master–servant relationship, on the basis of his analysis of colonial sources.[5] It was seen firstly as a labour arrangement founded on the deprivation of freedom and secondly, as being created and sustained by the indebtedness of the servant to his master. This view, according to Prakash, was based on the assumption that unfree labour was an aberration that stood in the way of social progress. Free labour would eventually also triumph in India and the administration had a duty to promote this process. In contrast to this colonial interpretation, Prakash claimed that although the bonded nature of the relationship between the farmhand and his master was an expression of an unequal relationship in the past, the need for labour must not be seen as the cause of bondage. According to him, halipratha institutionalized a state of dependence in agrarian society. The interaction between master and servant was the organizing principle of a form of servitude in which labour performance was only one aspect of a more comprehensive relationship revolving around domination and subordination. What should have been seen as a manifestation of social hierarchy was reduced in the colonial records to an economic transaction and classified as a form of debt bondage. In legal terms, the bonded labourer lost his freedom when he accepted the loan, expressed in monetary terms and sealed with a contract that robbed him of the power to decide how, where, and to whom he should sell his labour power for the duration of his servitude. The conclusion drawn by Prakash from this argument is that the history of bondage went back to the start of British domination, not earlier. His argument, presented in postmodern jargon, concludes with the statement that the alleged lack of freedom of groups like the halis in Surat district represented a break with the *ancien regime*, that '...far from being a relic of pre-modern times, was constructed by the colonial discourse of freedom' (Prakash 1990: 220).

Although I agree with Prakash that halipratha took on the character of a patron–client relationship, I tend to attach greater importance to the economic dimension and, more significantly, to emphasize that labourers were clearly attached to their masters in a state of bondage in the pre-colonial era. To suggest, as he does, that this perception is the result of colonial ignorance regarding how society was structured, denies the awareness on the part of both landowners and landless that the unequal relationship between them was clearly given an extra dimension by the subjugation that secured a far-reaching and permanent claim on the labour power of the hali.[6] As we have seen, neither party strove to terminate the relationship into which they had entered, nor were they eager to clear the 'debt' on which it was based. In this respect Prakash is right to correct early colonial reports which claimed that the master used the advance payment as a contract to force the labourer into servitude. I disagree, however, with his claim that the halis only became unfree labourers under British rule and, in the social and political order that preceded it, could be considered only as '...dependent servants of dominant landlords' (Prakash 1990: 81).

My view of halipratha in the early colonial economy of south Gujarat is the same as in the account on my first fieldwork study: in spite of the prominence I attribute to the patron–client aspect of the relationship, I still believe that the tie between master and servant was primarily driven by economic motives—for the master, it was the need for additional labour and for the labourer, it was maximum socio-economic security.

Landowners who could afford to do so took on a hali so that they themselves no longer had to perform manual work—engaging a servant was the first thing landowners did as soon as their economic condition improved. When the prices of agricultural products rose shortly after the middle of the nineteenth century, peasants displayed their greater well-being and leisure by taking on one or more attached labourers (*Gazetteer of the Bombay Presidency*, vol. ii, 1877: 197). Their motives were not entirely economic—they also aspired to a higher social status, but being able to command the labour power of others was a necessary condition for acquiring it. A primary consideration in assessing this situation is that the agrarian gentry that emerged in south Gujarat gradually extended the land for agricultural production by recruiting an army of farmhands from an underclass that had been kept in a state of landlessness. Opening up the area for cultivation was a historical process set in motion long before the colonial period and which generated an agrarian system based on servitude. After the land had been made fit for tilling, the labour power of the halis continued to be necessary to level out the higher and more extensively used *jarayat* land and prepare it for rice cultivation. In the slack season, the masters set their labourers to work on digging wells so that the irrigated area could be extended. These wells were known as *kachha*, indicating that they were little more than deep holes in the ground which had to be replaced at the end of each season.

The same applied to the ditches surrounding the fields, but the records have little to say about this gradual upgrading of agricultural resources by irrigating dry land. Lastly, the colonial sources make a clear link between the labour intensity of the crop schedule and the size of the hali population. Without the halis, the cultivation of sugarcane, an important commodity in the early colonial economy, would have been impossible.

From the perspective of the landless labourers the guarantee of sufficient work was an important motive for accepting their condition of servitude. Although a master was obliged to provide for his servants in the slack season, there was a greater chance of him failing to fulfil this duty if his client's labour power was not very productive. A patron with a lot of land and a wide variety of crops had little difficulty in finding halis prepared to bond themselves to him. The Deputy Collector of Surat went on record condemning the 'bad qualities' of the bonded labourers:

> If the master is a good cultivator, having wet crops such as sugarcane, ginger, potatoes, graft mangoes, etc., Halis are not inclined to run away as they get many opportunities to satisfy their thieving propensities (Deputy Collector of Surat N.M. Parikhji, *Census of India*, vol. viii, part I, 1922: 221).

As we have seen, the need for food security was the primary motive for the Dublas to enter into a relationship based on bondage and to see their master as a benefactor. They did so because there were no other, more attractive alternatives to enable them to meet their basic needs. But what prevented them from working and living as free labourers? According to the colonial sources a certain percentage of the Dublas did remain unbonded—a statement made all the more intriguing because the records provide no further details on the size of this minority or how they made a living. Were they independent in the sense that they did not have a permanent employer? Were they 'free' because they chose to avoid servitude or were they unable to find a master who was prepared to attach them to him. I conclude from the repeatedly heard claim made in colonial sources that they were worse off than the halis and that this choice was not made of their own free will. In other words, their 'freedom' was not a conscious and wilful decision on their part but due to the reluctance of landowners to take responsibility for them. This might simply have been because supply of labour exceeded demand, or because these individuals lacked the necessary qualities expected of halis: willingness to work, obedience, and loyalty accompanied by an explicit display of servility. However, declining prosperity among the landowners was also a significant factor. Servants taken on in boom periods would be released again when times were bad. According to the report on the revised survey and settlement in Chikhli taluka at the end of the nineteenth century, 'Halis are no longer maintained as the Anaolas find it hard enough to feed themselves, let alone their Halis' (Maconochie, *Revised Survey and Settlement Report on Chikhli taluka*, 1897).[7] The 1901 census report also stated that, during the serious famine of 1899–1900, many landowners were no longer able to support their farmhands (*Census of India 1901*, vol. xviii, Baroda, part I, 72–3). Such fluctuations indicate that the halis were part of a broader underclass of landless labourers, a segment of which were not even eligible for a life as bonded servants. As agricultural labourers and as clients, they were for too numerous and in excess to the demand for labour.

The landless were a social residue and were recorded as such in the colonial chronicles. Quotations in the preceding pages show that many officials tended not only to see the intense poverty of the halis as the reason for their servitude but also attributed their lack of basic security to their own shortcomings. In an early official report in response to a survey of the incidence of slavery commissioned by his superiors, the Collector of Surat district described the Dublas as a bunch of drunkards, blamed them for their immoral behaviour and their inability to live according to their means, and concluded his negative judgment by calling them an inferior species (Lumsden, 8 August 1825). This view had not changed by the end of the colonial era. The Census of 1931 gave the etymological meaning of the word Dubla as 'weak' (vol. xix, Baroda, part I, 1932: 460), and the derogatory meaning of the name survived after Independence too. P.G. Shah's ethnography of the Dublas begins with the comment that they worked considerably less hard than agricultural labourers from other castes. They were suitable as halis because they were so servile towards their masters.

…the Dubla is much in demand as a Hali by being a reliable and trustworthy employee even though he suffers from fits of laziness or dullness (P.G. Shah 1958: 24–5).

Internalization of Servitude?

The superiority of the master was validated by the subordinate behaviour he imposed on his halis. The well-being of the former contrasted sharply with the deprivation of the latter. The hali was in effect part of the property of the patron. Having no possessions of his own, he was the recipient of gifts from his benefactor, 'riches' that enabled him barely to survive. The great divide between them in material status was however mitigated by a way of life marked not only by their differences but also by how much they shared. The master, for example, ate the same food that he gave to his hali (*Gazetteer of the Bombay Presidency*, vol. II, 1877: 199) and allowed him, his wife, and children into the intimacy of the household. For his part, the hali could expect generosity if he showed his appreciation for his state of servitude.

The master on the other hand always appreciated this loyalty and put a premium on it by raising the status of his faithful Dubla. There was not much of material reward but the labourer was admitted more and more into the confidence of the master, given a freer hand in his work, allowed a sort of familiarity and intimacy with the master's family and was trusted with work of a more delicate nature than that of a purely agricultural labourer (Kishore 1924: 427).

The presentation of the master–servant relationship in this way concurs with the ideology of patronage which focuses on the desirable behaviour of both parties and their mutual affection. As I have mentioned earlier, this interpretation leads Prakash to define groups like the halis in south Gujarat not as bonded labourers but as the dependent servants of dominant lords. The same perception can be detected in the literature on my area of fieldwork. In the middle of the twentieth century, a close associate of Mahatma Gandhi spoke of halipratha in similar terms:

It has become a matter of prestige in the Dubla community to be a Hali, to work for a Dhaniamo. As a woman has no prestige in society without having married a husband, similarly a Halpati without a Dhaniamo as his master has no prestige in his community (Dave 1946: 18).

This statement implies that the halis internalized the dependence in which they lived and worked. Something of the power and status enjoyed by the master reflected on them. A Dubla who belonged to the entourage of a prominent Anavil was proud of being associated with such an influential figure and seemed to have no problem with the subservience that was expected of him. But, in my view, such stirring testimonies to vertical solidarity present an exaggerated picture of the patron as a benevolent and generous provider of wealth and welfare, while ignoring less attractive characteristics like the abuse of power, exploitation, and degradation. The domination of the patron was also expressed in the arbitrary fashion in which he granted or withheld favours. This capriciousness had its roots in the prerogative that comes with dominance and cannot be written off as a matter of personal preference. The patron was free to indulge his whims without being challenged to account for his arbitrariness. He could decide whether or not to provide a loan, and even the distribution of the grain allowance at the end of the day was not so much a ritual display of benevolence as an opportunity to express his displeasure at the quality of the work performed, and scorn for the neglect and absenteeism of the servants. I have already mentioned that Anavil Brahmans had a reputation for being abusive, suspicious, and stubborn, always looking out for their own interests and ready to start an argument. These are qualities that go with dominant behaviour. There is a popular saying that bears witness to their coarse and even filthy use of language: 'A Bhathela's mouth was opened with a hatchet' (Bellasis 1854). Their halis were the first victims of this treatment. Besides being kicked and hit, the labourers were browbeaten verbally. How did the labourers respond to this treatment? The obvious answer would be that they did their utmost to please their masters by being docile and obedient, and to do nothing that might cause them to take offence—in short, to act as exemplary clients. This would seem logical given their total dependence on the master for shelter, food, and credit. But if their basic needs were not minimally satisfied and the master withheld the support and protection to which they were entitled according to the code of patronage, the halis would also make it clear that there were limits to their servitude. The vulnerability of their situation did not prevent them from resorting to obstruction, sabotage, lethargy, displays of ignorance, evasion, and other weapons from the subaltern arsenal. Although the image of the relationship between master and servant presented to the outside world was one of generosity on the part of the former and gratitude on that of the latter, it was in many cases characterized by brutality on the one hand and tenacious resistance on the other. The veiled but obstinate refusal 'to behave' that typified the landless class did not escape the notice of outsiders.

· … obstinacy of temperament is a common feature of Dubla life whether it represents a man, a woman, or a child. If a Dubla has made up his mind not to work on a particular day, it is generally difficult to make him change his mind; also when he makes up his mind to do any work, it is equally difficult to divert his mind to other pursuits. If he is well fed and treated well, he can stand hours of work in the field and can turn out good crops; he is, however, sensitive to bad treatment and if jolted, the output of work is at once brought down (P.G. Shah 1958: 25).

The author of this passage tends to explain what is intended as a protest against the capriciousness of the dominant power as an expression of slavish subservience. Generations of servitude had supposedly robbed the Dublas of all vitality and reduced them to creatures without even the strength to stand on their own two feet. This confirmed the colonial view that the halis had only themselves to blame for the regime of bondage under which they lived.

Another aspect of domination, designed to keep those who are subservient at arm's length, also contradicts the portrayal of the patron-client relationship in terms of mutual affection and an intense concern with each other's welfare. In spite of the daily presence of the hali, his wife, and children in the master's household and the bond between their families that has often lasted generations, the Dublas were not admitted to the religious practices of Hinduism. Although the Anavil Brahmans needed halis to increase their ritual status, the latter continued to practise religious customs which caste Hindus considered inferior. Certainly, halis acquired a role in the ceremonies of their masters, but this was always in a way that demonstrated their servitude and confirmed the respectability of their benefactor. It was because they earned so little and their masters required that they be at their disposal at all hours of the day and night in a kind of beck-and-call relationship based on physical proximity, the labourers had neither the time nor the money to enable a recognition that they were true believers of the Hindu faith. Their poverty and lack of time to call their own were, however, not the only obstacles preventing them from living as fully fledged Hindus. Their exclusion was inextricably linked to the relationship of domination and subordination. After centuries in the immediate vicinity of Hindus who had raised their own religious status by subordinating the Dublas, the latter were classified in the colonial records as semi-Hindus. It was a 'half-way' label that left unclear what they had been and what they had not become.

The religious exclusion of the Dublas also had another aspect, however, which could be used to resist the regime of subordination in which they were confined. Like all tribal people, they indulged in animistic practices which the caste Hindus considered repugnant but to which the Dublas attributed magical powers to defend themselves if they felt threatened or aggrieved. Although a secretive source of resistance, it did not go unnoticed in the early colonial reports:

...they sometimes reverence a tree, sometimes a stone placed by nature in a curious position... and are much dreaded for their witchcraft by other classes of society (Bellasis 1854: 4)[8]; ...generally the higher classes fear the magic of the lower classes. The fear is often the only means a Mhar or a Mhang has of making the higher classes pay him his customary dues (Campbell 1885: 144–5).

If the halis did resist it was invariably on an individual basis. Nowhere in the colonial records did I find evidence of resistance against their servitude in the form of collective action. The social setting in which the halipratha was located did not provide the space in which such horizontal solidarity could flourish. The labourers and their families were bound to the master, were given permission or were even required to build their huts on his land and were at all times and in all respects within the direct reach of the dhaniamo. It could be said that the regime of subservience entailed a way of life which ensured that the halis had no regular or intensive contact with other members of their own community. Did this mean that they were under close and constant surveillance, and had no opportunity to compare their own experience with that of others, to discuss their grievances with them, or how they might improve the lot they all shared? Again, this interpretation is in line with the doctrine of domination which excludes the articulation of subordination in any collective form whatsoever. In my opinion, this view is too rigid; I suspect that the landless underclass from which the servants were recruited did actively resist the supremacy of their masters, who demanded complete submission and made no concession to resistance from below. Tanika Sarkar describes this culture of resistance as follows:

Within the outer arch of assimilation and hegemonization by the ideology of dominant groups, an inner, almost completely closed world, of primitive survival existed for slaves and bondsmen. This was their 'living space', an area of autonomy set apart from their master's domination and control. It was also a comprehension of their dark, helpless, primeval and precarious existence which they elliptically identified as their entire universe (Sarkar 1985: 122).[9]

Without doubt, living in the shadow of the village elite entailed avoiding behaviour that might cause offence. And that certainly included any demonstration in word or deed of collective awareness. Although the colonial reports contain little concrete information on the origins and history of the tribal ties that made them a distinct social group, the Dublas did have their own community, which was subdivided into clans. The members of each clan saw each other either as close or more distant family. These bonds of kinship safeguarded cohesion within the immediate circle, structured relationships between the members of the clan, ensured compliance with rules of conduct on the basis of a system of dos and don'ts, and designated leaders to represent the community and settle disputes within the group and with outsiders. Without going into further detail,[10] I wish to point out that halis also used the ties between themselves and with other Dublas to increase their distance from the landowners and protect themselves as individuals. But even retreat into the intimacy of the nuclear family and finding strength in their togetherness is denied to them by their ethnographer. He implied that the hali and his wife interacted more with their master than with each other and their children, sent to work already at very young age, grew up with no respect for their parents:

The parents and children behave without any restrictions among themselves and a general lack of discipline prevails, e.g. it is not considered improper for the children to speak obscene words, or smoke *bidi* in presence of the parents (P.G. Shah 1958: 42).

As I have already observed, the Dublas did not possess sufficient social consciousness to rise up en masse in protest first at their exclusion from the ownership of land and then at the yoke of servitude to which most of them were subjected. The conditions they lived in were not conducive to presenting a united front. Their resistance—the ultimate expression of which was deserting their master—was individual and not collective, incidental rather than systematic, spontaneous rather than organized or planned in advance. One aspect that must be emphasized is that the ultimate step of desertion was preceded by a whole range of signals indicating the hali's feelings of discontentment. The tension in the relationship with the master started with small, insignificant dis- agreements, rapidly progressing to more serious clashes, and ending with the breaking of the bond. Yet halis who actually took this final step were more the exception than the rule—not only because subordinates in general lose out to those who hold power over them, but also because desertion offered little prospect of a better life. Such acts of desperation were not inspired by the opportunity to escape bondage. At best the deserter could hope to find a master who was less brutal than his present one. Furthermore, there were many other considerations that would discourage him from taking the ultimate step. He was more likely to reconcile himself to his fate than allow it to come to a permanent break, with all the attendant risks and unpredictable consequences. In many cases, runaway halis would return to their masters of their own accord (Kishore 1924). It was a different matter of course if one of the hali's patron's rivals had persuaded him to leave, promising that he could enter into his service instead. In such cases, which were by no means rare, the hali was a pawn in a power game. Without external encouragement, clients found it difficult to break the tie with their patron. The code of patronage told them that to do so was a sin.

Loyalty to the master figured as an important item in their moral code. They looked down upon those who were not and very often would not have anything to do with such deserters (Kishore 1924: 427).

Other sources speak of the threat that the children of the runaway halis would be punished for the immoral conduct of their fathers.

...the Dhaniamas, belonging to the higher castes have sedulously developed a deep-rooted feeling among the Halis that running away from the master is a great sin for which God will punish the Hali's descendants (*Report of the Congress Agrarian Reforms Committee* 1951: 129).

Such threats are indicative of the pressure to which halis were exposed but to interpret them as proof that subjugation had been internalized would be a misconception. In my view, runaway halis were more afraid of the wrath of the master, Fearing that he would make every effort to track them down and bring them back. Remarkably often, runaways tried to flee to their wife's village, undoubtedly in the hope that the dhaniamo's influence would not reach so far. In this they were mistaken, since the landowners had agreed not to take on anyone who did not have the explicit permission of his former master. If a newly engaged hali proved to be a deserter, his new boss had no choice other than to send him back or compensate the lawful owner for his loss. It was certain that the deserter's disloyalty would not go unpunished.

Legal Constructions

The attitude of the colonial authorities to halipratha has already been discussed. From the beginning they left no doubt that they saw the halis as bonded labourers. Was this view justified? I share Prakash's view that the relationship between master and servant must not be seen as one based on indebtedness. It may have started with an advance payment, but the suggestion that it was sustained by the hali's inability to repay the debt was misplaced. Neither the provider nor the recipient of the 'loan' aspired to clear it with the intention of bringing the relationship to an end. The fact that it grew in the course of time was a direct consequence of a subsistence allowance that was too low for the hali to survive. But I differ from Prakash in that I do not see bondage as a pertinently inaccurate description of the regime under which these labourers lived.

Moreover, what Prakash observed in early colonial Bihar—the transformation of what had once been a manifestation of hierarchy into a labour relationship—did not apply in south Gujarat. As evidence for his interpretation, he claims that the landowners sealed the contract with a document in which the labourer stated that he had entered into a debt in exchange for his labour. Such a written contract, with which the master could force his employee to comply with their agreement, was not very common in Surat district, as the Deputy Collector observed:

Very few of the cultivators are in the habit of taking any documents or receipts from the Halis for amounts paid to them in advance as they have learnt by experience that such documents or receipts do not stand them in good stead in civil courts if the Hali elopes away (N.M. Parikhji, in *Census of India 1921*, vol. viii, 1922: 221).

The same source states that the courts tended to reject claims from landowners because the poor were not able to defend their interests in the same way that the rich are accustomed to do (see also *Gazetteer of the Bombay Presidency*, vol. ii, 1877: 200).

In my view, the fact that the British authorities took no action to release the halis from their state of bondage is more significant than the above-mentioned differentiation in treatment. The last quotation would appear to contradict this but there are ample records which give an opposite view. Generally speaking, the authorities seemed inclined to comply with the customs of the country. From that perspective, the halis had insufficient possessions to which the master could lay claim in payment for the credit he had provided. The only way for the master to get a return on his investment was to make use of the hali's labour. The government therefore felt obliged to return runaway halis to their creditor/master, as can be seen from an official instruction shortly after the beginning of colonial rule.

By a letter from Government, dated 19th April 1822, the Magistrates are authorized to apprehend and return to his master any Halee who may abscond (Vibart, quoted in Banaji 1933).

Subsequent reports contain no evidence to suggest that this official standpoint changed. At best, individual officials might have shown signs of sympathy for the miserable plight of the landless class. But the authorities too had adopted the view that the halis had only themselves to blame for their poverty and the debt that bound them to their master, a debt into which they entered of their own free will. According to the authorities, rather than standing on their own two feet, they lived off the wealth of the landowner and if they did not improve their work ethic, they were doomed to remain a residual social group. This standpoint is difficult to reconcile with that of Prakash, who claims that the colonial authorities wished to replace unfree labour with free labour. That transition would have necessitated the legal abolition of halipratha in south Gujarat and that was clearly not on the colonial agenda. From the beginning, the continued existence of the system was seen as a consequence of the halis' own lack of desire for emancipation. The belief that confining the Dublas in a regime of bondage was the only way to instil a work ethic that would enable them to prove their worth to society seemed to gain more and more ground. It was an argument that was applied much more widely to lower income groups than solely to the halis of south Gujarat.

In 1859 the Workman's Breach of Contract Act (WBCA) came into force. Under this Act, labourers who had entered into a contract with a European employer were compelled to fulfil specified obligations. From this perspective, when a labourer accepted an advance payment in exchange for a pledge that he would perform a specific task, he effectively entered into a contract. If he failed to perform that task, he could then be forced to comply with the agreement, if necessary by legal means. It was no coincidence that this first piece of colonial labour legislation was based on the assumption that native workers lacked the discipline to comply with agreements they had entered into of their own free will. Since labourers rarely had any possessions with which to repay the debt, there was little other choice than to impose penal sanctions on those who defaulted on the agreement. This solution had already been introduced for domestic servants and artisans in Calcutta earlier on, but in 1859 it was extended to include coolies who received earnest money on recruitment for work on a plantation. In this strategy, bonding was encouraged to instil a sense of duty to work on those who had opted out of the economic rules on which progress was based. Although, as far as I know, the WBCA was never applied to the relationship between landowners and agricultural labourers, the colonial administration did fail to put a stop to the servitude of groups like the halis. This suggests to me that replacing unfree labour with free labour was never one of the main tenets of colonial policy.[11] Labour relations were left to the free play of social forces, which in practice meant confirming the traditional dominance of the landlords.

Changes in the Rural Economy

In the course of the nineteenth and at the start of the twentieth centuries, the relationship between master and servant underwent radical changes. Before looking at the changes in detail, I will examine the factors that caused them. In one of the few studies devoted to the magnitude and composition of agricultural labour, S.J. Patel attributed the emergence of this class to the process of proletarianization in the rural economy that started to make itself felt around the middle of the nineteenth century. The former village community—consisting of castes of peasants, artisans, and service-providers which, according to him, existed up to that time—disintegrated under the influence of the commercial forces unleashed under colonial rule. The cohesion, homogeneity, and focus on subsistence that had dominated the local order until then made way for a process of social and economic differentiation which led to the emergence of a rapidly growing agrarian underclass. But what was the original identity of these landless or nearly landless labourers? Some had been artisans, like weavers, who could not compete against the import of new industrial products from the mother country of their foreign rulers, while others were peasants who had lost their land after falling into debt. This interpretation is in line with the image of rural impoverishment that became a prominent issue in nationalist literature from the early twentieth century onwards. Patel, who belonged to this school of thought, recognized that the traditional village community included a group of 'menials and domestic servants' who received a plot of land or grain to guarantee them a livelihood, in return for their servitude to landowning castes (S.J. Patel 1952: 32). His description could also apply to groups like the halis, but the author explained the presence of this subaltern segment, which he called the 'depressed classes', in a way that was fundamentally different to the position of the landless Dublas in south Gujarat. In his view, the menials and domestic servants as a group were in service to the other castes collectively. It was an institutionalized form of servitude founded on the communal character that he ascribed to the village economy and which was brought to an end by colonial rule. This process led to the emergence of a new form of bondage that was individual and based on a relationship of debt.

...the desintegration of the village communities brought about the 'liberation' of depressed classes from the *traditional* self-perpetuating form of bondage; but, in the process, it destroyed the basis of guaranteed livelihood. Because other alternatives for employment had not yet developed, they were forced to accept even the worst conditions of work for securing a livelihood. Their liberation from the traditional bondage, itself paved the way for the new type of economic bondage. They were no longer 'serfs' within the framework of the village communities, wherein, as a *group* of village menials and servants, they had accepted bondage to a *group* of cultivators. This relationship was replaced by a *new* form of bondage, wherein an individual in desperate economic need was forced into bondage to another individual. The traditional serfs were 'liberated' to be re-enserfed (S.J. Patel 1952: 88).

In my description and analysis of halipratha in the pre-colonial era, I found no confirmation of the existence of a village community as construed by Patel as the point of departure in his argument. Social groups like the Dublas were certainly 'depressed' but their servitude to the landowning elite was based not on collective but on individual arrangements. In my opinion, therefore, the attached farm servant dependent for his livelihood on working for others should not be seen as the product of foreign domination.

I do agree with Patel, however, that colonialism radically changed the way in which the halis were subjugated. This transformation was the result of complex, interrelated circumstances. A decisive factor was the gradual increase in production for the market, and the monetization of economic exchange that inevitably accompanied it. Although I have in a number of other publications criticized the view of a closed village household in which the members worked only to fulfil their own basic needs, the economic activity under the *ancien regime* had indeed a limited scope—it was largely restricted to the locality and its immediate surroundings, and there was only a small quantity of money in circulation. The exchange of goods and services more often took place in kind. From the middle of the nineteenth century, however, the sale of agricultural produce expanded to markets further away at the expense of those closer to home and the cropping pattern changed in response to the growing demand from outside. In the northern part of Surat district, cotton became increasingly important as a money crop in the agrarian cycle, while in the south it was sugarcane. Expansion of the total cultivated area and the conversion from dry to wet (that is, irrigated) land took place largely in the final decades of the nineteenth century. The increase in irrigation was largely achieved by digging more wells. As a result of population growth the pressure on agricultural resources increased without leading to a shift in the sectoral composition of the economy. Parallel to the now rapidly progressing trend towards commercialization, agriculture became much more labour-intensive during this period. The emergence of a new economic spirit manifested itself in the monetization of exchange relations between the villagers. The members of non-agricultural castes in particular took advantage of this change to settle in urban centres, a move that sometimes entailed them taking up new skills and trades.

...the complete equipment of artisans and menials with which the old type of village was furnished is being dissolved by the force of competitive tendencies. As villages become larger, the village barber, blacksmith, carpenter or potter seems to lose the definiteness of his circle of clientele. The influence of custom in fixing the remuneration for the hire of labour is also giving way gradually to the law of supply and demand. In many important directions, the village services are being depleted by the discontented village artisan or menial leaving for towns or large centres in the hope that with better wages and in newer surroundings his ambitions can be satisfied. The want of scavengers and village watchmen, who are gradually forsaking their traditional occupations, is now being generally felt; the decline among *luhars* and *hajams*—to mention two among the essential village occupations—and the emigration of *suthars* to towns, etc., are indications how the rural population which still forms about 80 per cent, is being gradually deprived of their ancestral facilities (*Census of India 1921*, vol. xvii, part I, 1922: 358).

Infrastructural projects gave economic development in the district a significant boost. In 1864 the north–south railway line from Bombay to Surat was completed, followed in 1898 by the west–east line along the Tapti river valley that linked Surat to Khandesh. The building of all-weather roads, such as that from Bilimora to Chikhli in 1878 and from Surat to Bardoli in 1884–5, helped break through the isolation at local level. As it became easier and less expensive to cover great distances, the labour market also expanded.

The agglomeration of Bombay, a major growth pole, came within reach of the rural population of south Gujarat. In addition to those who moved there permanently in search of a better life, seasonal migration evolved from the early twentieth century as the land-poor and the landless sought employment during the dry season in the salt-pans and brickyards that were growing up on the northern outskirts of the city.[12] Members of the higher castes increasingly acquired a secondary education which qualified them for jobs in the civil service or the professions. Migration within the district did not immediately lead to a major change in the customary way of life, but gradually the number of villagers who moved further afield and took up new occupations increased. Around the turn of the century there was even a moderate degree of emigration overseas, particularly to Africa. The crossing was often made in *dhows,* simple country boats sailing from small ports to the coast of East Africa. The dangerous voyage across the Gulf of Arabia depended on favourable winds and not all those who left reached their destinations. What they did when they arrived depended on their social background. Kolis and Kanbis found work as industrial labourers, the former perhaps also as coolies, Bohras became traders, and Anavils sought jobs as clerks in the colonial service (*Census of India 1921*, vol. xvii, Baroda State, part I, 1921: 105–6; *Revision Survey Settlement Jalalpur taluka* 1900: 85). By no means all of those who left in this period departed for good. Many returned sooner or later, and others kept in close contact with their families back at home.[13]

In addition to the fact that a much larger proportion of the agricultural produce was traded in distant markets, a wide range of new products entered the region for which there had previously been little or no demand. This led to a new style of consumption which threw the differences between rich and poor into sharper relief. Shortly before the turn of the century, the Collector of Surat described this new pattern of expenditure among the wealthier members of the farming population:

…the present men as they live less labourious lives,…have more expensive tastes than their forbears, and to gratify them will refer to the savkar, if there is no money in the house. Formerly the ordinary cultivators to a man wore country cloth; now they must have it of finer texture from Manchester. Cheap local rice, *dal* and *gul* were enough for the daily food; now vegetables, imported rice and refined sugar are in demand. A more luxurious generation seeks after *pan-supari*, *chiroots*, hired servants, sweetmeats, and American watches, and will borrow money to get them (Letter to Commissioner Northern Division, 27 January 1896 accompanying the *Bardoli Revised Survey Settlement Report* 1895, para 6).[14]

Erosion of the Master–Servant Relationship

The opening up of the countryside of south Gujarat and the advance of the capitalist mode of production in the economy resulted in a comprehensive process of social change. How did this affect halipratha? As we have seen, Surendra J. Patel believed that agricultural labourers as an occupational class emerged only under foreign rule and bonded themselves to landowners because they had no other way of fulfilling their basic needs. Their impoverishment, which he ascribed to the rapid decline of traditional crafts and services, was an expression of the underdeveloped and stagnated colonial economy. In the same way that Patel rejects the view that the cause of the bondage of the landless must be sought in the nature of the pre-colonial economy, in a study published much later, Sudipto Mundle also concludes that this mode of subjugation was a modern rather than a traditional phenomenon. His argument is based on the operation of the *kamiauti* system in south Bihar.[15] His explanation for agrarian servitude contradicts, however, the views of both S.J. Patel and G. Prakash—who, as we discussed earlier, elaborated on the *kamias* in pre-colonial as well as colonial times. While Patel claimed that a process of pauperization made bonding inevitable for labourers who had become superfluous in the rural economy in the colonial era, Mundle suggests that towards the end of the nineteenth century the exodus of labour from agriculture had reached such proportions that landowners could only be sure of keeping the landless in their employ, especially given the very low level of wages, by denying them the freedom to go in search of better paid work.

...the origin of the *kamiuti* system followed the penetration of capital into agriculture and was in fact a result of it. It was by no means a traditional pre-capitalist relationship which merely survived the penetration of capital into agriculture (Mundle 1979: 95).

Since I have already given my critical comments on the way in which Prakash explains the emergence of servitude in the agrarian economy, I will now respond to the arguments of Patel and Mundle. Both see bondage as a colonial phenomenon, but Patel considers it to have been caused by pauperization, while Mundle ascribes it to the emergence of new opportunities for employment outside agriculture. How do these interpretations concord with the changes in the master–servant relationship in rural south Gujarat? First of all, from what I have written earlier, it will be obvious that my views do not confirm those of Patel and Mundle—which are largely shared by Prakash, though from a very different perspective—that labour bondage did not exist in the pre-colonial era. In the report on my first fieldwork study, I gave due attention to the continuation and transformation of the halipratha system in the colonial period. The starting point of my argument was H.J. Nieboer's thesis that unfree labour disappears as pressure on the agricultural means of existence increases.[16] Yet the historical records that I consulted revealed no process of agrarian pauperization leading to a rise in the percentage of landless people. Nor was there any evidence of an exodus of labour from agriculture, as suggested by Mundle, which forced the landowners to use coercion to ensure that there were sufficient labourers for tilling the land. Neither argument, I concluded, can explain the radical changes that occurred in the system of agrarian labour relations.

Landless Dublas seized the opportunity presented by new work opportunities outside agriculture to escape from the clutches of the landowners. A clear example was the building of the railway line from Bombay to Surat across the plain of south Gujarat, which was completed in 1864. The construction of the line took several years and required a large army of unskilled labourers recruited on the spot by jobbers. Attracted by the high pay, many halis deserted their masters. Some of them opted out for good, starting new lives in the small towns along the railway line as navvies or porters. The opening up of the labour market was however temporary and of limited scale.

Between AD 1863 and 1866, when labour was dear, many Dublas left the families they formerly served and worked as free labourers. Since then they are said to have found their old position of ploughmen or halis securer and not more onerous (Enthoven, vol. i, 1920: 347).

During the First World War, several Dublas joined the colonial Labour Corps sent to Mesopotamia or managed to find work in the Bombay mills. From the start of the twentieth century, the halis became accustomed to migrating seasonally to the salt-pans and brickyards near

Bombay after the rainy season. That was the start of a slack period in agriculture and the farmers did not object to their labourers seeking work elsewhere, as Mukhtyar found during his village study in 1927.

...the average Hali (who) is often allowed to emigrate to industrial areas in the off season, when his master does not require his services and wants to effect a saving of so much wages, which he must pay without exacting any work, if the hali is kept at home (Mukhtyar 1930: 169).

This arrangement continued until after the middle of the twentieth century, as I observed during my own fieldwork in 1962–3.[17] I gave the name 'monsoon servants' to the Dublas in Chikhligam who went off as seasonal migrants to the brickyards after the Diwali festival. They only worked for their masters back in the village during the busy parts of the year, at the start, during, and at the end of the rainy season (Breman 1974: 129–33). There was, however, no mass exodus of labour from agriculture in the nineteenth and the first half of the twentieth centuries. Both urbanization and diversification of the economy were slow to take hold in south Gujarat. The major part of the workforce—and especially the landless labourers—continued, as before, to work in agriculture and live in the countryside.

During the period under review, the number of agricultural labourers increased rather than decreased. Was this because the agricultural economy had become more labour-intensive? This is true to a certain extent, and the expansion of cultivated land from the middle of the nineteenth century, undoubtedly, also had an impact. The extent to which the introduction of new crops like cotton gave employment a strong boost is, however, arguable. According to some reports, landowners did not switch to the new crops purely for economic reasons.

It is even asserted by careful observers that the keenness of cultivators to grow cotton is due not only to the fact that they can usually make good profits from it, but also to the fact that it is an easy crop to grow and leaves them plenty of leisure (Keatinge 1921: 145–6).

Another factor with probably a greater impact on the increase in the number of halis was the tendency of more and more farmers to follow the examples of the landlords and to refrain from manual work as soon as their economic position permitted it (Keatinge 1921: 146; *Census of India 1931*, vol. xix, Baroda, Part I, 1932: 267). For the same reason, the number of Dubla girls hired as domestic help to work in the household, clean the stalls, etc., increased. Shukla reported that the high price of cotton in the years preceding his study in Olpad (1929–32) had prompted more and more Kanbis to exempt themselves and their wives as far as possible from working in the fields, tending the cattle, cleaning the vessels, fetching water, etc. and to leave these demeaning and messy chores to the labourers, their wives, and children (Shukla 1937: 124; J.M. Mehta 1930: 132–3).

Did labour costs not present an obstacle for farmers wishing to indulge their desire for conspicuous leisure? In the course of time, the cost of upkeep for a hali had risen considerably. J.M. Mehta calculates that in 1930 it cost 122 rupees a year compared to 40 to 50 rupees four decades previously. In the same period, the advance that the master gave to the Dubla to be able to marry had risen from about 50 to 200 or even 300 rupees (J.M. Mehta 1930: 127). Yet it would be premature to deduce from these figures that the price of labour had more than doubled since the beginning of the twentieth century. What the hali received stayed the same, only its value in monetary terms increased over time. Because the payments to the labourers—both the advance and the daily wage— were made for the most part in kind, they did not come out of the money income earned by the landowner. The grain ration and the small cash emoluments received by the hali did not rise above the amount required for him and his family to barely survive. Wages remained at the lowest conceivable level from generation to generation. The degree of deprivation can be illustrated by the fact that the guests at a Dubla wedding would bring their own food so as not to embarrass their host. This custom, reported by C.H. Shah in his ethnography (1952: 67) was still in use at the time of my first round of fieldwork a decade later. In the middle of the twentieth century, the master of an attached labourer or maidservant spent little or no more on them than 150 years previously.

The loans in kind form a substantial portion of the total advance, as almost the entire quantity of foodgrains, pulses and vegetables required for the feasting on the occasion are advanced by the Dhaniamo. The other significant factor about the marriage loans is that as compared with the rise in the prices and the cost of living, the increase in the total computed expenses on the Hali's marriage has been much lower (RHLEC 1950: 26).

This passage is quoted from the 'Report of the Hali Labour Enquiry Committee' which was commissioned by the government some years after Independence and to which I will return in more detail. I can observe here, however, that the poverty in which the landless continued to live kept them firmly indebted to their employers. The state of dependence in which they lived did not allow them to exercise their own free will about how to utilize their labour power.

Nevertheless the argument that servitude on economic grounds was not justifiable gained ground. According to a district official in 1921:

The Hali labourer is notoriously inefficient, and with the present higher price it costs ever so much.to maintain a Hali. In short, the master also finds the system uneconomic. The Hali system is now day by day disappearing (*Census of India 1921*, vol. viii, 1922: 222).

Colonial officials went out of their way to convince farmers that it was much cheaper to employ free labourers on a casual basis. They might be paid a little more on a daily basis but the employers no longer had the responsibility to provide loans to enable their labourers to meet their non-daily needs. Furthermore, they would no longer have to pay them for days when there was no work. But it soon became apparent that the farmers were not open to these arguments. They insisted that their preference for permanent rather than casual employees was based on purely economic considerations.

At first sight this arrangement scarcely appears an economical one to the masters; but they have assured me that, everything considered, it is financially better than keeping no farm servants, and engaging labourers when they are wanted. For, when any of the principal agricultural operations, such as ploughing, reaping, & c., are in full swing, the demand for labourers is often far greater than the supply; and not to have sufficient hands at such seasons must mean a heavy loss. In the dull season these servants, or halis (cultivators) as they are called, are employed in various ways, such as repairing and building rice embankments, converting jirayat into rice land, carting manure, & c. (Fernandez 1895: 7).

The Call for Discipline

Halipratha continued to exist but the relationship between master and servant became more business-like. With the progressive monetization of economic production and the wider range of options for spending their money that it offered, and influenced by their more widespread exposure to the outside world, the landowners looked at the landless in a different light. They wanted to live a more comfortable life, with better housing, better food, and better clothing, and to prepare their children for a life beyond the village by investing in their education. The employment of one or more servants or maidservants fitted in with this new lifestyle. Taking on a labourer with a wife and children meant that the master no longer had to concern himself directly with the work in the fields or with tending the cattle. But the halis were no longer the object of the landowners' ambition to achieve more power and prestige. The time when they took servants on to emphasize their status as petty rajahs was past. The hali remained bonded to his master, but the element of patronage that had been so important in the past faded away. Little was left of the protection and support which the hali could depend on in difficult times. In his monograph, Shukla summed up the disappearance of this aspect of the relationship in no uncertain terms: 'If the master's work does not suffer in the event of the Hali's sickness, he may be allowed to rot in his cottage' (Shukla 1937: 123). Towards the end of the colonial era the halis had become a labour commodity which the employers exploited in a way that made it clear that economic motives were their main consideration in weighing up the costs and benefits of doing so. In that sense, replacing the labour power of themselves and their wives by a hali family was also an economic consideration.

Understandably, the bonded labourers responded to this change by no longer displaying the behaviour that had characterized their status as clients: loyalty and gratitude to the master, along with deference and docility to entice their benefactor to greater generosity. Once the dhaniamo no longer complied with the code of patronage the hali considered himself released from the obligation to be subordinate. More than before, they expressed their dissatisfaction by deserting their masters. They would take this step, as the report below shows, even without any hope of building a better life elsewhere.

The labourers run away not because they get better terms elsewhere but because the treatment given to them is not at all sympathetic. Most of the labourers are Dublas and Dhankas, members of the aboriginal classes, illiterate and ignorant. The employers sometimes maltreat them and to avoid further trouble they run away to some other places. To force these people to stick to the cultivators and sometimes work under degrading conditions would be cruel (*Baroda Economic Development Committee, 1918–19, Report*, 1920: 131–2).

For their part, the landowners saw the disloyalty of their subordinates as proof of their bad faith, their refusal to perform the duties they had committed themselves to on becoming bonded in exchange for the money the dhaniamos had invested in them in the form of 'loans'. In the masters' view, desertion was tantamount to breach of contract and, with the risk of this eventuality in mind, they became even less generous and forthcoming. Would this change in mentality on both sides mean the end of halipratha? Some commentators clearly thought so. Referring to the fact that bondage had worked to the satisfaction of both parties only thirty years previously, the Collector of Surat noted as early as the end of the nineteenth century:

The system has now broken down, not so much because the masters cannot afford to keep the 'halis', as because they will not stay. Imbued with the new sense of independence they run away to get higher wages, omitting to repay money that has been spent by their old master in marrying them or in other ways. The frequency of such instances has made the Anavla Brahmin chary of keeping them at all, at any rate on the old family footing (*Revision Survey Settlement Report of the Jalalpur Taluka*, 1900: 99).

In the late colonial period, the authorities declared themselves to be avid supporters of free labour. The belief, so strong in the past, that colonial rulers should adapt to the 'customs of the land' made way for an awareness that paying the landless Dublas a wage insufficient to live on forced them to accept advances for expenses that exceeded their daily earnings. The resulting relationship of bondage enabled the farmers to continue to keep the hali's wages at the minimum level required for the latter to reproduce. Yet the authorities in the area under direct British rule never went as far as introducing a ban on halipratha. Remarkably, the system was abolished in the part of south Gujarat that belonged to the princedom of Baroda. Abolition, however, did not have the intended effect.

In July 1923, the Government of the State by proclamation declared this whole system of forced indenture as illegal and allowed the Raniparaj serf to repudiate it if he chose to do so. But the intentions of the Government were not properly interpreted by subordinate revenue officials and the operation of the Government's order is therefore not effective (*Census of India 1931*, vol. xix Baroda, part 1, 1932: 255).

Without doubt, the landowning elite's close ties to the bureaucracy meant that halis could not call for the help of the police or the courts to put an end to their bondage—the very idea was beyond imagination and would meet with little success. Yet a new situation was gradually evolving which gave the landless underclass more room for manoeuvre. The continuing trend towards commercialization affected not only the relationship

▲   Dubla women used to wear low-grade metal ornaments on legs and
arms around 1920, a custom practised in many tribal communities
at the time.
Source: R.E. Enthoven (1920).

▲   A Dubla couple in the 1920s. The man's attire suggests that he is a
servant of a prominent landlord-cum-official.
Source: R.E. Enthoven (1920).

between master and servant but also eroded the closed ranks among the landowners which ensured that they did not engage a hali if he had deserted his dhaniamo. The rural elite seemed no longer to care for the code which had helped keep the halis immobile in previous generations. But the landowners had found new weapons to protect their own interests. In the late colonial era, they had become better versed in legal matters and tried to pressurize the government to take action against absconders. They claimed that labourers who deserted them had defaulted on the employment contract they had entered into voluntarily and which the employer had confirmed by payment of an advance. As argued before, it made little sense holding deserters accountable as they had no possessions to pay off their debts, but what the creditors wanted was to secure their labour power, and to achieve that they needed the help of the government.

To remedy this evil [i.e. runaway *halis*], some of the witnesses suggested that special legislation should be enacted by which the man could be prevented from avoiding the contract and that some kind of reciprocity may be established between the adjoining States by which these men could be brought back and made to fulfill the rest of their contract (*Baroda Economic Development Committee Report*, 1920: 131–2).

This demand was repeated some years later in an official memorandum presented to the Royal Commission on Agriculture. In the memo-randum, the Deputy Director of Agriculture—who represented landowners' interests in Gujarat—called for the introduction of an identity card with details of the labourer's work record, which he could show to a new master as proof that he had fulfilled his debt to the previous one.[18]

Despite persistent reports from the end of the nineteenth century onwards that halipratha was on the point of disappearing or had already disintegrated as a consequence of the dissatisfaction of both landless and landowners, this is not confirmed by observers who followed the situation in rural south Gujarat closely on the basis of investigations at the local level. Shukla, who reported on the pattern of agrarian labour relations during his fieldwork in Olpad taluka from 1929 to 1932, clearly concluded: 'We (too) have failed to observe any signs of disappearance of the system, at least in the near future' (1937: 132). This does not change the fact, however, that the relationship between master and servant was perceived very differently from the start of the twentieth century than at the beginning of the colonial era. This contrast may have been influenced to some extent by subjective judgements, but the social changes that occurred during that period were so widespread and far-reaching that they cannot be ignored. They altered the way in which the Dublas were perceived. Although these perceptions had always been negative, the landless labourers had previously also been seen as loyal clients who had performed their work for their patron with a sense of duty and had accepted the fact that he provided their basic needs with humble gratitude. Now they were condemned for their excessive laziness, improvidence, irresponsible behaviour, and lack of respect for their superiors. In this view, their bondage was founded on a pernicious inability and incapacity to work hard and to live within their means so that they could make life better for themselves. The custom of also giving the halis their grain allowance on days when there was no work, was now seen—despite the fact that not giving it could threaten their very survival—as encouraging an uneconomical mentality.

In the case of the Hali, there is one additional reason why his output is lower than that of the free labourer. It is that, as he is guaranteed every day's food whether he works or not, he becomes irresponsible and indifferent in his work (Mukhtyar 1930: 169).

The Dublas' carefree acceptance of their poverty-stricken lives was proverbial. During my first fieldwork study, I was told time and again the tale of the Dubla who lay on the floor of his hut all day, exploring the bottom of the pot with his toe to see whether there was still enough gruel to enable him to go another day without working. Their laziness and lack of concern were so striking that they were reflected in popular sayings, like: 'A Dubla will do no work while a grain is left in the pot' (Risley 1915: 325; also see Keatinge 1921: 150[19]). Equally condemning was the judgement Enthoven made.

The Dublas or weaklings as their name is said to mean, are feeble people, soon aged by their hard life and their fondness for liquor (Enthoven, vol. i, 1920: 341).

The report of the last census under colonial rule, in 1941, stated that they were perfectly content to go through their lives as weaklings and to remain subordinate to landlords like the Anavil Brahmans (*Census 1941*, vol. xvii, Baroda 1941: 74). According to this very negative view of the Dublas, the landowners had failed in teaching them the discipline they owed to themselves and to society. In the eyes of civilized people, the Dublas had remained economically and socially backward because of defects in their own behaviour.

Notes

1. The concept of 'voluntary' is debatable as N. Bhattacharya has quite rightly pointed out. In fact, he blames me for having under-theorized the dimension of contestation in the relationship between the hali and his master (2004: 13–14).
2. Until now, the desais have largely been portrayed as tax farmers. But the same name is used to describe the subcaste they had formed to articulate their higher status. When speaking of the subcaste, I refer to them as Desai.
3. Letter to David Greenhill, Acting Secretary to the Government of Bombay, consultation no. 108 of 1825, Judicial Department 1826, vol. 25–126, Bombay Record Department; Banaji 1933: 72.
4. The main documents are: *Parliamentary Papers*, House of Commons, 1828: *Slavery in India: Correspondence and Abstracts of Regulations and Proceedings*, 1831–2, *Report from the Select Committee on the Affairs of the East India Company; Minutes of Evidence, Appendix and Evidence*; 1834, *Slavery in India, Correspondence*, 1841, *Report from the Indian Law Commissioners Relating to Slavery in the East Indies*. For a summary of these reports, see Banaji, *Slavery in British India*.
5. *Bonded Histories*. Following this monograph Prakash published a collection of essays in which he summarized and discussed the work of various authors on agricultural labour in the past: *The World of the Rural Labourer in Colonial India*.
6. In an extensive and interesting essay on the position of labour under the *ancien regime* and the changes it underwent in the colonial era, Robb also rejects Prakash's proposition that '…the bondage described in pre-colonial or pre-capitalist India was just an imaginary Other of the capitalist West' (Robb 1993: 37).
7. Maconochie, E., *Settlement Report on Chikhli taluka, Surat district*.
8. Bellasis, no. 2, *Report on the Southern Districts of the Surat Collectorate*.
9. T. Sarkar, 'Bondage in the colonial context', p. 122.
10. For more information see the ethnography by P.G. Shah (1958) mentioned above.
11. For a discussion of the background and meaning of the WBCA see Mohapatra, 'Regulated Informality', pp. 65–95.
12. *Second Revision Survey Settlement of Kalyan taluka of Thana district* reported that there was no industrial activity at all until the end of the nineteenth century. After that, however, a number of brickyards had been opened (1927: 7).

13. The eminent sociologist I.P. Desai published a study on migration on the basis of research in his own village of origin in the Surat district, *The Patterns of Migration and Occupation in a South Gujarat Village.*

14. T.R. Fernandez, SBG, NS, no. 319, *Settlement Report on Bardoli taluk, Surat district,* 2 December 1895.

15. Mundle, *Backwardness and Bondage.*

16. Nieboer, *Slavery as an Industrial System.* In 1960, I published a study, together with my colleagues C. Baks and A.T.J. Nooij, in which we examined Nieboer's work: 'Slavery as a System of Production in Tribal Society', *Bijdragen tot de Taal-, Land- en Volkenkunde,* vol. 122, no. 1, 90–109.

17. Atgam, the village Mukhtyar selected for his local-level research is situated at a short distance, not more than 6 miles, from Chikhligam, which is the second village of my fieldwork in the early 1960s.

18. Memorandum by Rao Sahib B.M.Desai in *Report of the the Royal Commission on Agriculture,* vol. II, part 2, evidence taken in the Bombay Presidency, London, 1926: 577 and 601.

19. Keatinge, *Agricultural Progress in Western India;* Risley, *The People of India.*

3

The Agrarian Question in the Struggle for National Independence

The Wider Context

From beginning to end the Independence movement had a middle class character which, initially, had a strong urban bias. Nationalist thinking largely reflected the ideas and interests of the middle classes, who held prominent positions in the economies of the towns and cities. The leaders of the Indian National Congress were very aware of the need to achieve greater impact and legitimacy. Attempts in the early twentieth century to broaden the movement's social base inevitably brought to light the differences that separated the middle class from the working population. The logical response to this lack of unity was to emphasize the need to join forces, to refuse to accept that the interests of any one class were more important than those of any other, and to insist on the formation of a united front against the colonial state. Yet the Congress failed to develop a political·strategy that persuaded the organized workers in the non-agrarian economy, employed in new, urban-based industries, to join them in the struggle.[1] The much larger and more fragmented mass of people who depended for their livelihoods on work in what later came to be known as the informal sector were, however, not even targeted for mobilization by the liberation movement.[2] The policy of ignoring or even systematically excluding this broad urban underclass, comprising the self-employed and casual or regular wage-workers, by no means implied that they had no aspirations regarding representation. They may not have been included in the nationalist effort to resist colonial rule, but the culture of assertion and protest that evolved during the struggle for Independence also helped to increase the room for manoeuvre at the base of society and to move the issue of inclusion—but other than in the form of dependency and subjugation—to the fore.

The efforts of the Indian National Congress to extend its social base could not remain restricted to the urban milieu. After all, the large majority of colonial subjects on the South Asian subcontinent worked in agriculture and lived in rural areas. Since India was a peasant society, the Congress had to mobilize support in the villages. It was Gandhi who set out this political course ideologically and strategically around 1920. Evidently this movement met with success, given his resolute statement only ten years later, in 1931,[3] that the Indian National Congress was in fact a peasant organization. But of which peasants? For a movement aiming at unity, which had only recently turned its attention to the agrarian order and instinctively tended to see it as a homogenous mass of owner-cultivators, this was in itself a tricky issue. The movement's activities and the social debate that accompanied them show how the Congress leadership dealt with the agrarian question which occupied such a prominent place on the nationalist agenda in the late-colonial era. Two aspects stand out clearly: firstly, the inadequate attention paid to the differentiation within the agricultural population and, when it no longer proved possible to deny the dramatically unequal distribution of land, a resolute refusal to take account of the contradictions that it created. Secondly, the movement favoured the interests of the dominant caste-class of landowners. Shahid Amin explains this term, first used by Low,[4] as follows:

It is these peasants that dominate the agrarian movements which they initiate, and they essentially convert these movements into broad-based multi-class affairs by virtue of their political claims on the poor and the landless, or by virtue of support from their numerous caste fellows (Amin 1988: 104).[5]

I would add that this description refers to a social group that made up a minority of the village population (usually no more than 10 to 15 per cent) who owned a disproportionate share, around two-thirds, of the arable land.

Gujarat became an important stage for the agrarian agitation launched by the Congress to increase the pressure on the colonial authorities. The aim of the campaign, which Gandhi launched in central Gujarat in 1918, was to persuade landowners to refuse to pay the land tax. When it became obvious after several months that the campaign in the Kheda district was a dismal failure, the disappointed leaders had no choice but to wind it up. David Hardiman made a study of this first round of peasant militancy, in which he also examined how political mobilization in the Kheda district developed further.[6] He concluded that the campaign had failed because the land-poor farmers and landless labourers did not want to take part in a protest that would benefit only the better-off landowners. This was a schism which the colonial authorities were only too pleased to take advantage of. With this observation Hardiman not only exposed the tensions between the different agrarian classes but also showed that the Congress movement prioritized the interests of the dominant owners over those of the land-poor and landless peasants.

... property-owning peasants were, on the whole, far more welcome within the Congress than those without property. Congress became the party of the richer peasant communities not because these peasants had greater political awareness, but because in most cases the Congress shied away from supporting the more radical and more violent movements of the poorer peasantry (Hardiman 1981: 254).

His conclusion is in line with those of many other authors who have reported on agrarian protest elsewhere in India. In the light of the case study that follows—of the way in which the Indian National Congress operated in Bardoli—it is important to examine another aspect of Hardiman's argument. His analysis contradicts the established view that the initiative for the mobilization lay with the Congress leadership. He makes a convincing argument that the roots of the agitation must be seen in the aspirations of the Patidars in Kheda to expand their local power base by seeking affiliation to the movement for national independence: 'time and time again it was the peasants who took the initiative' (Hardiman 1981: 245). Given what happened only a few years later in south Gujarat, I myself tend to take the more nuanced view that the agendas of local leaders among the dominant farmers coincided with that of the Congress, in an atmosphere of collusion and brought together by what Bhatt called 'link men' (Bhatt 1970: 336) so that they could be mutually adjusted and elaborated.

The lessons learned in Kheda were useful when it was decided to hold a subsequent satyagraha in Bardoli. The decision reflected the strong pressure that the regional spokesmen of the agrarian elite exercised on Gandhi. But the Congress leadership had made sure that the factors that had led to the fiasco in Kheda were not present in this subdistrict of south Gujarat. First of all the dominant farmers were a much more homogeneous group here than in central Gujarat. The Patidars in Bardoli had just emerged from a past in which they were known for their simple way of life. There was also far less differentiation in the scale of the property they owned than among their fellow caste members in Kheda, which made the ties between them stronger. In addition, the landless Dublas were subjugated to the landowning class as halis. The dependence of the farm labourers was expressed in a docility which guaranteed that the antagonism between the upper and lower classes, which had caused the Kheda campaign to fail, was either absent or not likely to result in overt resistance or disturbances of the public order.[7]

I will describe the course chosen by the Indian National Congress regarding the agrarian question by referring to the events in Bardoli in the 1920s. That point of departure fits in with my interest in the way in which the nationalist movement devoted (or failed to devote) attention to the fate of the broad mass of the land-poor and landless peasants in rural areas. The regional focus also permits me to study how the Congress, whose aim was to free the country from colonial rule, responded to the practice of unfree labour in the political economy of rural south Gujarat. The system of unfree labour inevitably came to light as knowledge about the agrarian structure and landscape increased, in and through the programme of agitation. Lastly, Bardoli is attractive as a case study because the two leading Congress leaders, that is, Mahatma Gandhi and Vallabhbhai Patel, had such an emphatic impact on political mobilization in the region. Both came from Gujarat and that background is an indelible and integral part of the views they held. It is important to note that Patel was far more familiar with the agrarian milieu, even before he entered public life, than Gandhi.

There is a broad range of literature on the campaigns in Bardoli, first in 1922 and then in 1928. The preparations, progress, and results were recorded in detail in the Congress movement's own history. The source material on which this history is based has also been largely preserved. The value of this material lies not only in its objective significance. Without doubt, the insight it provides into the chain of events, sometimes on a day-to-day basis, and the role of the actors who took part in them is a key element in our understanding of the situation on the ground. The second Bardoli campaign was turned into an epic that was intended to bring the peasant assertion to the attention of the entire nation. In May 1928, after he had adroitly succeeded in the run-up to the campaign in preventing VIPs from visiting what had become his personal stamping ground, Sardar Patel got a resolution passed at a meeting of the Congress Working Committee in Bombay which congratulated the peasants of Bardoli on their struggle and complimented its leader and his colleagues for their boundless energy (Shirin Mehta 1984: 136). The whole country was to be made aware of the imminent victory and the motto became 'Bardolise India' (Dutt 1986: 77).[8] There is good reason why later studies speak of myth construction, the conscious compilation of a record presenting only those facts and opinions which fit in with the authorized version of the struggle. The distorted view that this produces itself merits closer study and I look at this in more detail in the chronicle of events in Bardoli which follows here. My starting point was the statement with which Shahid Amin concludes his historiographic review of agrarian protests under the nationalist banner:

Parallel to the history of dominance and subordination in the quotidian existence of the subaltern, there is also a history of dominance, resistance, subordination, and appropriation within nationalist agitation itself (Amin 1988: 121).

The Story of Bardoli by Mahadev Desai—who was Gandhi's secretary and who served as the chronicler of the campaign—is the most striking example of the wave of hagiographic publications which appeared immediately at the time.[9] The main theme is the admiration for the resolute and shrewd style of operation of Vallabhbhai Patel, who succeeded in winning over the people of Bardoli for the cause and meting out a sensitive defeat for the colonial authorities. The fame he acquired earned him the title 'Lion of Bardoli', which Gandhi awarded him in public. The honorary name Sardar which he used from then on had already been adopted earlier by his peasant supporters. It was not until after Independence that more balanced and even downright critical appraisals appeared of the civil disobedience campaigns in Bardoli in 1922 and 1928.[10] My examination of what was left unsaid in the official documents is based—in addition to the information I gathered from the original sources—on these later assessments. As such it is not intended to repeat or review these earlier studies. My main concerns are whether and in what way the very large landless underclass was involved in the political mobilization, at what point the local and national leaders of Congress became aware of the halipratha system and how they responded to it, the consequences this 'discovery' had for the continuing debate on the agrarian issue and the question that inevitably followed: how the lack of freedom within the movement's own ranks could be brought to an end as part of the struggle for Independence.

Prologue

At the beginning of the twentieth century, the Kanbi Patels were as yet hardly visible as the dominant caste in Bardoli and the surrounding area. They were of *shudra* (low caste) origin and held a position that was only slightly higher than that of the Kolis. They had gradually become somewhat better off by growing cotton, which had been introduced as a cash crop into the northern part of Surat district shortly after the middle of the nineteenth century. In the course of time, cotton cultivation had expanded considerably. This was partly achieved by cultivating new land, but it also occurred at the expense of the area under food grains. In 1923–4 cotton occupied one third of the cultivated area (Charlesworth 1985: 287).[11]

Table 3.1: Shift from Foodgrains to Cash Crops in the Late Colonial Era

	1894	*1923–24*
cotton	25,000 acres	40,099 acres
jowar	27,554 acres	18,642 acres

Source: Shankardass (1988: 65).

The expansion was driven by the price hike of cotton, the commercial crop which dominated in the central plain of south Gujarat.

After 1890 the price rise in Bardoli cotton accelerated, roughly doubling by 1910 and reaching new levels twice as high again in the best years between 1917 and 1924, when Japanese demand for Indian cotton was so intense (Charlesworth 1985: 287).

The increased prosperity of the main landowners led to a radical change in the way they lived and worked. Instead of tending the fields and the cattle themselves, together with their wives, they now employed farm servants. This trend was already discussed in the previous chapter. The changing lifestyle was reflected in the new and larger houses they built for themselves. The cattle were no longer kept in the house, but in a separate stall. The money to make their lives more comfortable did not come only from the higher income from agriculture. Around the turn of the century, Kanbi Patels started to emigrate to countries in Africa and America, a trend which was to reach even greater proportions in the second half of the twentieth century. At first, the emigrants were mainly men who would return after a few years abroad. The money they saved was used to benefit the family back home. They would send it or bring it with them and it would be invested in the farm (to buy land or cattle) or just used to make daily life more dignified.[12] A growing segment of the Kanbi Patels developed themselves from self-working cultivators into agrarian managers. A significant indication of this changing identity was that local-level leaders took the initiative to set up cooperatives, first to purchase cotton and later to process it. The cotton gins, the first of which dates from the early 1920s, broke the monopoly of the urban-based merchants who had kept the producers in a state of dependency by providing them with advances (Breman 1985: 22–3).[13]

The improvement in their economic situation acted as a lever for social mobility. This meant giving up various caste customs which were seen as inferior. The motivation for purifying their conduct and introducing religious reforms—which testified to the growing influence of the Arya Samaj sect—paved the way for upward mobility and the transition of the Kanbi Patels from a Shudra to a Kshatriya identity. The self-elevation to the status of Patidars was accompanied by playing down the differentiation between the various Kanbi sub-castes. Without doubt, the leading advocate of this variant of the Sanskritization process was Kunvarji Mehta, a social activist who, was forced to resign as a teacher at a village school because of his activism. This setback did not stop him from showing his fellow caste members, with renewed vigour, the way to achieve greater respectability. In 1908 he set up the Patidar Yuvak Mandal, a caste association which formalized what was already an informal network. From this platform, he published a caste periodical, organized conferences to propagate caste unity, and collected money for the opening of a caste hostel in Surat which, from 1911, provided accommodation for students attending school and college in the city. The hostel evolved into a centre from which the new ideology of the Patidars was diffused in the surrounding countryside. This mission included the appointment of an *updeshak*, a paid social worker who visited caste members in the villages and instilled in them the importance of social reforms and of educating their children. As well as working to unite all of his fellow caste members in a single association, Kunvarji Mehta also established contact with Patidars in the Kheda district. The first conference of Gujarat Patidars was held in 1910, but he had his sights set further afield, as became obvious when he took part in the All India Kurmi Parishad in 1913. He saw this as bringing together at the national level dominant landowners who were separated at the regional level but who had similar backgrounds. For him, the peasant was the role model for the identity of his caste.

The ground gained by the Kanbi Patidars in economic, social, and cultural terms also expressed itself in aspirations to political power. The obvious vehicle to achieve this was the Indian National Congress. In the early years of the twentieth century the *swadeshi* movement intensified Mehta's nationalistic feelings and he was among the delegates to the meeting of the All India Congress Committee in Surat in 1907. Mehta had already established contact with Gandhi while the latter was still in South Africa, which came about because of the presence of a considerable number of Gujaratis from Surat in the Indian community to which Gandhi directed his activities. When Gandhi returned to India in 1915 Kunvarji Mehta was among those who welcomed him in Bombay and invited him to visit the Patidar *ashram*. Early the following year Gandhi went to Surat to attend the opening of an Arya Samaj temple. During his stay in the city he travelled to outlying villages to visit many people he had previously worked with in South Africa. In addition to Kunvarji Mehta, Gandhi was accompanied on this first tour of the Surat district by social worker Dayalji Desai. While Mehta was concerned with promoting caste consciousness among the Patidars, Desai was doing the same among the Anavil Brahmans of south Gujarat. The two social workers knew each other well and Desai chose the same course that Mehta had already followed: setting up a caste association, publishing a journal for the caste members, and establishing an ashram in Surat where the sons of the Anavils could stay while attending school in the city. Yet Mehta proved more successful in these endeavours than Desai. I believe that this was due to the different positions of the two castes in the hierarchy. Unlike the Patidars, who had risen above their lowly status as Kanbi Patels, the Anavil Brahmans were not so much concerned with upward social mobility as with maintaining their elite position. The more individualistic behaviour of the latter prevented them from closing ranks in the same way as the Patidars and focusing on their shared interests (Bhatt 1970: 330). This difference in caste identity, however, had no detrimental effect on the close relationship between the leaders of the dominant landowners in Surat district.

The Background to the Civil
Disobedience Movement in Bardoli

The goal of the non-cooperation movement set up in 1920 was *swaraj*,
self-rule. When he presented the programme Gandhi promised that, if
it was implemented, India would be free within a year. A month later,
he visited Surat to see how and where the campaign of civil disobedience
could be initiated. Kunvarji Mehta did not hesitate for a moment to
recommend Bardoli as the most appropriate place, rather than Kheda,
which had been the original first choice.[14] The plan was to put the
boycott of the colonial government into practice by persuading the
landowners to refuse to pay the land tax. At the end of 1921, Gandhi
visited Bardoli to acquaint himself with the state of affairs. He attracted
large crowds and, during one of his speeches—in front of an audience
of several tens of thousands—he saw a group of people standing
separately at some distance from the rest. When he asked who they
might be, he was told that they were 'untouchables'. He invited them to
join the main ujliparaj crowd, who allowed this to happen without
protest. A committee had already been set up to coordinate the campaign
in the subdistrict. The eleven members of this panel were all from high
Hindu castes and more than half were Patidars or Anavil Brahmans.
These hand-picked frontmen represented no more than a third of the
total population. Gandhi himself led the boycott, which started in
February 1922. After all the preparatory work, the response was
overwhelming, especially among the Patidars. It was clear that they would
comply with the appeal not to pay the land tax. In half of the 137
villages in Bardoli the village headman was a Patidar. But the sharp
dividing lines running through the population of the subdistrict could
not remain hidden to Gandhi. When he asked how many children from
Bhangi or Dhed castes had been admitted to the national schools that
had been opened, he was told that only a few such youngsters had gained
access to this alternative from of primary education (part of the boycott
had involved calling on schoolchildren not to attend the government
schools) (Shirin Mehta 1984: 86). When Gandhi further probed what
proportion of the population would take an active part in the civil
disobedience, he was shocked to hear that participation would be
restricted to the ujliparaj. The others, he was told, belonged to the
kaliparaj who were not traditionally counted as part of the population,

although they made up three-quarters of it. Half of them were Dublas, more than twice as many as the Patidars and Anavil Brahmans put together. In their shack colonies on the edge of the villages, the members of this landless caste were outside the public eye. The question asked was that the campaign could surely not be intended for them. A week later, Gandhi decided to abandon the campaign and told the peasants to immediately resume paying the land tax. The formal reason for this dramatic decision was the eruption of violence in Uttar Pradesh, an incident in the market town of Chauri-Chaura, when an angry mob stormed a police station and burned it to the ground, with the constables still inside. This violation of the principle of non-violence was opportune for Gandhi, whose promise of freedom within a year was clearly not feasible. Equally important was his realization after his encounter with the peasantry of Bardoli that to continue to campaign would mean that 'half of our body could not be mobilised, as it was crippled', as Gandhi wrote in his *Navjivan* column. This was standpoint which the committee of landowners set up to support him could neither understand nor appreciate.[15]

Gandhi returned to Ahmedabad, but not without leaving instructions on what to do next. A few trusted workers stayed behind with orders to uplift the tribal population from their state of backwardness. Earlier attempts by Congress workers under the leadership of Kunvarji Mehta to persuade the kaliparaj to take part in the civil disobedience against the colonial government had met with little success. This seemed to change when Mehta told the people of the rural hinterland that Gandhi was the avatar of their tribal god (Hardiman 1987: 168–9). He was very successful with this ploy, until Gandhi himself told him to stop. Instead of getting support under false pretences, he told his disciples to take constructive steps to tackle the deprivation among the tribals. By spinning and weaving, and abstaining from alcohol, non-vegetarian food, and many other harmful and unclean practices they would be able to gain a rightful place in mainstream society. Implementation of this programme, which had a strong Hinduist bias, was supervised by social workers operating from six ashrams, centres for constructive activities spread around the outlying rural areas, with the one in Bardoli town as the main focal point. The staff provided information and training, distributed spinning wheels, collected the yarn and the khadi made from it, and set up *bhajan mandlis*, small singing clubs that strengthened community feeling with edifying and nationalist songs. In disseminating this new morality, the Gandhian workers encountered a way of life that was new to them. The sympathy and compassion they felt for the people who constituted their primary target group could not disguise the fact that they had no affinity with the tribal culture and tended to see it as the very reason why these people lagged behind in their development. These social reformers reported on the progress they made and a wider public became aware of their experiences when they were published in the chronicles of the Independence movement. Gandhi himself wrote the introduction to an article, translated by his secretary Mahadev Desai, that had appeared earlier in the Gujarati magazine *Navjivan*. Under the title 'Face to Face with the Pauper', the author describes a visit to a Dubla one evening. Sitting in front of her hut, the woman willingly answered questions, narrating how she and her seven children had survived the day with so little food. The conversation continued:

'Where is your man? Gone out?' 'The master has summoned him and he has gone there.' The master happened to be known to one of us. The family were servants (or slaves?) of this master who had ill-treated them and the poor man had fled from his clutches. But the master had traced him out and one might well imagine what had happened to the wretch. As though this was not enough, we asked one more question before we left her in peace. 'Did you go to work today?' 'How could I go? Who would take care of these children?' We were silenced, but in a moment we mustered courage to say to her: 'If you have a wheel, the children can playfully spin on it, and you can earn a few coppers' (*Young India*, 31 March 1927).

The staff of the six centres brought a large band of proselytes with them to the annual conference to demonstrate the success of their activities. The first kaliparaj conference in 1923 was chaired by Vallabhbhai Patel who, as Gandhi's deputy, had been appointed president of the Swaraj Ashram Sangh. A crowd of 20,000 tribals listened to speeches by Patel and Gandhi's wife, Kasturba. A month later, Kasturba presided over a follow-up meeting at which a message from Patel was read out. Praising the kaliparaj for their response to the appeal to mobilize, Patel also warned them not to turn against those who had stood in the way of their advancement.

Everyone is surprised to see the awakening in your community. But you should be careful. If you try to run too fast, you are likely to fall. Your decision not to work for Parsis and Muslims is very serious. Whatever steps you take should be well thought out (Hardiman 1987: 193).

Elaborating on the same subject Hardiman notes that in her speech, Kasturba Gandhi was even more explicit in calling on the kaliparaj to temper their radicalism. She cautioned the tribals for the strike they had started and called on them not to persist in their refusal to work any longer for the Parsis. It was a sign of the changing times that the tribals took no notice of these instructions given by their well-wishers.

In a richly documented analysis of colonial records combined with oral accounts based on fieldwork, Hardiman challenges the accuracy of the customary view that Gandhian activists had liberated the tribals from their ignorance and deprivation. The starting point of his study is the Devi movement which spread through the tribal communities of south Gujarat like a tidal wave in the early 1920s. What had originally emerged as an exorcism cult in the face of a smallpox epidemic gradually changed into a purification movement—its followers broke with elements of their tribal culture which were seen by outsiders as proof of their inferiority. The reforms they practised included taking a bath each day, bodily hygiene, decent clothing and housing, chaste relationships between men and women, and a taboo on licentious behaviour, avoiding non-vegetarian food, and total abstinence. The way of life that the goddess Devi prescribed for her followers was strikingly similar to the reforms preached a little later by Gandhian missionaries. Hardiman does not deny that, with this message, the latter succeeded in penetrating the tribal communities. He believes, however, that Gandhi became popular in these circles—indeed, achieved almost divine status—because the ideas that were propagated in his name had already been introduced to the tribals by reformers in their midst. Nationalist activists and tribal reformers proved to have the same agenda, although the activists did not act as mentors with a brief to awaken a still slumbering mass. In Hardiman's argument the struggle for emancipation originated in assertiveness from below. In this scenario too, the Independence movement provided a channel for the expression of social aspirations that had already been lying dormant for some time and which had grown steadily in strength. He opposes the tendency to interpret the desire for emancipation expressed by the Devi movement as an example of the transition 'from tribe to caste'. The purification called for by the reformers, was not to make themselves acceptable as pure Hindus that had to be integrated a little higher above the base of the caste system. Their ambitions reached further; they wanted equality with the higher castes, and gaining self-respect was a primary condition for achieving that goal. Relevant in this context is Hardiman's comment that disciples of the new lifestyle were mostly to be found among the tribal landowners, while the landless members of the tribe showed little interest (1987: 151–2). His findings show clearly that Dhodhias and Chodhras were more easily persuaded than Dublas. Still, other colonial sources insisted that the Mata movement gained support in particular among tribal communities, such as Dublas, who already had long-standing contact with caste Hindus (*Census of India 1941*, vol. xvii: 62–3). It was not for the first time that their resistance to subordination took a religious turn. A segment of Dublas in the neighbouring Broach district called in the late 19th century for emancipation from domination along with the promise that the goddess Mata would make the enemies' bullets melt (Dosabhai 1894: 299, 301 and Hunter 1892: 413, both quoted in Breman 1985: 124).

The followers of the Devi movement proved more radical in their desire for reform than the Gandhian activists and exceeded limits which the latter took care to respect. That applied in particular to the idea that progress could be achieved by rejecting impurities in one's lifestyle. Although the tribal reformers also recognized the necessity of self-purification, *atmashuddhi*, in contrast to the advocates of Gandhi's teaching, they had no hesitation in attributing the shortcomings in their existence to the social abuse to which they were subjected: the regime of exploitation and repression that was the prime cause of their state of backwardness. Hardiman observes that the Devi movement did not call on its followers to adopt Hindu customs and rites, and did not, therefore, aim to achieve religious conversion, but in the final phase of its development displayed resistance to the established order by demanding higher wages and calling for a ban on all work for distillers and traders (1987: 46). It has already been mentioned that Congress leaders were displeased at these displays of militancy. Docile obedience was, and remained, the message that Gandhian shepherds preached to their flock. Defiance, not to mention resistance against the ingrained hierarchical structure, was considered inappropriate and the traditional distinction between ujliparaj and kaliparaj was not up for discussion.

Agitation became more and more violent, but the religious interests were organised on a more permanent basis under Hindu influence. *Bhajan* meetings were held everywhere and became a regular feature of aboriginal life; attempts to give *dikshu* to educated tribesmen were made and advantage was taken of the anti-drink movement to introduce changes in food, dress, habit, etc. While the anti-drink fury and the class-war subsided, as they were bound to, these changes in religion and social attitude have persisted and tended to become more permanent (*Census of India 1931*, vol. xix, 386).

By the time the campaign of civil disobedience had started, the Devi cult had already passed its peak and, a short time later, the storm had blown over. Many tribals no longer adhered to the reforms that had brought about such far-reaching changes in their way of life in such a short time. They reverted in particular to the excessive consumption of alcohol. This is not to say that the assertiveness and struggle for self-respect that had been the main driving forces of the purification movement in south Gujarat had left no traces. This impact, to which Hardiman rightly attracts attention at the end of his study, will be discussed in the following chapter.

Clearly, the Congress movement lacked sufficient insight into the intricate fabric of rural society. To recruit support among the tribals it needed more knowledge of these communities and the problems confronting them. In addition it had to explore the best way to ensure that this mission to civilize the mass at the base of society was a success. At the first kaliparaj conference in 1923, Vallabhbhai Patel set up a committee to investigate these issues. Gandhi summarized an interim report and published it in the magazine *Young India*. During its tour of forty-seven villages in Chikhli and Bulsar taluka, the committee was constantly confronted with complaints and talks about the consumption of alcohol. Addiction to strong drink was related to local superstition, as drinking played a central role in tribal ceremonies. The remedy was in the constructive work advocated by Gandhi: anti-drinking propaganda to save money together with the distribution of spinning wheels and instruction in their use, so that people could supplement their meagre incomes. But surely the main obstacle to tribal upliftment was their subaltern position in the social structure? In his own typical way, Gandhi addressed this issue in his summary:

There is no hope for this land so long as the upper and well-to-do classes do not realise their duty by their unfortunate and ignorant brothers who after all the backbone of the country (*Young India*, 16 June 1927: 200).

It was an appeal to the better-off people to familiarize themselves with the destitution in which their less fortunate compatriots were living and to do something about it. But what exactly he meant by 'their duty' is not clear. The constructive work that Gandhi saw as the key to liberation from backwardness started and ended with removing the defects in the tribal way of life. However, not all social workers trained in the Gandhian school of thought were as reserved or conservative as their leader. After becoming acquainted with the suffering of the tribal population, some of them displayed a more critical viewpoint and supported a more progressive course of action. One of the best known of these activists was Sumant Mehta. As a medical doctor he held an official position in the civil service in the principality of Baroda as sanitary commissioner, but stepped down to devote his efforts, together with his wife, to the Independence movement. It was at his suggestion that Gandhi announced—at the kaliparaj conference in 1927 chaired by Mehta—that the name 'kaliparaj' would no longer be used. While studying in England, Mehta had often been called 'nigger' or 'blackie', and this had inspired him to oppose the identification of tribals as 'black people'. The term *raniparaj* which he introduced emphasized in a more positive light that these people had originally lived in the forests.[16] Gandhi gave his blessing to the new name.

What I have said so far could create the impression that the campaign of civil disobedience did not challenge halipratha in any way. This impression is not entirely accurate. There was indeed no systematic action taken to end this form of unfree labour in the agricultural economy in Bardoli and the surrounding area. It was of course remarkable enough in itself that this dark stain on the fabric of society could be ignored in the campaign to liberate the nation. A small number of exceptions that prove the rule show clearly what interests inspired the Congress leadership and how they decided to pursue these priorities in practice. At the end of 1960, as part of the record of the struggle for Independence in the region, the Surat district authorities commissioned a special publication devoted to the social history of the tribal communities in the late-colonial era. The author, I.I. Desai, needed no more than a few sentences to describe the insignificant role of the Dublas. The effort to mobilize them within the framework of the movement for national Independence extended no further than a few events aimed especially at this segment, all of which resulted in a fiasco. One of these meetings, held in a mango orchard alongside the road from Navsari to Palsana, was attended by Vallabhbhai Patel himself. The reforms called for at such occasions always related to ways in which the Dublas should improve their indolent and lethargic lifestyle: not to go into debt to get married, to avoid large-scale expenses and, of course, to give up their addiction to alcohol. The resolutions to which all those present committed themselves by raising their hands were not worth the paper they were written on, as they were never put into practice. In fact, the social workers were of the opinion that all effort was a waste of time because the Dublas were lethargic and had no self-respect. Because they were unaware of the total lack of prospects offered by the situation in which they lived, they also had no desire to improve their ways. Their deprivation was so great compared to that of the other tribal groups that Gandhian activists could find no starting point to arouse their latent aspirations for a better life. Whenever there appeared to be the slightest spark of vitality among them, it was extinguished again in no time. This widely shared view held the Dublas themselves accountable for their inactivity. Twenty years after the start of the reform movement, this community remained—to use one of Gandhi's expressions— 'untouched like a lotus in the water' (I.I. Desai 1971: 157).[17]

But now and then a stone would disturb the still water, as can be seen from an incident that occurred in the Sarbhon ashram in early 1924. Gandhi had appointed Narhari Parikh, a trusted supporter, as leader of the ashram, which had been set up shortly before to conduct constructive work in the area to the south of Bardoli. His daily work consisted of propagating spinning and collection of the yarn in the local villages. On his own initiative he opened an evening school for Dubla children from a slum on the outskirts of the village. His intention was to teach them the basic principles of the alphabet, which fitted in with the Gandhian programme of tribal upliftment. The Patidar landowners immediately expressed their strong displeasure at his interference in their domain and told him to stop. After all, what need had the children of the landless for education, when they would be spending their lives tending to their master's cattle and working in his fields? When Parikh did not respond to their demands, the peasants adopted harder measures. The Dublas were informed that they were not to send their children to the ashram. As a true disciple of Gandhi, Parikh went on a hunger strike, first for three days and then for seven. But the Patidars were not impressed by his protest, announced a boycott on the social worker and repossessed household articles he had borrowed in the hope that he would decide to leave. Gandhi had heard about the conflict and sent Vallabhbhai Patel to Bardoli to prevent further escalation and to reconcile the conflicting parties. Patel persuaded Parikh to give up his hunger strike and the Patidars to allow the school to be reopened. However, in the darkness and silence behind the scenes of this public drama, the dominant landowners had applied so much pressure on their hali servants that not a single child attended the school again. Thus ended the attempt of one Gandhian activist to uplift the Dublas around him. The school remained open formally, but informally it closed for ever.

In 1946, Jugatram Dave published a booklet, for which Narhari Parikh wrote the foreword, describing and criticizing the halipratha system.[18] Dave, who was a trusted lieutenenant of Gandhi, explained frankly how, after the incident in 1924, no further action was taken that might jeopardize the confidence of the main landowning class in the Independence movement.

We could recognise that to serve the Halpatis [note: the new name for the Dublas introduced in 1939] was not so simple a task, as it appeared to be. It involved an age-long economic tradition. *We should first patiently secure the confidence of the farmers' community. Only by a long service of years together we shall be in a position to awaken in them the feeling of human sympathy and justice for Halpatis. So from 1924 to 1938 we, the volunteers never raised this issue* [my italics] (Dave 1946: 35).

In the next chapter I will discuss why this policy of non-intervention came to an end in 1938 and with what consequences. But in the preceding period, Gandhi showed that he was very well aware of the yoke under which the Dublas laboured as servants of the landowners. A speech in 1922 at the Swaraj ashram in Bardoli made his position very clear: 'The *ujliparaj* should understand that in the present condition of India we are all Dublas' (I.I. Desai 1971: 127). It was quite clear that the stalwarts of the nationalist movement had become aware of the lack of freedom in agrarian society. Suman Mehta did not mince words when he blamed the vested interests for the misery of the landless underclass in and around Bardoli.

The condition of these Dublas is indeed pitiable. It is shameful on the part of the high-cast Hindus who have used them as mere slaves. These people have no access to education, or any good values. The stories of Ram and Sita never fall on their ears. They start working as labourers from the tender age of eight. They are slaves, they live as *halis* or landless agriculturists on the farm of well-to-do farmers. When they marry, they incur debts of Rs 50 to 200 and provide drinks to their relatives. They begin to work for people they borrow money from and sign letters to repay the debt. The debt, of course, is never over. Both the landowner and the Dubla are aware of this. The landowner maintains accounts in such a way that interest multiplies and there is more credit than debit in the accounts. This whole issue has become quite knotty now because the landowners (*dhaniyama*)-claim that they do not benefit from hiring a Dubla instead of a casual labourer. I don't believe this. If hiring Dublas was not economically advantageous, thousands of men would not be engaging Dublas. They are certainly not being hired for altruistic reasons (S.B. Mehta n.d.: 234).[19]

The Success of 1928

During one of the periodical reviews of the land tax, the most important source of revenue for the colonial state, the authorities announced that they had decided to increase the tax rate in the subdistrict of Bardoli by 30 per cent. They justified this on the basis of the rapid development of the agricultural sector and the greater prosperity of the cultivators. In his report, the official in charge of the revised survey and settlement operation listed a number of improvements that supported this claim: the larger and better houses the farmers had built in recent years, thriving trade, increased land prices and tenancy rates, and high incomes from cotton, the main cash crop.[20] There was no doubt that Surat district, and Bardoli in particular, had experienced more rapid economic growth than most other areas in west India. While the government was still discussing the increases, the landowners in the subdistrict already had some idea of what was in store. Early in 1926, the Bardoli Taluka Congress Committee published a pamphlet calling on its members to not to comply with the new tax rates and to prepare themselves for a campaign of public agitation if the protest was not successful. But that option had to be investigated, so an enquiry committee was set up to respond to the official proposals. The committee produced a report debunking all the arguments supporting the increase. It was shown that only emigrants to Africa who transferred their savings home or brought them back with them had achieved any real material progress and that, after a number of good years, the cotton prices had crashed to just half the level reached in 1924. Moreover, the positive impact of the earlier increase in income had been more than cancelled out by a sharp rise in production costs. In short, far from making a profit, the argument was that most peasants were suffering heavy losses.

The findings of the Bardoli Enquiry Committee were published in two magazines, both edited by Gandhi. An English version appeared in *Young India*,[21] and the committee's chairman, Narhari Parikh, wrote a series of eight articles for Gujarati readers in *Navjivan*, which came out weekly.[22] Parikh provided an overview of the agrarian population of Bardoli: 11,000 were tribal peasants (Chodhra, Dhodhia, and Gamit) who were owners or tenants of small and low-quality plots. Half of the remaining 76,000 were ujliparaj (Kanbis, Brahmans, Baniyas, and Muslims), and the other half were Dublas, who owned no land but worked as farm servants for the high-caste peasants. Most were halis, with only a few working as free labourers. Parikh provided this overview to show clearly that agriculture in Bardoli entailed high production costs. This was largely due to the fact that the ujliparaj landowners were unwilling to work their land themselves.

Among the farmers the inclination to rely on their own labour has gradually gone down. In the Anavil caste self-cultivating farmers are very few. Among them the womenfolk don't work at all.... The Kanbi would hardly work if he could get a farm labourer (Dubla) to whom he could assign the work. The practice of farm labour (Dubla) in Surat is of a special kind. The real tillers of the land are these farm labourers. But their condition is almost like that of slaves. Whether the crop yields are good or poor, whether prices realised are more or less, the remunerations they receive are the same, as they have been over the ages. Therefore they have no personal interest of any kind in the cultivation. Work done under compulsion can never be good and hence the condition of agriculture is deteriorating by the day. Still the farmers believe genuinely that their interest lies in the preservation of *halipratha*. This system has lowered the Dubla community from human existence to the state of animals. Morally the practice is harmful even to farmers who are considered as masters of the Dublas. But these masters believe that the *hali* system is economically beneficial to them. It is not.[23]

In the subsequent article in the series Parikh explained that the costs of agricultural production were much higher than the government had assumed because the high-caste landowners insisted on keeping halis. He also explained what this meant. Dubla boys would start tending their master's cattle from the early age of seven or eight. As cattle boys they would get a morning meal, a pair of pants and a pair of shoes once a year, and a wage of 6 to 12 rupees a year. When the Dubla was 18 to 20 years old, his master would pay for his marriage, which would cost some 150 to 200 rupees. That debt obliged him to work for the master, for which he was paid in the form of breakfast, a midday meal and, at the end of the day, a grain allowance that would have to suffice as an evening meal for his wife and children. The Dubla's wife was permitted to work elsewhere but only after she had spent a few hours in the morning working in the master's household and cleaning the stall. For these chores she would get a little food, two to three rupees a year and a *sari* with a blouse piece. Altogether this would amount to about eight to ten rupees a year. The labourer himself cost only six annas per day (n.b.: 16 annas = 1 rupee)—this was the value of his food and the grain allowance—yet he was expensive for the master to maintain. The latter had to give him his grain allowance every day, even when he was too ill or too lazy too work, otherwise he would have no food. Any expenses incurred by the master for which the labourer did not work in return were added to the original debt. This also applied to the small amounts of money the master gave him to buy alcohol. That would happen if someone in the hali's household died—for when visitors came to pay their respects and for the funeral—but also on other occasions; for example, if the labourer had continued to work during the rain, or had done some extra jobs. The debt gradually increased and was, of course, never paid off. Parikh calculated that the total wage bill for the master was nine annas a day, or at least 150 rupees a year. To this he added several tens of rupees for what he called interest on his investment in labour and an amount for depreciation. After all, the master did not get back the money that he had invested in the servant, and it was necessary to take account of the risk that the latter might die or run away after some time. I have described the argument of the committee chairman in detail to show how he managed to raise the cost price of a hali so considerably. His reason for doing this was to show that unfree labour was not cheap for the employers but actually very expensive. He added that the arrangement was also less than perfect because it gave the Dubla no reason at all to work hard.

This system makes the farm labourer free from the worries as to from where tomorrow's meals would come and, consequently, the attached servant becomes totally irresponsible and careless and he does much less work than a free labourer.[24]

Without doubt, Parikh initially criticized the halipratha system because he thought it immoral. When the high-caste landowners proved unresponsive to this argument, he tried to convince them that it was economically inefficient. But in fact, his line of reasoning confirmed what the masters themselves always said: the Dublas had no sense of responsibility, cared for nothing, and were endlessly lazy. In a different way, he actually took sides with the landowners by suggesting with his calculations that their costs outweighed their profit.

The authorities proved unresponsive to this interpretation. They rejected the protest against the higher land revenue and the factual evidence on which it was based, but as a sign of goodwill, agreed to restrict the increase to a maximum of 22 per cent. For the hard core of the dominant landowners, this concession did not go far enough. They discussed the matter amongst themselves to bring their widely varying opinions into one line. The advocates of a more confrontational course of action visited Vallabhbhai Patel in Ahmedabad to get him on their side. The delegation returned to Bardoli with the message that he supported their demands. The Congress committee then called a meeting to consult with the members. The landowners who attended the meeting—who represented almost half of all the villages in the subdistrict—agreed to ask Patel to lead the campaign against the authorities. Patel consented to do so, but also asked the leaders of the protest to meet Gandhi and inform him of the situation in detail. Gandhi gave the farmers' protest his blessing.[25] The authorized records of the satyagraha are not clear on why Patel led the campaign instead of Gandhi. Reading between the lines it is clear that the lobby of landowners preferred Patel, not only because Gandhi had called off the campaign in 1922, against their wishes, but also because they suspected that he was biased in favour of the tribals, including the poor peasants and the landless labourers. They were certain that Patel, from Patidar stock, would allow himself to be led by the interests of the dominant landlowners. The possible differences of opinion between the two Congress leaders on the agrarian question did not mean that they expressed their differences in public. Patel wanted a free hand in Bardoli and to make it clear that, as the landowners wanted, his word was law. Dinkar Mehta said this in as many words—and as a member of Patel's entourage during campaign, he was in a position to know.

From outside, the Sardar was not allowing others to come. Gandhiji never came. Everything had been left to the Sardar. He used to give daily reports to Gandhiji (interview with Dinkar Mehta 1975: 34).

Gandhi had appointed Patel leader of the Congress movement in Gujarat and given him the name Sardar in 1924 to show his appreciation for the courage, zeal, and stamina of his lieutenant.[26] In return, Patel made sure never to criticize his chief in public.

Sardar Patel arrived in Bardoli in February 1928 and immediately organized a meeting with local leaders to determine their willingness to take action. He ran the campaign like a military operation. He divided the subdistrict into four zones and set up camps in each one, with a staff of volunteers. The staff carried out orders from the headquarters, visited the villages in their area and reported their findings and questions to the central command. These lines of communication ensured that the top and the base remained in close contact and were able to keep a sharp eye on new developments. Patel arrived on the date that the first tax return was due and the authorities were taking steps to effect mandatory payment—together with a very substantial fine for refusal to pay. An information network was set up by posting observers at government offices and following officials as they went about their business. A lot of attention was devoted to publicity. During the four months that the campaign lasted, the department in charge of public relations published a newsletter, *Satyagraha Patrika*, giving news on activities, when and where meetings would be held and who would be speaking at them, what the government was planning to do, and so on. This incessant flow of information served to keep the rank and file motivated and ensure that they did not desert the cause. Jugatram Dave edited the newsletter, which was published daily with a circulation of between 9000 and 12,000.

The *Patrika* had two to six pages of news, abstracts of speeches, and specific instructions and directions for anticipating official moves in the localities and being prepared to oppose them. Its language was simple and colloquial, replete with familiar analogies and charged with satire. Each issue was full of exciting reportage of events as well as poems, stories and humorous skits lampooning government officers (G. Shah 1974: 104).

Although the newsletter was primarily intended to keep the people informed of the campaign's progress, it was also used to mobilize public opinion in the country. Sardar Patel had brought along a whole team of activists, who were staff members of Gandhi's Sabarmati ashram in Ahmedabad and students from Gujarat Vidyapith, the college, based on his principles, which he had established in the city. Among the latter group was Dinkar Mehta, whose job it was to record Sardar Patel's speeches and prepare them for publication in the bulletin.[27] The Bardoli campaign was critical to Patel's political reputation and he took personal charge of ensuring that the progress and results achieved, as well as his role, were recorded in detail. Gandhi's secretary, Mahadev Desai, was also released from his duties in Ahmedabad to act as official chronicler for the duration of the agitation. Activists from outside the subdistrict came to reinforce the local campaign staff. These volunteers were recruited by the workers of the six ashrams that had been involved in Gandhi's efforts to achieve tribal upliftment in the preceding years.

A committee of peasants' leaders set up by Sardar Patel adopted a resolution that rejected the new tax demand and called on the farmers to refuse to pay. The meeting at which this occurred was solemn, and included Hindu hymns and readings from the Koran. The struggle about to be embarked upon was referred to as *Maha Yagna*, a great sacrificial offering. The religious symbolism was intended to present participation in the satyagraha as a holy and inescapable duty. As with the action committee set up by Gandhi in 1922, all twelve members of the new committee came from the agrarian elite: there were no less than five Patidars, three Anavil Brahmans, two Muslims, one Bania, and one Parsi. Once again, two-thirds of the local population were not represented in this core group which was to decide on the course of the campaign, under the leadership of Sardar Patel. What measures were taken to create the impression that the entire population had been mobilized? The most decisive factor was to bring the landowners together in a united front.

... initially there was very little Anavil support to the movement. However, once the atmosphere of the satyagraha was under way, Dayalji (note: Desai) successfully provoked his caste members to come forward and support the movement by reproaching them through his caste magazine *Anavil Sevak* for their loyalty to the government. He put them to shame by showing that lower castes like Patidars and even the Scheduled Tribes had fearlessly joined the movement. Upon this Anavils were also mobilised into the movement (Bhatt 1970: 330).

Although the tax increase would primarily affect the well-to-do landowners it was to be expected that the government would try to create division and to isolate the hard core of the protesters from those peasants who would either not have to pay very much or who were prepared to pay the higher tax for fear of the sanctions. The members of the peasants' committee may have owned the lion's share of all cultivable land between them, but getting them to agree was difficult enough. The Baniyas, Parsis, Muslims, and even the Anavils were considered likely to give in soon enough when the government started to apply pressure (M. Desai 1929: 36–7). Sardar Patel could count on the Patidars, but their support alone was not enough to keep the resistance campaign afloat. The solution to this problem was to declare that all those who made a living in agriculture qualified as *khedut*, peasants. Widely varying groups were brought together under this label: large and small landowners, tenants and sharecroppers, and the largest class of all, the agricultural labourers. Even artisans and members of service castes were included in this wide-ranging definition, since they too were seen as depending on agriculture for their livelihood. The fact that only a minority of this heterogeneous mass were affected by the new land tax did not prevent the campaign from being made into a common interest that acquired the character of something of a holy war that all 'farmers' were obliged to fight against the colonial state.

The term was applied to not only all cultivators but to virtually all inhabitants of the taluka as all of them depended on agriculture as a source of livelihood. Hindus and Muslims, Patidars and Baniyas, caste Hindus and adivasis were all equal in so far as they were connected with agriculture (G. Shah 1974: 97).

In the fight between good and evil, Gandhi as holy leader and Sardar Patel as his high priest led the good side, that of the people. Heroically, they stood up to the government, which was demonized as evil incarnate. In the light of this Manichaeist dichotomy it was natural to condemn any form of collaboration with the authorities as consorting with the enemy. Village chiefs and petty officials in charge of local-level administration were placed under considerable pressure and, faced with growing hostility, many patels and talatis resigned their positions for fear of even worse reprisals. As a result, the higher echelons of the government were cut off from the base of society and could no longer count on the loyalty of the staff that did not resign. As they increasingly lost touch with the situation, the authorities became less alert and less able to respond adequately to events. This created a power vacuum that only strengthened the determination of the activists.

The campaign leaders and their staff of volunteers tried other ways of closing the ranks, especially by appealing to caste loyalties. Landowners who vacillated or who refused to comply with the call not to pay the tax were called to order by the members of their own caste and others, who imposed a wide range of sanctions.

A Baniya of Valod paid a heavy price for his payment of land revenue. Following a decision of the village council, the shopkeepers refused to sell anything to him, the barber refused to shave him, and the potter denied him vessels. His daughter was sent back to him by his son-in-law. Nobody even talked with him. So much so that the indigenous midwife refused to render her services while his wife was in labour. Only after the intercession of the village headman, who took pity on him, did the midwife attend to his wife. Consequently, the Baniya had to yield, apologize for his action, and pay a fine to the village fund. Thereafter, he was taken back into the fold of the caste and village community (G. Shah 1974: 99).

It was not only outsiders who threatened disloyal landowners with a social boycott, but also members of their own family. Few were able to withstand this intimidation and were forced to toe the line. The public explanation for redressing their wayward behaviour was that these sinners had seen the error of their ways and had returned voluntarily to the fold.

For its part, the government also increased the pressure. In July 1928, a little over half the land to which the higher tax rate applied had been possessed, with the accompanying threat that it would shortly be auctioned to outsiders at a low price. In response to this, Sardar Patel emphasized that the campaign was part of the struggle for freedom. He told the peasants not to be afraid: their land would still be there when the foreign rulers had gone. The government tried to create a division by telling tribal landowners that the higher tax rate did not apply to them. This tactic also failed. Not because the rules and customs of the caste hierarchy were not effective in their case and the threat of a boycott would therefore have little impact, but because the tribal groups believed that their desire for emancipation would best be served by supporting the nationalist movement. The reform work of the Gandhians had reinforced this belief. They supported the ujliparaj not out of of weakness or fear but because it strengthened their bargaining position in the agrarian economy of the region.

On the whole it was the more prosperous adivasis who participated directly, for most of the poorer adivasis were tenants who were not directly responsible for paying the land-tax. In Vedchi the leading reformer, Jivan Patel, was beaten up by the police for refusing to pay his tax. In Bedkuva the big landowner Panabhai Gamit took the lead in refusing his tax, and several advisasis were punished by having their buffaloes and furniture confiscated by the government. In all eighty-two adivasis were arrested during the course of the struggle. Chodhri women played a notable part, being to the fore in demonstrations, courting imprisonment and persuading their menfolk to refuse their tax (Hardiman 1987: 203).

The authorities were frustrated in all manner of ways in their efforts to confiscate the property of those who were due to pay tax. Village headmen who decided to stay on were urged—by appealing to their dignity and self-respect—to at least refuse to cooperate with the government. 'Otherwise he is no better than Dubla or a bonded slave of the Government', said Sardar Patel caustically (Shirin Mehta 1984: 123). The subordination of lower to higher castes was exploited by ordering the former not to provide any form of assistance in confiscating the property of landowners. 'Non-tax payers, like Adivasis and Harijans, stood by their masters, deciding that none of them would help a government officer in carrying the forfeited property' (G. Shah 1974: 98). They showed the courage to which Sardar Patel spurred them on in a poignant reference to their reputation as Dublas.

'You fear that you will be called upon to assist in a *japti* (note: confiscation). Shake off that fear. You are men, you are not *dublas*. Spurn that appellation of degradation. *Dubla* means weak and cowardly. Weak and cowardly are they who would exact labour from you. You are strong enough to labour in the fields, strong enough to carry burdens for yourself and for others, how can you be called weak?' (Chopra 1991: 132).[28]

Landowners evaded the long arm of the government by leaving the village if a raid by the tax inspectors was imminent. Moving tales appeared in *Satyagraha Patrika* about how their faithful Dubla servant watched over the household effects and the cattle they had to leave behind. Control over agricultural labour was also a weapon that could be used to call a whole village to order if the landowners remained recalcitrant.

The village Kadod, the stronghold of the Banias, had remained aloof. To make the village join the movement, the surrounding villages like Rayam, Sankli Akoti, Balda, Bamni and Nani Falod organised a boycott of Kadod and decided not to supply any farm labour to till the land. At last the village gave in on April 1928, regretted its action, pledged its support to the movement, and assured Vallabhbhai that 'nobody from us will pay land revenue dues from henceward' (Shirin Mehta 1984: 122).

Mobilization drives based on pretensions of vertical solidarity are suspect. In contrast to the harmonious unity that it implied, there was in practice a long-standing tradition of discrimination and denigration of the low by the high. This stigmatization was also reflected in the appeal of the campaign leaders to the ujliparaj to conduct themselves decently or to run the risk of turning into inferior people. A warning given by Kunvarji Mehta to his Patidar audience in the village of Mota illustrates this attitude.

Narrating a 'historical' episode he said that a hundred years ago a 'religious' war took place between the local people and foreign aggressors in which the brave men of the time went to protect their motherland. They were Kshatriyas. But a few cowardly and selfish persons betrayed their community by keeping away from the war. They were subsequently out-casted by the community, forced to settle outside the village, and were obliged to carry dead animals and village sewage as punishment for their 'sinful behaviour'. Those were the Dheds, the untouchables, who were suffering for the act of cowardice of their ancestors. They were lucky that now Gandhi had come to their rescue and tried to bring them out of their misery. Mehta implied that the persons who were 'throwing bones' (not cooperating in the satyagraha) would be treated like untouchables. Raising his emotional tone, he asked the women in his audience, 'Would you like your husbands and sons to do this job?' Turning to the men, he asked, 'Are you ready to do such a job. If you say no, then you should dismiss the idea of paying land revenue and be ready to help to raise the prestige of the Patidars' (G. Shah 1974: 99–100).

After almost half a year it became clear that the united front was not going to be breached and both parties felt that the time had come to attempt a compromise. Finding a solution that was acceptable to both sides took a long time, but the colonial authorities and the campaign leaders had an interest in finding common ground. The authorities had only managed to collect a sixth of the taxes due and were alarmed that a local issue had achieved such popularity across the country. For his part, Sardar Patel had to take account of the vulnerability of his peasants' alliance and prominent voices within the Congress movement which did not want the agrarian question to be brought to a head. Political developments at the national level reinforced calls to scale down the conflict in Bardoli. One condition for an agreement was that owners whose land had been confiscated would get it back. In addition, village officials who had resigned would be considered for reappointment and peasants taken into custody for refusing to pay the tax would be released. Once all this had been agreed satisfactorily, the way was clear to agree on a lower tax rate. Early in August 1928, in the expectation that this problem would be solved, too, it was decided to end the campaign. The government appointed two officials, R.S. Broomfield and R.M. Maxwell, to conduct an investigation into the rate of the land tax. They were given permission to talk to the peasants and to listen to the opinions of their representatives. They also took note of the report of the Bardoli Enquiry Committee, which had signalled the start of the farmers' resistance in 1926. During their tour lasting more than two months,

Broomfield and Maxwell gathered information in forty-nine villages in Bardoli taluka. Their report, published in April 1929, recommended increasing the land tax by 6 per cent, a quarter of the original increase proposed by the authorities.[29] There was no doubt that the satyagraha had been a resounding success. The colonial authorities had suffered a sensitive defeat, and the Congress movement had succeeded in presenting itself as a diligent and effective representative of the peasants' interests. But the question remained: of which peasants?

Consolidation of Agrarian Dominance and Subordination

Behind the campaign banner of 'each and every one', it was the dominant landowners who were at the forefront of the agitation. The support of the entire population was, however, required to fight for the interests of this agrarian elite, who owned between six and 25 acres. As ujliparaj this segment represented no more than 13 per cent of the population in the subdistrict and, to ensure that the demands of this minority were met, the remaining massive majority of the landpoor and the landless underclasses belonging to low castes and tribal communities had to be mobilized. Their interests, in as far as they were considered separately at all, were taken to coincide—or at least run parallel to—those of the dominant landowners. An excuse that may have held some water earlier, namely that the leaders of the Independence movement had little insight into the social structure of the agrarian economy, was no longer valid in 1928. The image invoked in the early nationalist literature of a village community with a simple hierarchy in which self-employed cultivators exchanged part of their harvest with non-agrarian specialists in a relationship of reciprocity was at variance with the dynamics of the rural economy in the late-colonial era. In addition, it should have become clear that the social differentiation inherent to rural society could not be exclusively, or even largely, attributed to the effects of foreign rule. The presence of a cadre of Congress workers in Bardoli from the early 1920s had put them into direct contact with tribal cultivators and landless labourers. As they implemented their programme of constructive activities, the Gandhian social workers had observed their clients' subordination in servitude to the dominant landowners at first hand. Mahadev Desai's *Story of Bardoli* portrayed the tribals as 'the meekest of the meek' (M. Desai 1929: 54–5). The halipratha system became a regular subject of discussion in periodicals linked to the Congress movement. And yet, in the run-up to the agrarian campaign, the leaders of the movement did not hesitate for a moment in siding with the economically and socially strong elite while completely ignoring the excessive poverty and subalternity in which the landless half of the population of Bardoli lived.

The Independence movement not only took cognizance of the inequality that existed, but also used it for political ends. According to Sardar Patel, the broad alliance he forged expressed the harmonious solidarity between high and low castes. He consciously paid no attention to reports implying that unity had only been achieved with much more than persuasion and a little insistence. As already noted, according to a police source, the decision to hold the satyagraha in Bardoli was partly because the lower agrarian classes in the area were known for their docility.[30] Where, ten years previously, a similar campaign in the Kheda district had failed because the landpoor peasants and landless labourers refused to take part or were even hostile towards it, it was assumed that this antagonism between high and low, through which economic contradictions were sharpened by caste conflicts, did not exist in south Gujarat. Here the disprivileged and propertyless classes seemed to have accepted or even internalized their fate. That they would join rather than resist or sabotage a struggle meant to benefit the better off was taken for granted and only served to make the campaign leaders even more determined to succeed. According to Mahadev Desai, by taking part in the campaign they would achieve higher esteem from their masters.

... the refusal, on the other hand of the ordinary Dublas to help in the *japti* work (note: confiscation) was bound to have a wholesome effect on the relations between the landholders and the Dublas who worked for them. Those who had been up to now no better than menials and slaves came now to be looked upon as friends and brothers who had their share in the fight no less important than that of the landholders themselves (M. Desai 1929: 64).

The caste awareness to which the campaign strategists appealed not only related to the code of good conduct to which all were obliged irrespective of their communal identity, but also reaffirmed the subservience which the lower caste members owed to their superiors.

Patel told untouchables, Dublas and artisans that it was their dharma to be loyal to their masters. 'The government wants to divide you and the *shahukar* [note: moneylender], but for you, your shahukar is everything. You should laugh at and consider him a fool if somebody says that you should change your shahukar. It is just like saying to a *pativrata* [note: chaste and dutiful wife] that she should change her husband. How can you leave your shahukar who has helped you in your difficulties?' (G. Shah 1974: 101).

The campaign's chronicler saw this display of primordial solidarity as evidence of the benign power of tradition. The caste association of the Kanbis, he wrote, showed that their communal awareness had not been lost in the modern era (M. Desai 1929: 6). In this expression of contentment and pride in the resilience of the past there was no room for dissenting voices: for example, the fact that the caste association was hardly twenty years old and should be seen more as an expression of modernity than of tradition. Some Gandhian activists were critical of the way in which vertical dependence was manipulated to achieve a united front which concealed serious inequality and division. Gandhi received a number of complaints about this lack of scruples.

One can easily see that but for the organisation of the subcastes and castes we would never have won the battle of Bardoli. But it is immoral and improper. When philosophers of the world consider even nationalism as narrow, has not the Sardar of Bardoli given new life to communalism? Have we not committed immorality in defeating the enemy by throwing at them the mud of casteism? (Bhatt 1970: 333).

The peasants' leaders dismissed these complaints sarcastically as ideologically motivated and Gandhi did not respond to the accusations. But there was of course something contradictory in his unremitting campaign to combat discrimination against the untouchables and to advocate the emancipation of the Dublas, while Sardar Patel and notable Patidars like Kunvarji Mehta made condescending statements about the lower social segments. As one of the main spokesmen of the Bardoli campaign, Mehta encouraged the Patidars to show resolve and courage so as not to be degraded to Bhangis, while Patel castigated the Dublas for their weak and cowardly behaviour. Gandhi was well aware of the insincerity of the ujliparaj, who feigned to support his struggle to end discrimination against the untouchables in public but who stubbornly held on to a lifestyle based on abhorrence and disregard for the subaltern castes.

What leaders preached in public differed from what they practised in their private lives; 'those who met (or hugged) untouchables in public meetings before Gandhi bathed with their clothes on when they returned home' (Dhanagare 1983: 102–3).

In support of this statement the author added that, until 1936, not a single student from the untouchable castes was admitted to the ashram schools and hostels run by the Patidar Mandal in Bardoli and the surrounding area.

The leaders and supporters of the satyagraha had every reason to be proud of what it had achieved. The Congress had indeed succeeded in being recognized as a peasant organization. That the party had achieved this by allying themselves with the rural segment that controlled a disproportionate share of the cultivated land had been dictated by political opportunism. By seeking their support exclusively among the local elite, the nationalist leaders consciously avoided tackling the issue of the unequal distribution of land and the widespread existence of unfree labour in the agrarian economy. In the mildest interpretation these major problems remained unchallenged because to do so would inevitably have exposed the sharp class divisions in the primary sector of the economy. Although Sardar Patel insisted that the Bardoli campaign had no political objectives and was driven purely by economic motives, it was clear to everyone that recruiting support among the rural population was a high priority for the nationalist movement in its struggle against the colonial government. In this interpretation, the choice of the Congress to support vested interests was a strategic decision. In any case, the consequence was that the mass of landpoor farmers and landless labourers remained invisible and unrepresented. This bias would not change in subsequent agrarian campaigns supported by the Congress elsewhere in the country. It led Indulal Yagnik to comment scornfully on what he quite understandably considered to be a policy line favouring the rural elite:

While a lot of activity has been promoted in recent years to carry on temperance and spinning activities among these unfortunate people, nothing has been done to snap or even relax the unique chain of slavery in which thousands of these Dublas, men and women, live under the oppressive yoke of the so-called higher classes (Yagnik 1943).

The well-to-do peasants in Bardoli were satisfied with the considerable reduction in the land tax. For the Patidar majority among them it was possibly more important that, by taking a leading position in the struggle, they had increased their power and status. The aspirations which had inspired their leaders to join forces with the nationalist movement at an early stage had been fulfilled. The members of this caste would benefit even more, in economic and political terms, from their upward mobility after Independence, as I have described in another study based on fieldwork in the region of Bardoli (Breman 1985). But the hegemony of the Patidars evolved at the expense of the continued subordination of the Dublas, an outcome to which the Congress leaders were prepared to give their full support. Dhanagare summarized this scenario as follows:

> The Bardoli *satyagraha* thus symbolised agrarian class alliance against the government, but the co-operative endeavour was encouraged only insofar as it did not give rise to consciousness along class lines, and only to the extent it did not disturb the traditional social structure. The structural dependence of the lower castes on the superior had not weakened, but on the contrary was reinforced by the Gandhian political ethic that aimed at establishing a *gemeinschaft* solidarity among various castes and classes to fight against the British (Dhanagare 1983: 107).

In the historiography of the Bardoli satygraha the class conflict within the peasantry has been consistently underplayed. Sardar Patel, and not Gandhi, became lionized by the dominant landowners who were the main beneficiaries of the anti-colonial protest movement. The statue erected at the entrance of the town is not of the Father of the Nation but of the peasant leader, who happens to be a member of the same caste of Kanbi Patels now dignified as Patidars throughout Gujarat. And the national museum which has come up in the grounds of the Swaraj ashram also carries not the name of its founding father Mahatma Gandhi but that of his disciple Sardar Patel venerated until today as the one and only hero of 'the people of Bardoli'.

What explanation was given for tolerating the ongoing exploitation and oppression of the Dublas? Two motives are prominent in the accounts of the agitators. Firstly, that releasing the Dublas from their bondage in the halipratha system was a difficult problem for which an immediate solution could not be found because it would require a change in mentality among the landowners. I have already noted the comment of prominent social worker Jugatram Dave that it would take a long time for the masters to allow their code of conduct to be infused by feelings of humanity and justice. This was the target he had set for himself but it was no easy task. As evidence of this, in his series of articles on the investigation by the Bardoli Enquiry Committee, Narhari Parikh cited the example of a master who was forced by his fellow caste members to take back land that he had given to his servant on a sharecropping basis. The Patidar himself was too busy as a trader to cultivate his land, so he had decided to leave it to his hali, who received half of the yield. He had to cancel the agreement under pressure because Dublas were agricultural labourers and the other landowners saw the promotion of even one of them to the status of sharecropper as an unacceptable provocation (N. Parikh in *Navjivan*, 3 October 1926). As a genuine disciple of Gandhi, the author himself resolutely rejected the radical approach to accelerating the process of emancipation advocated by a number of hotheads. In his foreword to Jugatram Dave's booklet on halipratha, he showed that he was true to the Gandhian faith.

Some old social workers of the Bardoli taluka sense an attempt to create class conflict in the activities of workers to bring about an awakening among the Halpatis. But Jugatrambhai has made one thing very clear in this booklet, that efforts to secure human treatment and justice to the Halpatis should be made on the basis of truth and non-violence and never in a manner which would breed class conflict (Dave 1946: 10).

What Gandhi had in mind was that the dominant landowners would give up their newly acquired distaste for physical labour and return to a more simple life as self-working peasants, as former generations had done. But the Patidars, happy to have escaped such a way of life, had no intention of fulfilling the ideal of 'plain living and high thinking'. They engaged farm servants not only to do the work in the fields and tend the cattle but also so that they had subordinates to order around as they saw fit. Was Gandhi really so naive that he believed he could persuade the agrarian elite to put a stop to the regime of poverty and subordination in which the landless were imprisoned?

The second reason that social activists did not make a special effort to free the Dublas from bondage was because they believed that the latter owed their deprived status to shortcomings in their lifestyle. The reforms required to change this could not be achieved in the short term and were therefore not urgent. In fact they called on the landless to improve their behaviour by purging themselves of a wide range of vices: alcohol abuse, the ease with which they got themselves into debt, their inability to think ahead, and their indolence. It was because of all this that they were unable to extract themselves from the burden imposed on them by their masters. Even observers who commiserated with the landless—as, for example, Sumant Mehta did repeatedly—held the Dublas accountable for their misery.

A Dubla lived in the *wadi* (field) behind my house. His chief occupation was to smoke *bidi* and drink *toddy*. His wife was tall and emaciated. She would leave for earning her daily wages (*majoori*) every morning. She bore a child every twelve months, hence there was an army of starving children in her hut. One of her children was three months old. When the mother left for work, all the children would cry their lungs out and fall into silence out of exhaustion. The mother would extract milk from her breasts and leave it for the young child in a dirty saucer. The young child would be fed this milk by his six year old sister. The family ate only *jowar* (millet) gruel for food and nothing else.... I tried hard to drive some sense into that Dubla's head. I offered to employ him for sundry tasks so that the children would have at least something to eat. He was simply not ready to give up smoking and fooling around with women of his age. Never mind if he also starved, but he would simply not work. He finally took up the responsibility of working at a *toddy* shop so that he could have some *toddy* on the sly (S.B. Mehta n.d.: 233–4).

In this manner the Dublas themselves were blamed for their status as bonded servants. What it boiled down to was that they were halis because they wanted to be. It is the well-worn argument that slaves become slaves because they lack the resolve to live and work in freedom. Servitude had made the Dublas improvident and lazy but the reverse was equally true. Work or no work, they were assured that their master would provide all their basic needs. The virtues of diligence, moderation, and sobriety were unknown to them and only by learning them could they shake off their bonds of debt. This argument meant that outsiders, no matter how well-intentioned, could honestly say that they simply were unable to achieve what the Dublas themselves apparently did not seek: to be free labourers.

It was not difficult to find examples of Sardar Patel's prejudices against Dublas. But he came closer to peasant life than Gandhi ever was. Although the latter tended to romanticize the rural existence, Patel was aware of its less attractive aspects. In a speech during the campaign he spoke of the need to clean up the village and get rid of the filth and stench. He accused the peasants of being untidy and unclean, showing a lack of respect for women and negligence towards environmental degradation. Radical changes were needed in all these aspects and the imminent independence would bring the ideal village, as he envisaged it, closer to reality. Further, there would be no place in that ideal for the impure behaviour that he saw as being embodied in the Dublas.

What type of Dubla have you appointed? Who don't have the manners to go to latrine, who are drunkards and who themselves are so dirty! I feel so wretched while drinking water from a farmer's house when I go to a village. But where should I go? All these dirty people are my brethren, therefore I have to drink water somehow or the other. What is bad in doing the work with your own hands instead of keeping Dubla so dirty and getting work from him? I shall prefer to draw water myself instead of asking such a dirty man to draw water for me. Reform him if you want to get work from him. Make him give up drinking and set him right. Your fears are baseless; a reformed labourer can give you 12 hours work done in just four hours. And if he continues to be illiterate, he will whimper about the whole of the day and his work shall lack cleverness. Such a foolish person does not listen to what you say, does not carry out your orders properly and runs away as and when it comes to his mind. If he is a bit sensible, you can make him understand what you want him to do. But you yourself give him money for drinking and turn him into an animal (Chopra 1991: 302).

Another example that illustrates Sardar Patel's stigmatization of the Dublas can be found in an interview with Dinkar Mehta. Mehta was one of the students from Gujarat Vidyapith in Ahmedabad who came to Bardoli as a volunteer to work for the leader of the campaign. In the interview Mehta describes how upset he felt about the destitution of the Dublas. When he mentioned this to Patel, the latter curtly replied that the time was not yet ripe to solve this problem. The hero of Bardoli reacted sharply when Mehta insisted, telling him plainly not to raise the issue again. The young activist noted that Patel's reluctance was more than just a matter of priorities.

We also got the impression that he and some others were not very sympathetic to them. We came to know this when Narharibhai [note: Parikh] and myself went to the areas called Dublawadas (the area where the Dublas stayed). None else tried to go there... I used to write to Kaka Kalelkar [note: a close colleague and confidant of Gandhi] that the condition of Halis and Dublas was horrible; but that issue was not taken up by anybody. But we did not complain about that. That was our discipline (interview, Dinkar Mehta 1975: 33).

Compared to Patel, Gandhi was mild-mannered and patient, and more willing not to denigrate values different to his own. He told his followers that they should practise humility in their endeavour to achieve tribal upliftment. Persuading these people to adopt a better lifestyle should not, in his opinion, be inspired by contempt and arrogance. It was precisely these feelings with which Jugatram Dave, the founder and leader of the Vedchi ashram in the hinterland of Bardoli, rejected the accusation that he showed no respect for tribal culture. 'You want us to preserve what we want them to forget!', was his indignant response to this reproach. Gandhi neglected to temper the self-satisfied zeal of his disciples and gave them the free hand in what he saw as the fulfilment of a civilizing mission (Hardiman 2003: 146). On the other hand he did not shrink from expressing his aversion to the hard-hearted way in which the high-caste farmers treated the Dublas. In no uncertain terms, he referred to the abrupt and cruel way in which the masters browbeat their servants as 'Dyerism'.[31] But even then Gandhi did not stand in Sardar Patel's way and break the silent agreement that the Lion of Bardoli could lead the campaign in the area as he wished: on the side of the ujliparaj landowners, and subjugating everyone and everything to their interests. The outcome of the struggle was to further strengthen the existing pattern of domination and subordination. Gandhi never wavered from the stand he took on the need to maintain non-antagonistic class relations in solving the agrarian question. As he wrote in *Young India* in May 1931:

Whilst we will not hesitate to advise the *Kisans* when the moment comes to suspend payment of taxes to the government, it is not contemplated that at any stage of Non-Cooperation we would seek to deprive the *Zamindars* of their rent. The *Kisan* movement must be confined to the improvement of the status of the *Kisans* and the betterment of the relations between the *Zamindars* and them. The *Kisans* must be advised scrupulously to abide by the terms of their agreement with the Zamindars whether such is written or inferred from custom. Where a custom or even a written contract is bad, they may not try to uproot it by violence or without previous reference to the *Zamindars*. In every case there should be a friendly discussion with the *Zamindars* and an attempt made to arrive at a settlement (Tagore in Sharma 2006: 340).

The political strategy that led to victory in Bardoli was the subject of much critical discussion after Independence. These analyses suggest that the landless were held in bondage in a relationship of dependence and had no other choice than to remain loyal to their masters.

Thus, the control of the higher castes on the lower strata was absolute and in the context of the traditional social and economic structure, the latter perceived their support to the dominant groups as advantageous to themselves (Shirin Mehta 1984: 187; Shankardass 1988: 85).

Dhanagare shares this standpoint and adds to his conclusion, which is in the same vein, that 'probably the poor trusted their masters as being their only hope of improving their conditions' (Dhanagare 1983: 104– 7). The impression created in these accounts is that the Dublas were sensible in accepting their fate and remaining faithful to their superiors, be they landowners or campaign leaders. But were they as passive and docile as these perceptions seem to suggest?

Notes

1. See, among others, Low (ed.), *The Congress and the Raj*; Bhattacharya, 'Swaraj and the Kamgar: the Indian National Congress and the Bombay Working Class', pp. 223–49; Chandravarkar, *The Origins of Industrial Capitalism in India*, pp. 411–20; Breman, *The Making and Unmaking of an Industrial Working Class*.
2. Gooptu, *The Politics of the Urban Poor in Early Twentieth Century India.*
3. Quoted in Hardiman 1981, p. 1.
4. Low 1977, pp. 22–3.
5. Amin, 'Agrarian Bases of Nationalist Agitations in India: An Historiographical Survey'.
6. Hardiman, *Peasant Nationalists of Gujarat.*
7. Hardiman refers to a police report which shows that this may have been the reason for choosing Bardoli as the location for the satyagraha in 1921, (Hardiman 1981: 152, fn. 94).
8. Dutt, *Sardar Patel in the Bardoli Movement.*
9. Published in 1929 by Navjivan, the in-house publishers for the Gandhian movement in Ahmedabad, and subsequently reprinted many times. Mahadev Desai was an Anavil Brahman and was appointed by Gandhi as his secretary at the request of the leader of his caste, Dayalji Desai (Shirin Mehta 1984: 72–3).
10. The main publications are as follows, in chronological order: Bhatt, 'Caste and Political Mobilisation in a Gujarat District', pp. 299–339; G. Shah, 'Traditional Society and Political Mobilization, pp. 89–107; Dhanagare, *Peasant Movements in India,* 1920–1950, especially chapter IV; Shirin Mehta, *The Peasantry and Nationalism*; Hardiman, *The Coming of the Devi*; Epstein, *The Earthy Soil*; Shankardass, 'Provincial Consolidation: 1928', pp. 60–91.
11. Charlesworth, *Peasants and Imperial Rule.*
12. N. Patel described this early emigration and its effects on those who stayed at home in an interesting article published in an American magazine, 'A Passage from India'.
13. Breman, *Of Peasants, Migrants and Paupers*, pp. 21–2.
14. See fn. 7 of this chapter for details.
15. In 1924, Gandhi lamented that his moral appeal had not been heeded by the Bardoli landowners. He wrote: I long to go to Bardoli and ask the people there to satisfy me in all those complaints. My heart holds firmly even now the promise which the representatives gave me with God as witness. They took a pledge to eradicate untouchability, to uplift the Kalipraj community, to put an end to the sufferings of the Dublas, and to spread khadi throughout Bardoli...

I know Bardoli is not quite prepared for this. The question of course is, will it ever be prepared? When will it be? What have they to say? (*Navjivan*, 15 June 1924).

16. S.B. Mehta, 'Kaliparaj ke Raniparaj', p. 446. See also Hardiman 1987: 188.
17. I.I. Desai, *Raniparajma Jagruti*. Swatantra Itihas Samiti.
18. Dave, 'Halpati-Mukti'. On the same subject, see also I.I. Desai, ibid., 158–9.
19. S.B. Mehta, *Atmakatha* (*Autobiography*).
20. M.S. Jayakar, SBG no. 647, *Settlement Report on Bardoli Taluk*, Surat district, 30 June 1925.
21. Malkani, 'The Agricultural Condition of Bardoli'.
22. Parikh, Bardolina Kheduto in *Navjivan*.
23. *Navjivan*, 26 September 1926.
24. *Navjivan*, 3 October 1926.
25. See Mahadev Desai 1929, pp. 43–5.
26. Gandhi, *Letters to Sardar Vallabhbhai Patel*, p. 7.
27. Oral history interview with Shri Dinkar Mehta, Ahmedabad, 27 July 1975 by Dr Hari Dev Sharma for the Nehru Memorial Museum and Library.
28. Chopra (ed.), *The Collected Works of Sardar Vallabhbhai Patel*, pp. 132. The same quotation can also be found in M. Desai (1929: 64).
29. Broomfield and Maxwell (1929).
30. See fn. 7 of this chapter.
31. Dyer was the British general who in 1919 had ordered his troops to open fire on an unruly crowd in Amritsar. Because of the brutal and excessive violence he resorted to, several hundreds of people were killed.

4

The Rising and Falling Tide of Radical Agitation

Signs of a Counter-strategy

The story of Bardoli was publicized to illustrate the vigour and valour with which the rural population resisted foreign domination. Its high propaganda content must be seen in the context of the struggle for national independence. This applies, too, to the claim that landowners and landless were united in vertical solidarity against the common enemy. But were the Dublas as tractable as the record of the campaign of civil disobedience suggests? I searched in the sources available to me for any indications of resistance, on the part of the agrarian underclass, to a hegemonic culture that took their subordinate position for granted. Claims of the existence of a counter-strategy must be supported by empirical evidence if the criticism of wishful thinking is to be convincingly denied. The following observation by Shahid Amin is relevant in this respect:

A priori formulations in such matters often turn out, on closer scrutiny, to be based on ignorance of the complex relationship between popular culture, religiosity and inchoate political consciousness. The analysis of popular participation in nationalist agitation should, therefore, leave some room for the thoughts, feelings and aspirations of the subordinated, even if they appear only to follow their 'usual masters' (Amin 1988: 105).

The problem is of course that the satyagraha in Bardoli was recorded in such a way that did not permit consideration of any form of separate social consciousness, antagonistic or not, for the Dublas. Even critical observers like Sumant Mehta, Dinkar Mehta, and Indulal Yagnik— whose roles will be described in detail later—were too far removed from the world of the agrarian underclass to realize that the campaign of civil disobedience offered more scope for 'the weapons of the weak', which could be used to increase their resilience and articulate their resistance to oppression.

The previous chapter described the change in the position of the tribal cultivators. While the Gandhian social workers created the impression that, thanks to their programme of constructive work, there was a mentality shift among the Chodhras, Gamits, and Dhodhias, Hardiman argues in his study of the Devi movement that the initiative for reform came from within the group and not from outside. The new identity adopted by these tribal communities was part of their ambition to join mainstream society without becoming stuck as a low caste at the base of the Hindu hierarchy. They proved receptive to certain aspects of the Gandhian mission of so-called upliftment which were compatible with these ambitions, without succumbing to the pressure exercised on them to acquiesce in the loss of their land rights to moneylenders and drink dealers. They did not heed the call to avoid confrontation with these vested interests and to accept their degradation to the status of indebted tenants and sharecroppers. This militancy led to their reinstatement as owner-cultivators after Independence. The purification movement at the start of the 1920s gave expression to an assertiveness and self-respect as markers of the reborn tribal culture. Ideas in Gandhian thought that corresponded with these traits were adopted, and led to Gandhi himself being accepted as a prophetic figure. A rumour spread through the region that his face could be seen at the bottom of the well, and the number of his followers grew with each alleged sighting. Thanks to the activities of the social workers in the six ashrams that were set up in the area, Gandhi achieved even greater fame in the tribal villages in later years, his popularity by far exceeding that of Sardar Patel. The kaliparaj farmers—now renamed raniparaj—may have joined the Bardoli campaign in 1928, but they did so with their own agenda and not in subservience to the ujliparaj.

As mentioned before, the tribal peasants had their own habitat and they had succeeded as a community in remaining at a distance from Hindu culture. By contrast, the Dublas—most of whom were landless and bonded to high-caste landowners as halis—lacked their own physical and social space. Living and working in the shadow of their masters made it very difficult for them to develop a collective identity and sense of solidarity. For these land labourers, the obstacles to the development of assertiveness and self-respect were much greater than in the case of the landowning tribals, who may have been marginalized, but—with the exception of a small minority—had not become the bonded servants of the dominant castes. It was no coincidence that the Devi movement, which called for reform of an impure way of life, received less support among the Dublas than among other tribal groups. They did not appear to fulfil the conditions for an emancipation process inspired by self-improvement. But was this stimulus not provided by the Gandhian activists? As we have seen they made a conscious decision not to try and change the state of exploitation and bondage in which the Dublas lived. This policy of non-intervention was based not only on fear of the dominant castes, who stubbornly resisted any improvement in the lot of their subordinates, but also on the conclusion that the landless did not qualify for self-improvement as long as they refused to fulfil the minimum requirements for virtuousness.

This does not, however, lead me to conclude that the Dublas remained docile and obedient in the Bardoli satyagraha in the expectation that a display of loyalty towards their masters would achieve what seemed impossible along horizontal lines of solidarity: economic and social emancipation. Reading between the lines of the campaign chronicles and reports, a different picture emerges of resentment and recalcitrance against the coalition of the dominant castes and Congress leadership. While the records of the nationalist movement laid heavy emphasis on the traditional solidarity between high and low castes, the harmonious unity of landowners and the landless, it was clear that—under the impact of a capitalist mode of production—the agrarian regime had undergone far-reaching changes. This led to a change in attitude that hardened the relationship between master and servant. Illustrative of the degradation of the Dublas to a labour commodity, pure and simple, was the inclusion of the items 'interest' and 'depreciation' in the calculation of labour costs in the *Report of the Bardoli Enquiry Committee* (1926). Two years later Broomfield and Maxwell criticized this method of inflated accounting, with which the landowners and their spokesmen tried to reject the arguments in favour of raising the tax rate.

It is a difficult matter to reduce that rather uncertain quantity, the Dubla, to rupees and annas. But anyhow we cannot regard this method of accounting for him as satisfactory (Broomfield and Maxwell 1929: 63).

The Patidars were infuriated at what they consistently saw as the lethargy of the Dublas, but which in fact was the latter's resolute unwillingness to conduct themselves as hard-working and devoted farmhands for a wage that was insufficient to enable them to survive. Why should they work longer than a few hours and not just spend the rest of the time lazing around if their masters sent them away at the end of the day with so little? The landowners insisted that they fulfilled all their obligations to the halis, the most important of which being the issue of the daily grain ration. But they cheated their subordinates by giving them less than they were entitled to. For their part, the servants responded obstinately, by refusing to carry out orders, not turning up for work the following day, adopting a negligent atittude to whatever they were told to do and other acts of sabotage. In short, there was reason enough to interpret the notion of the 'good master' and the 'loyal servant' as a construction to which the Gandhian social workers in particular held tightly as evidence of a unifying tradition. Their appeal to landowners and landless alike to work closely together was based on the spurious idea of past harmony that needed only to be restored. The tension in the master–servant relationship sometimes surfaced at unexpected moments, as can be seen from an incident described by Mahadev Desai in *The Story of Bardoli*:

During our tour with the Broomfield Committee, we went to a village to collect preliminary information. We were asking about the condition of the Dublas, and whether the Kanbis gave them the proper measure of rice. The men said, 'Yes.' One of the women who were carefully listening to us from inside, rushed out an exclaimed: 'No lies before these friends. Let us confess that we do not give the proper measure. The Dublas trouble us a lot, and we also do not deal with them fairly. That is why we are in such a wretched plight' (M. Desai 1929: 138).

There are indications that the farm servants resorted to 'the weapons of the weak' in their low-profile resistance against the landowners. From generation to generation, halis and masters must have developed a routine how to deal with each other. But the steady trend towards commercialization that resulted from the transition to a capitalist agricultural economy brought new tensions that created further imbalance in a relationship that was already extremely unequal. The Dublas were dependent on their masters for their every need and that made them vulnerable to the occasional or indefinite denial of perquisites, such as their right to *chas*, the buttermilk that the hali was given for free in the early morning and which was an indispensable ingredient in his diet. He may have taken fallen and damaged fruit home from the field, gleaned the remnants of the grain after the harvest, or gathered a little firewood on the master's land without asking his permission. These were favours which the master could withhold at his whim. If the labourer then continued these practices, which had been customary, he was accused of theft. Halis would respond to such expressions of their master's displeasure less and less frequently by humbly pleading for forgiveness and promising to mend their ways. Instead, they would stay at home, claiming to be ill, or worse still, seek casual work elsewhere. This refusal to behave with 'propriety' led increasingly to confrontation. The master would go to his labourer's quarters to try and persuade him to work and would find him still sleeping inside his hut. On being aroused by his master's shouts the hali, while still lying on the ground, would then put his toe in a pot of *bhadku* (gruel made of chas and grain) to see if he had enough food for that day. If he did, he just turned his back to the master. Stories like this were proverbial among the high-caste agriculturalists and, during my fieldwork several decades later, they were still very common (Breman 1985). I suspected then that, behind the complaints about the indescribable laziness of the Dublas, there was another frustration—the inability of the masters to enforce obedience from these inferior workers, even under the threat of severe sanctions.

Did this defiance become more frequent and intense over time? I assume that to be so, but I can base that assumption only on the complaints of landowners recorded in reports and other documents. Amin's comment that we seem to know more about the interests of the subordinated than about their social consciousness is pertinent (Amin 1988: 118). There are almost no examples of direct oral accounts by agricultural labourers themselves, including in the testimonies of Gandhian social workers. In so far as they came into contact with the Dublas, and that was in itself sporadic and also only fleetingly, they reported more from the perspective of their own mission of upliftment than from that of their informants. In the previous chapter I referred to sources that showed that, from the beginning of the twentieth century, the landowners—irritated at the growing disloyalty among the landless— insisted that the government introduce measures to force them into obedience to their masters and honour their employment contracts dutifully.

The interpretation I put forward here contradicts the view that the Bardoli campaign of 1928 was pursued on the basis of maintaining the traditional 'vertical solidarity' that supposedly existed between the high-caste agriculturalists and the farm servants. The few indications I could find that are not founded on bias and prejudice do not confirm the notion that the labourers indeed placed their hope in unconditional subordination to their masters. From what Dinkar Mehta describes in a few sentences, a completely different attitude emerges, namely an antagonism that was expressed in a steadfast refusal to side with the landowners.

The Dublas and Halis neither joined the movement nor attended our meetings. They complained, 'This movement is of the Dhaniamas, our masters. What have we got to do with it? We won't get more than four annas even if their revenue is reduced; we don't get more than five annas.' That was the way they used to complain. So they did not participate; they did not sympathize with the movement, because they realised that their condition was not going to change (interview, Dinkar Mehta 1975: 32).

This refusal to become involved in the movement is a symptom of resistance, but passive rather than active. Attempting to evade calls to be loyal to the objectives of the campaign and not to collaborate with the colonial authorities is, from my point of view, still one of the weapons in the arsenal of the weak. Yet I believe that the agitation that took place in the sole interest of the landowners certainly gave the landless more scope to express their own protest. At the end of the day, the Bardoli agitation served a wider goal: freedom from foreign domination. During the swaraj movement of 1921–2, Gandhi had told the high-caste agriculturalists of Bardoli flatly that they could only consider themselves fighters for national Independence if they put a stop to the exclusion and repression in their own society. The message fell on deaf ears among the ujliparaj but it must have penetrated the milieu of the landless to some extent. Certainly enough to strengthen their social consciousness and allow them, on occasion, to resort to collective action. There are no references to any such feelings of solidarity among the Dublas in the annals of the campaign, but the colonial authorities were less timid, as can be seen from the following passage from the report by Broomfield and Maxwell.

Then the Dublas are undoubtedly becoming more independent, and more capable of combining in defence of their rights or interests. If they think they are stinted of their food ration and not paid a fair wage they will desert their village in a body, as happened this year in Afva[1], Vankaner, Timberva and other places (Broomfield and Maxwell 1929: 15).

The almost casual remark at the end of this passage ('and other places') shows that, while the satyagraha was in progress, the Dublas had developed their own agenda of resistance which, only a few years later, would become more organized and more public.

Advocates of a Radical Policy

Two disciples detached themselves from Gandhi's entourage because they saw the agrarian question first and foremost as the need to improve the position of the landpoor and landless peasants. Both devoted considerable attention to the plight of the Dublas in south Gujarat. Indulal Yagnik and Dinkar Mehta came from the urban bourgeoisie, but broke away from this privileged milieu at an early age to join the Congress movement.[2] The political experience they gathered persuaded them to pursue reforms that would benefit the agrarian underclass. They opposed the choice of the nationalist high command, which essentially voiced the interests of the well-to-do landowners. Their radical views were not welcome and both found themselves in conflict with the party line, which allowed no space for the mobilization of the landpoor peasants and agricultural labourers. In the following pages I will give a brief description of these two leftist activists and then look in more detail at an initiative in which they were both involved: setting up the Kisan Sabha in 1935 and the agitation that was implemented in south Gujarat under the auspices of this organization.

The elder of the two, Indulal Yagnik, was born in Nadiad in 1907. He was a Nagar Brahman, one of the highest castes in Gujarat. When he was studying medicine in Bombay, his father died. Indulal then decided to study law and in 1913 he began a legal practice in Bombay. His interests lay, however, in social work and he became active in the Servants of India Society. In that period he started to take an interest in improving the lot of the untouchable castes and tribal communities in Gujarat. He published a magazine which, with its name shortened to *Navjivan*, later became the weekly mouthpiece through which Gandhi dissiminated his nationalist and socialist ideas to a wide public. In 1917, Yagnik settled in Ahmedabad and joined the small core of faithful disciples with which Gandhi surrounded himself. A year later Yagnik played an important role in the Kheda satyagraha and was appointed secretary of the Gujarat Provincial Congress Committee. Establishing regional branches of the nationalist movement was Gandhi's idea and, under the leadership of Sardar Patel—who became its president in 1921—the Gujarat branch soon proved itself to be the strongest in the country.

Deeply convinced of the need for far-reaching social reform Gandhi drafted his constructive programme, which he gave a strong rural focus. An important feature of that initiative was the appointment of village workers, *gram sevak*, who—through their exemplary lifestyle and by organizing a wide range of activities—had to launch at the grassroots, social reforms which at the dawn of Independence would result in a society free from poverty and discrimination. The Gujarat Vidyapith in Ahmedabad became the action centre for spreading Gandhi's ideas and in 1921 it was given the responsibility of training village workers and teachers. After a course of several months the gram sevak, under Yagnik's supervision, put what they had learned into practice in the rural areas of Gujarat. Yagnik came into contact with the tribals in Panch Mahals while engaged in relief work during a famine caused by successive harvest failures. In Bombay he collected money for food to distribute to the victims in this backward district. This experience prompted Yagnik to propose setting up boarding schools for tribal and untouchable children. He believed that they could be trained to relieve the misery and deprivation in their own communities:

I presented arguments for the institutions of the untouchables. How can we uplift the untouchables by merely mixing with them in our meetings and processions? In the present meetings when untouchables arrive, except when Gandhi makes a special insistence, how close are they invited to sit? Besides, by making them sit for a while or by touching them a little bit, how can their progress be achieved? (*Atmakatha*, vol. III: 10).

Although Gandhi approved the suggestion, Sardar Patel and other Congress leaders in Gujarat refused to make any funds available. In their view, the time was not yet ripe for such ambitious changes, which should be left until after Independence. In 1921, disappointed at the lack of support, Yagnik offered to step down as secretary of the Gujarat wing of the Congress movement. He was even more disillusioned when Gandhi sided with Sardar Patel by accepting his letter of resignation.

In 1922–3 Yagnik spent a year in prison for agitation. After his release he moved to Bombay to earn a living as a journalist. His break with the Congress movement and its ideological programme was irreparable and in 1930 he went to Great Britain and travelled in Europe for some years. The agrarian question continued to interest him, as can be seen from his vivid concern for the Irish peasantry and the struggle for independence in that country. In 1935, Yagnik returned to India and found work as a journalist on a daily newspaper in Bombay, but because of his reputation as an agitator, he was banned from British Gujarat. He came into contact with the Congress Socialist Party, which had been set up while he was abroad, but did not want to join it because it still operated within the framework of the Congress movement, which he saw as following a capitalist course.[3] A short time later, he became involved in setting up the Kisan Sabha, which we will look at in the next section.

Dinkar Mehta was born in 1907 as the son of a Brahman clerk in Surat. His mother died young and an uncle, who was part-owner of the textile factory in which his father was employed, showed him the way out of the orthodox milieu to the reform-minded Arya Samaj. His early interest in nationalist ideas received a strong boost when, as a secondary school student, he moved to the Anavil ashram in Surat. Gandhi, who visited this institution in 1922, deeply impressed the boy with his message for simplicity and concern for social reform and he resolved to devote his life to the service of the poor. Mehta's political development was strengthened when he became active in the non-cooperation movement in the early 1920s. Support for the Congress came almost exclusively from the middle classes. Young people were in charge of the Congress committees which were set up in smaller towns like Bardoli, Jalalpur, Gandevi, and Bulsar. When Mehta joined the Gujarat Vidyapith in 1926 he distinguished himself from the majority of his fellow students by the purity of his Gandhian lifestyle. He took part in the Bardoli satyagraha of 1928 as a volunteer and was a member of Sardar Patel's staff of helpers. He was arrested for stopping people from paying their taxes at the office of the *mamlatdar*, and sent to prison for three months. After that he completed his study in Ahmedabad and was appointed as a teacher at Gujarat Vidyapith. He acquired experience in organizational work as secretary of the Surat District Congress Committee. The supporters with whom he had most contact were predominantly students and members of the urban bourgeoisie. Agricultural labourers were not members of the Congress and no effort was made at all to extend recruitment activities to include them.

During a second spell in prison Mehta became more critical of Gandhian teaching and, after his release, found himself increasingly irritated by the political compromises Gandhi was prepared to make. But he was sill hesitant to abandon the political line founded on harmony of interests and reconciliation of contradictions between various classes:

I had completely accepted the Gandhian outlook that the upper class could be appealed to and then they would behave better, and in course of time the Gandhian outlook would be accepted and there would be thousands of people believing in it. They would preach and influence others. Then the inequality would be removed (interview, Dinkar Mehta 1975: 85).

Under the influence of Marxist literature and radical activists in his circle of friends, Mehta adopted a more left-wing approach, without this leading to a break in his personal relationship with Gandhi. In 1934, together with several dozen other young Congress members, he set up the Congress Socialist Party. In the years that followed, the party pressurized the nationalist leadership—usually without success—to introduce far-reaching economic and social reforms. Dinkar Mehta was not only one of the founders of the new organization, but was also a member of the executive, with labour as his special portfolio. From the start, the members were divided into two camps: communists and a more moderate faction that enjoyed the support of Nehru. At the first conference, which preceded the Congress meeting in Bombay at the end of 1934, land reform was high on the agenda. A year later, the Provincial Congress Socialist Party in Gujarat held its first conference. It was a great success, much to the displeasure of Sardar Patel, who severely condemned the radical wing and successfully opposed the merger between the Gandhian trade union in Ahmedabad with the labour movement in Bombay, which was under communist leadership. In preparation for the birth of the Kisan Sabha a year later, Mehta wrote a pamphlet on the agrarian class composition in Gujarat—subdivided by him into large landowners, middle class agriculturists, landpoor peasants, and landless labourers—and drafted a resolution in which he called for the abolition of the halipratha system. The second All India Conference of the Congress Socialist Party in 1936 in Meerut led to the expulsion of the more moderate elements, who called for the party to be disbanded to prevent divisions within the nationalist movement. The prominent activist Ishwar Desai, an Anavil Brahman from Valsad district, was one of those who resigned from the Gujarat Congress

Socialist Party which he had helped to set up only one year before (Desai and Desai 1997: 48). The divergence between socialists and communists continued and Dinkar Mehta became the linkman for the latter in the CSP. He was among those who wrote to Indulal Yagnik to persuade him to return to India and join an organization of radical activists (which had not existed when he had left the country), to oppose the reactionary course that the Congress movement had adopted.

The Kisan Sabha and the Nationalist Movement

The initiative to set up the Kisan Sabha came from within the Congress Socialist Party and its programme was drafted in the CSP's shadow.[4] After his return, Yagnik sought contact with leaders of agrarian pressure groups that had become active elsewhere in India. He established close relations with the movement in Bihar where, from the end of the 1920s, Swami Sahajanand Saraswati had been pressing for improvement in the position of peasants who were dependent on zamindars. As a young Brahman, the Swami had entered a religious order, but decided to give his life a more worldly purpose by concerning himself with the fate of the rural masses. Initially he followed a Gandhian approach in addressing the agrarian question but he became disappointed with the persistent failure of the Bihar section of the Congress movement to put the spotlight on the contradictions between the landlords and cultivating peasants. Rejecting the eagerness of the nationalists to reach a compromise between the polar ends of the agrarian spectre, he decided to mobilize the peasant masses outside the Congress. In these years, he focused mainly on the abolition of landlordism and recognition of the occupancy rights of tenants. Joining the CSP gave him the opportunity to operate from a countrywide platform of like-minded activists. In 1928, in Andhra Pradesh, Professor N.G. Ranga, belonging to a family of wealthy landowners, founded the Andhra Ryots' Association. The name intentionally implied that it represented the entire agrarian population and that its agenda entailed the radical reconstruction of rural society. These leaders corresponded with each other, planning to join forces, and Yagnik wrote a number of pamphlets in which he specified the issues that they would be discussing. After Yagnik read in a newspaper that Sahajanand had said in a speech that bread was more central to the life of *kisans* than God was, he started sending articles to him on the agrarian question which he had written in Bombay.

A meeting in Lucknow in April 1936 resulted in the setting up of the All-India Kisan Sabha (AIKS). The choice of Sahajanand as president of the association had been decided in advance. Ranga was appointed general secretary of the executive board, of which Yagnik was also a member. Their deliberations were preceded by a session of the All-India Congress Committee, also in Lucknow, which was chaired by Jawaharlal Nehru and in which Sahajanand and Ranga took part as delegates. The Congress had approved the first meeting of the AIKS and Nehru himself had addressed the meeting, wishing them luck with the initiative. Yagnik had drafted a list of demands that was discussed by a small group before being submitted to the plenary meeting as resolutions. On top of the agenda was the abolition of zamindari and other forms of landlordism without compensation and a halving of the land tax. The only proposal which addressed the problem of agricultural labourers was that all land still available for cultivation should be set aside for them. Yagnik wrote a short report for the Congress Socialist Party on the results of the first conference and took on the editorship of a new bulletin, *Kisan Patrika*, in which the AIKS would report regularly on its aims and activities throughout the country. In the months that followed he devoted a great deal of time to setting up provincial committees. He himself took charge of the Gujarat branch and Dinkar Mehta became a member of its working committee.

At the Congress session in Lucknow the nationalist leadership had conceded to the request of the provincial divisions to conduct a survey of the agrarian situation and submit proposals for land reforms. The AIKS leaders had little confidence in the outcome of the survey and, several months later at a working meeting in Bombay, criticized the leadership for doing too little. They were particularly critical of the fact that the Congress leadership refused to call for abolition of the zamindari system. That was the start of a dispute on how to approach the agrarian question. The conflict was to become more heated as the years passed. Sardar Patel in particular had voiced his opposition to the AIKS even before it was formally launched and openly expressed his lack of confidence in its frontmen. At the Congress meeting in Faizpur at the end of 1936, the drafting of an agrarian programme was at the top of the agenda. The AIKS had submitted a peasants' manifesto but the radical demands it contained had no chance at all of being adopted. The call by the left-wing for far-reaching changes in landownership went unheeded. The proposal to halve the tenancy rate and the land tax was amended to a 'substantial reduction' and the demand for a minimum wage for land workers, which would have made it possible for them to improve the quality of their lives, was diluted to a call for a 'living wage' (set at a level that only just allowed them to meet their basic needs). The AIKS also failed to receive formal affiliation as part of the Congress movement.

The activists who had joined the AIKS were divided into three political factions: Congress supporters, socialists, and communists. The last two were tolerated in the nationalist movement in the mid-1930s but little more than that. They were at best the spokesmen of the interests of the subaltern agrarian classes, but they seldom came from that milieu themselves. Despite the suspicion of radicalism and militancy that the AIKS immediately invoked, it was a typical multi-class association, in which the sharp segmentation within the agrarian order remained underexposed. Attention was focused one-sidedly on the interests of the cultivating classes, and the grievances they felt as agriculturalists against landlords, moneylenders, merchants, and the colonial authorities. The mass of landless labourers hardly came into the picture and calls for improvements in their lot were mostly restricted to recommendations that would not adversely affect landowning peasants and which seemed designed to include them in the ranks of owner-cultivators. That applied, for example, to the suggestion to allocate waste land to the landless or to accept them as members of agricultural cooperatives to which the surplus land taken away from zamindars would be donated. The communists in particular toyed with the idea that, as waged workers, agricultural labourers did not belong in the AIKS but should be organized in trade unions, along with industrial workers. That idea found little support and was superseded by the belief that as landless peasants, the labourers' place was in the rural-agrarian rather than in the urban-industrial economy.

In the second half of the 1930s, the AIKS leadership split when, to Yagnik's great pleasure, Swami Sahajanand began to devote more attention to the deprivation of the agrarian underclass. This inevitably led to a shift in the political course in a more radical direction. Although the three leaders decided together at the end of 1936 to initiate a survey on the plight of agricultural labourers across the country, Ranga did not follow the two others in pressing for reforms that would benefit the landpoor and landless peasants. He retained his position in the union without compromising on his class bias in favour of the more substantial landowners. The loss of unity among its leaders inevitably affected the organizational strength of the AIKS. Its appeal to the Congress leadership at the Faizpur meeting not to take any active part in government had no effect. After the elections early in 1937, the Congress formed ministries in several provinces, including Bombay. After these ministries had been installed later in the year, the AIKS submitted a memorandum to the newly appointed political leaders containing three urgent demands: lower land taxes, cancellation of debts, and abolition of the zamindari system.

The Congress leaders resisted the pressure to introduce radical agrarian reforms and grew more irritated when, instead of descaling their activity in the provinces where representatives of the nationalist movement had come to power, the radicals in their midst pursued the agrarian agitation with even greater vigour. A proposal to incorporate the AIKS into the Congress, as had occurred with the Congress Socialist Party, was intended not to express approval of the movement but to keep agrarian activism under tight control. Forewarned by Yagnik, Swami Sahajanand opposed this merger on the grounds that the union cherished its independence, so that it could also protest against the actions of a Congress government, if necessary. The appeal to the AIKS by Nehru and others in mid-1937 to avoid, or at least temper, its policy of confrontation, simply had a counter-productive effect.

He had said that for the protection of the interests of the kisans there is a general need of an association, but, in the villages in which the Congress is serving the kisans effectively, there is no need to start a Kisan Sabha. Reading those words, our anger flared up. In many of the states where Congress ministries were formed their ambiguous policies had come out in the open; we passed a special resolution in opposition to them. Maintaining our opposition to the acceptance of ministerships even now that Congress had actually accepted political power, we advised strengthening our voice in every state regarding our fundamental rights and urgent demands (Yagnik, vol. v, 1971: 95).

A meeting of activists was held, at which Nehru's speech was discussed. The activists were so enraged at his call for non-action that they decided to add the hammer and sickle to the red flag of the Kisan Sabha.

When in a gesture of goodwill the home minister of the Congress government in the Bombay Province cancelled the order banning Yagnik from entering Gujarat, he took advantage of his restored freedom of movement to become involved, together with Dinkar Metha, in an industrial labour conflict that had broken out shortly before in

Ahmedabad. The textile workers of the city had gone on strike in protest at a wage cut that the employers had introduced two years previously with the support of the Majur Mahajan Sangh, the Gandhian trade union that was affiliated to the Congress movement. The Mill Mazdoor Mandal, set up in 1933 by Mehta and his supporters in the GCSP and immediately banned as a left-wing union, led the agitation and succeeded in getting the wage cut turned into a rise.[5] The campaign made it clear that radical organizations of peasants and workers had grown up in the margins of the nationalist movement and were dead set in their refusal to toe the political line Congress. It was evident that a coalition of these radical forces—personified by Dinkar Mehta and Indulal Yagnik—could place the Congress leadership in an embarrassing position.

Hali Pratha Murdabad

Dinkar Mehta had already began to mobilize the halis in south Gujarat from within the GCSP around the end of 1934 and the start of 1935 (Interview, 1975: 108). He had become aware of their situation during his participation in the Bardoli satyagraha in 1928 and he was undoubtedly able to build on the contacts he had made at that time. He had drafted the resolution calling on the GCSP to abolish the halipratha system. A number of large parades and meetings held in different places of the Surat district in 1936–7 aimed at achieving the end of labour bondage (Interview, 1975: 135). The newly set-up Gujarat branch of the Kisan Sabha would undoubtedly have taken part in these events. Although he lacked Mehta's familiarity with the region, Indulal Yagnik was aware of the regime of unfree labour in south Gujarat. During his stay in England he read what a colonial official had written about the way the landless Dublas were bonded to the dominant landowners in the report on the 1921 census. In his description of the system, Sedgwick, the author of the report, compared the halis with the slaves on American plantations before the Civil War and stated that it was the government's responsibility to effect their liberation. He added detailed statements from district authorities and specified the total number of halis in Surat district: 57,010 (*Census of India 1921*, vol. viii, part I, Bombay 1922: 219–23).[6]

An excellent opportunity to draw public attention to the existence of widespread labour bondage presented itself in February 1938 when the annual session of the AICC was held in Haripura, a village close to

Bardoli. In preparation for the agitation that was to accompany the meeting Yagnik gave Sumant Mehta a copy of the census report that he had brought with him from England. Mehta, who had joined the Gandhian movement at the time of the Bardoli satyagraha, had since become involved in the activities of the GCSP.[7] On the basis of his familiarity with the landless milieu and making use of the document he had received from Yagnik, Mehta wrote a short article for *National Front* in which he explained that the halis' masters were capitalist farmers, and that even the smallest landowners held Dublas in bondage on the basis of loans varying from 75 to 500 rupees. He estimated the number of halis in south Gujarat at a hundred thousand, and called for a ban on this form of serfdom and a penalty for landowners who persisted in engaging landless labourers through debt-based servitude.[8] His article was published in the daily newspapers in English and Gujarati. To maintain the interest of the media, Yagnik arranged the re-publication of the census report describing the halipratha system in detail. The AIKS central committee decided to organize a large-scale protest during the Haripura meeting to increase the pressure on the Congress leadership.

Spending several days and nights [my note: in Surat] we prepared a proclamation of the rights of the tribal peasants, the *halis*, and the farmers of Gujarat; we published it and distributed it widely. We also formed a plan for the march of thousands of kisans and halis from the area of Vyara, Bardoli, Mandvi, Mangrol, etc., on the main road of the Congress Nagar [my note: camp], and for a big meeting which would be addressed by Swamiji, Dr Sumant and local workers to give the message of the Kisan Sabha. Naturally, since Pangarkar[9] was very well known in the area of Songadh-Vyara, he undertook to take as many kisans and halis as possible in a procession on the appointed day to the Congress Nagar. We asked Swamiji to travel for a few days in Gujarat and especially in the villages near Mandvi before the Haripura Congress. Besides, we also decided to distribute copies of the kisan manifesto and the programme of the procession in the newspaper and to distribute copies at Surat, Navsari, Bulsar and other towns (Yagnik, vol. v, 1971: 108).

Swami Sahajanand's tour of Surat district before the AICC meeting in Haripura was a great success. He was met everywhere by large groups of tribals and in his speeches, prepared or off the cuff, he expressed fierce criticism of the agrarian policy of the Congress government that had taken power in various parts of the country. In his political work, Dinkar Mehta was largely concerned with the problems of the urban-industrial workforce, but he participated enthusiastically in the mobilization of the land-poor and landless peasants in south Gujarat. When asked about his impressions of the agitation, he mentioned the large number of tribal women who were not at all afraid to appear at the public meetings.

... from amongst the *adivasis* in particular, Dublas and Bhils of Panch Mahals, a large number of women used to attend the meetings. That was an experience which was not witnessed in the kisan movement in other areas. For instance, among the Kshatriyas of Kheda district, women were not participating because they were observing *purdah*, some sort of (*Laj*), and amongst the Kshatriyas there was a system of minor *purdah* (they would drop their *saree* below their eyes in the presence of males). But *adivasi* women were free. So a very large number of women were attending meetings of the Kisan Sabha (interview, Dinkar Mehta 1975: 139).

Prior to the meeting in Haripura, Yagnik led another procession through Bombay and asked the Congress government to meet the demands of the peasantry, which the AIKS had put into writing. The petition was presented in the presence of Ambedkar and communist leaders like Dange and Parulekar. Chief Minister Balasaheb Kher replied by saying that he had only just been appointed and that he would comply with what was agreed in the Congress agrarian programme. The Kisan Sabha flag flew at the head of the procession, in which around 50,000 people took part. The AIKS were clearly not afraid to make life difficult for the Congress politicians who had gained positions of power. The newly formulated Bombay Tenancy Act protected the rights of cultivators who had worked the land leased to them at least six years before the Act came into force in 1939. On an experimental basis the Act was to be introduced in Surat district two years later. No provisions were made, however, for the largely tribal peasants who were sharecroppers on their ancestral land, which had become the property of moneylenders and traders. In south Gujarat it was customary for them to give half of the harvest to the legal owner of the land. The agrarian agitation therefore aimed not only to abolish halipratha, but also to put end to this system of *adhbhag* and reduce the share of the harvest that had to be given to the landlord to one third.

Holding an AICC meeting in a rural location meant that all kinds of facilities had to be laid on to cater for such a large number of people. The committee charged with making these arrangements issued an order to requisition the help of several thousand Dublas from the area around Haripura[10] in the months leading up to the meeting to perform a wide range of work: setting up a tent camp for the meeting and to accommodate the guests, arranging the supply of food, water, and other necessities, digging latrines, and making the simple country road suitable for the carts that would be used to carry the guests. A completely new road was even built for the motor cars that would be used to transport the prominent Congress leaders from the railway station in Surat or Navsari. The landowners did not approve of the recruitment of this army of workers, and many allowed their Dublas to go under protest. Some went to fetch the labourers back, because the latter had decided to go and do the work—which paid higher daily wages than they normally received—without first asking the master's permission. The workers were supervised by staff and volunteers from the nationalist movement, who had been long before mobilized to prepare for the meeting. For this special occasion, there was also a temporary ban on alcohol, which would later become definite. Social workers from the Gandhian ashrams in the region were in charge of the whole operation. They informed the Dublas about the purpose of the meeting, to seek liberation from foreign domination, and told them about the Congress leaders who would be attending. I will look at the strategy behind this in more detail in the following section but it is important to understand that the Gandhian workers were instructed not to have any contact with the activists of the Kisan Sabha and to warn the workers whom they supervised against these troublemakers. According to the Congress officials and their Gandhian allies, the left-wing elements were out to mislead the Dublas and incite them to action against the Mahatma and the Congress.

The Kisan Sabha activists were given to understand that they would not be allowed to hold any parades or demonstrations on the road that led to the Congress camp. A group led by comrade Bukhari decided to find out if there was any truth in these informal reports and started a procession, waving the red union flag and shouting slogans: *Inquilab Zindabad* (long live the revolution), *Adh Bhagni Pratha Nabud Karo* (abolish the system of half share), *Hali Pratha Murdabad* (death to the hali system), and *Kisan Sabha Zindabad* (long live the Kisan Sabha). This went on for two consecutive days, and their spontaneous protest attracted a growing number of demonstrators. The news reached the Congress leadership while they were in session. Sardar Patel was furious and fiercely condemned what he called 'extraparliamentary incitement' by the Kisan Sabha. Congress president Subash Bose urged him to calm down and said that the peasants' union had time and again proved that it served the interests of the rural masses and that no politician had a right to dispute its existence.[11] On 18 February the long-awaited march to the AICC meeting took place. The report on the event in *National Front* started with a biting comment on the call made by supporters of Sardar Patel in the days leading up to the march asking people not to listen to the speeches of the AIKS and especially not to take part in the demonstration. The appeal was in vain and the march was a great success.

Bands of Kisans started from different centres. They walked ten, twenty and thirty miles carrying with them the Red Flag and the national tricolour and Kisan and anti-imperialist slogans. They held meetings all over the route. Their numbers swelled to thousands. All the processions merged at a distance of two miles from Haripura. From there a mighty procession started for the Congress Nagar. It was a wonderful sight. Five thousand peasants, shabbily dressed, covered with dust, worn out from the long march, yet full of enthusiasm formed themselves into a procession. The procession marched through Vithalnagar with hundreds of banners and slogans and terminated in a rally attended by over ten thousand peasants. At the rally resolutions were passed condemning the action of the Viceroy in interfering with the orders of the popular ministers of Behar and U.P., congratulating the Ministers on their bold stand, and calling upon the Congress to reply to this challenge by resorting to mass action, endorsing the Kisan Sabha demands. Swami Sahajanand, comrade Yagnik, Lalji Pendse, Dinkar Mehta and Professor Ranga among others addressed the vast peasant gathering (Bukhari 1938: 8–11; for another report on this meeting see Yagnik, vol. v, 1971: 117–18).

After the AICC meeting in Haripura the leaders of the peasants' union continued their campaign in the area. From what Yagnik wrote about this in his autobiography it would appear that the tribal sharecroppers in the northern part of Surat district had participated in the mobilization drive en masse. In July 1937 they had already protested in the Mandvi and Bulsar talukas against the customary sharecropping contracts which required them to hand over half of their yield to the landlords.[12] When activists from the Gujarat Kisan Sabha appeared on the scene a year later, the sharecroppers called on these outsiders to help them in their efforts to get the landlords' share reduced. In addition to having to pay all the costs of working the land themselves—buying seed, keeping draught cattle to till the land, tools, and their own labour cost—the sharecroppers were also vulnerable because the landlords could terminate the annual contract if the harvest did not come up to their expectations. Towards the end of March 1938, a meeting was organized in the village of Lavet, which was attended by 7000 land-poor cultivators from the Mandvi and Mangrol talukas. In the days that followed, the protest escalated. The governor of the prince of Baroda, who resided in Navsari, visited the area to try and de-escalate the conflict. His intervention failed and he called in the help of the Kisan Sabha leaders. Yagnik described the situation in *National Front*.

It is instructive to note that all this happened in the absence of the Kisan Sabha leaders. It was as well that the officials saw the mettle of the local Kisan Sabha leaders who initiated the whole struggle. But officialdom could not do without the Kisan leaders for long. So Comrade Pangarkar, the secretary of the Gujarat Kisan Sabha was, soon afterwards, summoned by the Subha of Navsari for an interview. Their talks were friendly and conclusive on many points. While the Subha could not easily fix the measure of rent, he readily agreed that, with monsoon in sight, no landlords could forcibly dispossess their tenants. Comrade Pangarkar promptly issued a handbill to this effect and gave fresh encouragement to the militant kisans (Yagnik 1938a: 12).

This first step was not the end of the story. Encouraged by what the sharecroppers had already achieved, the halis now agitated against their masters. They demanded cancellation of their debts, higher wages and, above all, the right to work in freedom. They went on strike to strengthen their case. It was of enormous significance to the agitation that it received the support of the sharecroppers. Yagnik continued his report as follows:

The months of April and May witnessed a series of these labourers' strikes against their bosses. There were sporadic scuffles and struggles. Some serfs were beaten up by the Pathans and other servants hired by their masters. And the kisan leaders of Lavet promptly repaired to the scenes of these little rebellions, backed the cause of the serfs and tried to secure freedom of service and adequate wages for them. Thus was the united front of the small tenants and agrarian workers realised in the course of the struggle (ibid.: 12).

The demonstrations and protest meetings continued. In the last week of May 1938, the Governor of Baroda summoned representatives of the landowners, sharecroppers, and agricultural labourers to his office in Navsari to bring the conflict to an end, and the protestors turned up *en masse* to express their determination. The Governor said that he had not been aware of the existence of unfree labour in the princedom of Baroda and asked for more details.

Comrade Pangarkar called up some Halis, including a young lad of 14 who testified in moving tones to their conditions of abject slavery. At this the good official promptly agreed that the system should be wiped out root and branch and that no man could be impressed into service irrespective of any debt owing to his master. This term was written out and signed by Comrade Pangarkar on behalf of the peasants and labourers (ibid.: 13).

Initially, the landowners appeared to give in. They agreed that the Dublas would no longer be employed as halis but as daily wage workers. No agreement was reached in the tenancy dispute—the differences between the parties were too great—but it was confirmed that the landlords could not expel the sharecroppers from the land they worked. Yagnik welcomed the outcome as a victory and predicted that the revolt that had started in the princely state of Baroda would soon spread to the adjacent territory of British Gujarat. The battle was not yet over and the success proved shortlived. The dominant landowners refused to meet the demands of their halis in spite of the agreement with the Governor of Navsari district. The masters exerted considerable pressure to force the labourers to return to work under the old regime, including the use of physical force. Halis who persisted and offered their services to another landowner were blacklisted. The monsoon started and the agriculturalists tried to recruit outside labour but were only partially successful in their efforts. Now it was the landowners who appealed to the government, first to the Governor in Navsari and then to the Dewan in Baroda, to break the agricultural labour's strike and force the sharecroppers to see reason by threatening them with eviction. Unimpressed, the Gujarat Kisan Sabha called for a new demonstration, to which the authorities responded by sending armed police to the area and banning the leaders of the peasants' union from coming to the area. Yagnik was convinced that all this turbulence had shaken the agrarian system to its foundations and announced the start of the final battle in *National Front*:

For three days I went around Kosamba, Surat and Navsari, interviewing merchants, lawyers, peasants and tenants. To my surprise, I found that the *halis* were in ferment in the whole of South Gujarat—in Broach, Navsari and Surat Districts. I also heard the *hali* question being discussed in the railway train, streets, newspaper offices, and private drawing-rooms. I was satisfied that *a few hundred Raniparaj and Dublas (Halis) of Mangrol had ignited a fire of freedom that was destined to envelope the whole area from the River Mahi to the outskirts of Salsettee...*

At the moment of writing the air is full of wild threats and evil forebodings. 'Tenants will be ejected', 'Standing crops will be attached', 'Halis will be beaten into submission'—these are some samples. But in great struggles the spirit of man can rise to heights of courage and heroism unknown hitherto. *No power on earth can again enslave a people who are awakened to their right of life and who are determined to be free* (Yagnik 1938b: 5, 15).

In the meantime, Yagnik had gone to East Bengal to take part in a conference, together with Swami Sahajanand and other AIKS leaders, against the zamindari system. In south Gujarat, the protests continued. Under threat of having their crops impounded, the tribal cultivators in Mangrol did not shirk from using physical violence against the landlords or their agents, and even turned on the police when they arrived with warrants to seize their land. Local agitators were arrested, together with a number of sharecroppers who refused to bow to the pressure from the government and the landlords.

... in all 29 kisans were arrested, 22 for the theft of a crop share that was being taken away in a cart by a landlord and 7 on a charge of assaulting a Parsi landlord. In the latter case one kisan leader has been sentenced to three months' rigorous imprisonment and a fine of Rs. 50/- and this is expected to lead to an improvement in the situation. The movement for the non-payment of rent continues and attempts are being made to spread it to other talukas of the district (Government of Bombay, S.D. 115,, first half of January 1939, p. 3).

A couple of months later the Gujarat Kisan committee came together and passed resolutions calling on the tribal peasants and the halis to persevere in their brave struggle. The activists set up a Volunteer Corps to prevent obstruction by landlords at kisan meetings (S.D. 3264, first half of December 1938, p. 3). Swami Sahajanand made another visit to Surat district to express his sympathy and solidarity. He urged the sharecroppers to be resolute in their demand that the landlords should claim no more than a third of the yield. After a speech in Mandvi a number of halis of large landowners came to meet to him.

When they described their slavery Swamiji gave them a motto that if you would remove slavery from your mind and stop performing free labour you are independent from today onwards. These words had a magic effect on the *halis*. From the next day onwards the *halis* struck work at several places in Mandvi taluka and a joint front of the *halis* was forged (Yagnik, vol. v, 1971: 136–7).

By the end of 1938 the euphoric mood of half a year earlier had been tempered. A new article in *National Front*, unsigned, but probably written by Yagnik, praised the local agitators and waxed on the fear they had struck in the hearts of the landlords. Had the district court not decreed in December 1938 that the hali system was illegal? Under the headline 'The *raniparaj* are stirring', the article claimed that the resistance that had been initiated in a small number of villages seemed to be spreading throughout south Gujarat like an oil slick and the agricultural labourers were on the point of breaking their chains (25 December 1938: 7, 13–14). Although by now the zeal and the confidence that had dominated earlier in the year had been dampened somewhat, the agitator remained optimistic. After all, a revolutionary politician can do little more than repeat endlessly that there was light at the end of the tunnel. Unfortunately this assessment turned out to be another instance of wishful thinking.

The Gandhian Solution: The Long Road to Self-improvement

Firstly I would like to recall that, since the fiasco surrounding the opening of the evening school for Dublas in the village of Sarbhon by one of its most prominent social workers, the Gandhian movement of tribal upliftment had steered clear from mobilizing the Dublas. The explanation for this decision not to initiate a programme of constructive work among the agrarian underclass, which accounted for half the population in the area around Bardoli, tended to downplay the strong resistance of the landlords. Although these dominant peasants made it clear that they would not tolerate any external interference with their halis and showed no signs at all of being uncomfortable with the system of unfree labour, the Gandhian workers justified their inactivity by suggesting that the landless themselves were no less attached to the system of bonded labour than their employers. Subordination to a master gave them the security they needed by providing their simple basic needs and vitiated the need to take their fate in their own hands. Such a mentality, which suggests indifference or downright indolence, was considered a major obstacle to well-intended efforts to raise the Dublas to a higher economic and social plane.

What happened in 1938 to change this view that the halis felt no urge to be free? No reference at all was made to the agitation campaign initiated by the Kisan Sabha. Remarkably, the Gandhian records which I have used as a source for my study, make no mention at all of the very important part played by Yagnik and his supporters in addressing the agrarian question. While the colonial authorities, alarmed by the growing number of agrarian conflicts in south Gujarat, had started to monitor in fortnightly reports the threat that peasant agitation posed to political and social stability, the Gandhians ignored in their bulletins and documents the penetration of radical activists into their domain. The impression is created that the protests were stage-managed solely by the social reformers who adhered to Gandhi's teachings and were staunch political supporters of the Congress. These writings essentially suggest that the excitement in the run-up to the AICC meeting in Haripura created an atmosphere in the surrounding villages in which the Dublas came to understand the aim of the meeting—national independence—as the announcement of their own independence. The preparatory work for setting up Congress Nagar, the meeting ground together with the tent camp, lasted six months and took place with a huge army of labourers. The social reformers in charge of the operation had to answer incessant questions from the workers they had recruited and who, in their eyes, had no political awareness whatsoever.

...the big advantage was that in this way a sense of togetherness developed among them. A mentality to work in a group was born and they got an idea of the advantages that could be gained. What is Congress and why such a large congregation takes place, were the things they slowly came to learn about. Thousands of men and women and children of this community attended the meetings held by Congress to spread information on what was going to happen. As a result, awakening to a considerable extent took place in this class and the dissatisfaction about their own condition grew simultaneously. Thus the deep roots of uplift were planted and the spirit of this community woke up, which was before totally ignorant of their state, life or the world at large and which had remained content for so long in their backward and down-trodden condition (I.I. Desai 1971: 161–2).

How can the people who were ignorant, distressed and caught in slavery, grasp the understanding of *Hind Swaraj* all of a sudden? In fact they could follow the simple and straight meaning of *Swaraj* as freedom from the bondage of *halipratha*. Hundreds of Halpaties[13] began to dance with eagerness inspired by two thoughts—hope of freedom and journey to Haripura Congress. Had the Propaganda Committee not made efforts, these people would have hardly realised up to the last moment that there was something like Congress and that a *Maha-Yajna* [great sacrifice] of *Swaraj* was going to be performed. All this for securing human rights for people like them (Dave 1946: 36).

There was a clear divide between the approach of the Kisan Sabha agitators and the Gandhian social workers. I will look more closely at the strategic consequences of this later, but there was also a difference in their use of language. While the left-wing political activists spoke in a style that invoked solidarity in their efforts to mobilize the landpoor and landless peasants, and considered the struggle that they had to embark upon as inevitable on the road to emancipation, the text quoted above shows that the Gandhian reformers distanced themselves much more from their target group. The Dublas were seen as ignorant, and not only politically; they appeared to respond childishly to reports that they did not understand and which they saw as announcing their immediate liberation. This freedom would be provided by benefactors who remained invisible and about whom they knew very little. This impression of a magical metamorphosis was strengthened because it was so unexpected, a sudden reversal of their fortunes rather than the result of gradual changes in the agrarian regime spread out over a number of years.

As a reward for their hard work in the months leading up to the AICC meeting and their contribution to its success, Sardar Patel had promised the Dublas that they would be given their freedom if they promised to stop using alcohol. In the Swaraj ashram located in Bardoli he called on the dominant landowners of the subdistrict—each village was represented by a small number of them—to abandon the system of halipratha. In separate talks he informed spokesmen for the halis that the system was to be abolished. The sources do not identify those who took part in these discussions on behalf of the landless labourers. My guess is that they were represented not by members of their own class, but by Gandhian social workers. On 15 December 1937, Sardar Patel addressed a crowd of Dublas from twenty villages in the area, in which he indicated that the forthcoming liberation of the country from colonial rule made it intolerable that the slavery that persisted here in the countryside, and which he claimed occurred nowhere else in India, should be permitted to continue. In plain peasant language he condemned the masters, who looked after their cattle better than their servants.

The custom of Dublas (bonded labourers) is a shame on us, because it deprives us of human rights and reduces us to the state of animals. I told you when I came here last time [n.b.: in 1928], that it is better to be animals in the houses of farmowners than to be bonded labourers ... because special place is provided for the animals in farmowners' house. When the animal is hungry at night the farmowner or somebody from his house gives food and water to the animals and caresses them. Then when farmowner provides dwelling place to animals it is a sin to keep human beings in bondage. But though we are men, we have lost our rights as human beings, not only that but alas! We have lost rights as animals also. See your dwelling houses, even animals can't be kept there. Your huts are made of grass, that is not painful, but the huts are in very bad condition. The tenderness with which the animals are given grass and other cattlefood, who gives you bread with such tenderness? They give you bread but it is thrown in your face, because it is not given out of love but out of disgust. That is the reason why I tell you that your condition is worst than that of animals (Chopra and Chopra 1996: 65).

There is nothing wrong with this outburst of indignation about the inhuman treatment of the labourers and the way in which the Congress leader spoke bears witness to his intimate knowledge of the lives these peasants led. Swami Sahajanand could not have expressed it better. The difference was that Swami Sahajanand was not only more familiar with the lives of the landless but also, like Yagnik, knew how to approach them as equals. This was decidedly not the case with Sardar Patel. After expressing his compassion at the inhuman treatment the Dublas were subjected to, he carried on to lecture them on the way their lived their lives. If a man marries he must support his wife and children without getting himself into debt. If he cannot do that, he should not marry in the first place. And then he scolded the halis for ensuring the persistence of their bondage themselves and for being so utterly stupid that they would not even be able to understand the gist of what he told them.

But you will not be able to understand all this. The bird which is habituated to live in a cage, if it is made free by the person who maintains it, then it gets scared, and returns again to the cage. Similarly if the farmowners free the labourers, they will return to the masters because they have no hatred towards slavery (ibid.: 65).

After this stiff reprimand, Sardar urged the labourers to work loyally and adopt a decent and civilized lifestyle. He clearly felt that he was far superior to those he was addressing, as a father correcting his foolish and wayward children. He not only summed up the failings that stood in the way of the emancipation of the Dublas, but also appeared to see these failings a justification of their backwardness.

As we have knowledge about our rights similarly we must have knowledge about our duties also. What type of behaviour one who wants to enjoy should have? He should not use abusive language nor he should use indecent words, but he should utter words which are decent. He should not insult anybody, he should not scold anyone, nor should he use foul words. He should learn how to use decent language. You should change your names if the names are not decent. It does not behove to give the names of dogs and cats to human beings. As soon as you enter schools, get your names changed by the teachers and call everybody with respect. Similarly you keep your body clean. As soon as you return from work take bath. You keep your looks clean. Similarly you also keep your mouth clean. The mouth from which you offer sweet words and pray *Ram* should not be used to gulp down wine or toddy. It is sin to do so. It has done most of the damage. If you think it relieves you from fatigue, however that is not a fact. It deprives you of money as well as energy (ibid.: 66).

Patel continued his harangue to the Dublas in subsequent public lectures. He undoubtedly felt this was necessary in response to the more aggressive and more successful agitation adopted by the Kisan Sabha before and after the Congress meeting in Haripura. The Congress leader continued to stubbornly avoid mentioning the Kisan Sabha's role in his public appearances. He did, however, warn the Dublas that they must be patient because small children who want to learn to walk, run too fast and break a leg when they fall. In reply to pleas from landless labourers to be freed from their bondage he answered coolly that they must no longer borrow from the landlords to get married. The amount they needed to pay for this and other major life events had to be reduced and they had to earn it themselves. They could do that by saving the extra income they made during the harvest period. After all, Sardar Patel continued, they needed little money for their daily requirements. 'If you get enough food to eat, open space to live in, and clothes to cover your body, all needs are fulfilled' (Speech of Sardar Patel at the Halpati conference held at Varod village in Bardoli taluka, 15 December 1937). At another meeting he remarked: 'You require only one *dhoti* and one shirt, nothing more. You can get your cloth, even from the cotton which is blown away from the field. It is not at all difficult' (Speech at the Halpati conference held at Bardoli on 26 April 1938).

At the same meeting, Sardar Patel commented that the only thing bonding his listeners to their employers was their own weakness. He advised them to maintain cordial relations with the landowners. Just as a pair of oxen are required to pull the plough, farming requires cooperation between landowner and worker. If they quarrel, both will be hungry. So they should stay calm and not cause trouble, he said, in a veiled reference to the confrontational attitude that the Kisan Sabha activists were taking at that time. 'If any farmer gets angry and slaps you, do not return the slap. If you do that you will be suppressed.'[14]

The Halpatis are Free!

After lengthy consultations with the dominant landowners on one side and with the landless, or their representatives on the other, the final outcome contained the following points:

1. Abolition of halipratha, including cancellation of the debt. Halis who had worked for the same landowner for twelve years or more could no longer be expected to pay off the debt. Those who had been employed for a shorter time had to pay back a twelfth part of the debt for each year less than the twelve years.

2. The daily wage was set at 4 annas and 8 paisa, and at 80 rupees a year for annual contracts. If the labourer had a debt to pay, 1 anna or 15 rupees would be deducted from these amounts, respectively. These rates applied to the men. The daily wage for women was 3 annas and in addition, women and boys received a small amount for working in the household or taking care of the cattle.

3. These wages had to be paid in money. The custom of providing meals was discontinued and the other payments in kind, of which the daily grain ration was the most important, would also be stopped.

4. A *panch* of supervisors was to be appointed by employers and employees to ensure that these rules were implemented and complied with. Each village had such a council to settle disputes, and if that failed the cases were submitted for arbitration at a higher level.

The formal declaration that the Dublas would henceforth live in freedom and that the landowners would have to comply with this condition was without doubt the crux of the whole agreement. Wages stayed at the same level as before, and were therefore far too low to live on. That the daily wage was set at 4–5 annas (at best) showed that Narhari Parikh had grossly exaggerated ten years earlier, during the time of the Bardoli satyagraha, when as representative of the peasant-owners he had calculated the costs of a hali at 9 annas a day.[15] The reasoning behind scrapping the daily allowance in the form of payment in kind for a cash wage was that this would encourage the Dublas to be more independent. By providing his own food and sharing the fruits of his labour with his wife and children in his own hut, the land labourer could retire into a homely atmosphere at the end of the day and learn to take responsibility for those who were dependent on him. The agreement reached was also attractive to the farmers' wives who no longer had to provide meals for one or more labourers.

Sardar Patel announced the setting up of the panch in a speech on 21 August 1938 and the other points were gradually introduced. Problems arose immediately and were not only related to lack of experience in the initial stages. Firstly, the dominant landowners were only prepared to cooperate with the appointment of a panch in a few villages. After all, they had traditionally been the ones to set the terms and conditions of engagement and they did not like the idea at all of having to negotiate them with representatives of the landless peasants. It was even more difficult to persuade them to pay the labourers' wages in cash. They said that the arrangement had been made without them being consulted, and that they therefore did not have to comply with it. The labourers responded by only reporting for work if the farmers showed that they were willing to abide by the agreement. But this impasse did not last long, because the landless did not have the resources to maintain their protest for more than a couple of days. As a consequence, the old practice of payment in kind often just continued.

How was supply and demand intended to work under this new labour regime? Dublas who had always worked for the same landowner were expected to give him priority before offering their labour to another employer. The farmers were, however, afraid that the labourers would ignore this unwritten rule just out of spite. What other options were available? By way of experiment, one village agreed on a meeting place where the Dublas would assemble early in the morning to wait for a landowner who needed one or more labourers. It was also expected that, at the end of the day, employer and labourer would make arrangements for the following day. When drawing up the rules for an eight-hour working day, Sardar Patel had allowed for it to be extended to ten hours if necessary. But the farmers complained that the Dublas were not punctual, arriving for work much later than agreed and leaving much earlier. For their part, the labourers said that the bosses kept them back until long after the end of the agreed working day. This bone of contention was solved by sounding a bell at the start and end of the working day.

In the presence of Gandhi, Sardar Patel announced the formal end of the halipratha system on 26 January 1939. He chose to do this on what was celebrated in Bombay Province already as Independence Day in the hope that, in the collective memory of the nation, this date would also come to be known as 'bonded labourers' liberation day'. Ironically enough, the ceremony was held at the headquarters of Patidar Gin, the cooperative enterprise in Bardoli that was the bulwark of the dominant landowners (Breman 1985: 21). Here too he entreated the Dublas to do what they had always refused to do: work hard and live in frugality. Sardar Patel pointed out that the supply of labour in agriculture was greater than the demand, and that the landless would therefore have to search for other ways to earn a living. He told them that they could earn 2 to 4 annas extra by spinning and weaving. Emphasizing the importance of harmonious relations with the landlords, he called on the landless not to steal standing crops from the land, even if they were hungry. For their part, the landowners must stop protecting their property with security guards who were notorious for the hardhanded way in which they treated the Dublas.[16]

The proclamation designed by Patel was submitted to Gandhi for his approval. The Father of the Nation gave the agreement his blessing at the meeting in Bardoli, at which Nehru and five ministers from Bombay Province were also present, but not without commenting that the labourers' wages were unjust. In Gandhi's view the farmers had proved themselves hard businessmen by fixing the wage level for men and women far too low. He said that both were entitled to a wage of at least 8 annas for an eight-hour working day. But he qualified his criticism by rhetorically asking why he should veto an agreement that landowners and labourers had entered into on their own accord? His comments were shocking because they implied that he was unaware that the landless had no bargaining power and had no say at all in the level at which the wages were set. He also suggested, like Sardar Patel before him, that an eight-hour working day would leave the Dublas plenty of time to supplement their meagre income by spinning and weaving. Mahatma Gandhi thus gave his blessing to the liberation of the halis and, on this auspicious day, gave them a new name. The suggestion of weakness that their identity as Dublas implied, demanded that they be called something else. Gandhi decided that they should be known as *Halpatis*, lords of the plough, a name meant to dignify their work and which would erase the abuse they had suffered in the past. The traditional name for the landlord, dhaniamo, he who endows riches, would also no longer be used as it referred to a time that was gone forever. The festive celebration ended with a song and even those landlords who had maintained their resistance to the abolition of the halipratha to the very end, joined in with the chorus at the tops of their voices: *Chhuta thaya re, chhuta thaya, Halpatis chhuta thaya re* (the Halpatis will be free).

The joyful mood was shortlived, however, and disagreement soon regained the upper hand. It was the landowners who first distanced themselves from the agreements that their spokesmen had made with Sardar Patel. In response, the Halpatis refused to continue working under the old regime. The bosses counted on the fact that the landless did not have the resilience to go on strike or stay away for longer than a few days. But as the unrest escalated, the next step came from the weakest side: the halis' wives refused to perform the tasks that they had always done: domestic chores such as fetching water, caring for the cattle, and cleaning the stables. This enraged the masters and their wives, who were not accustomed to doing such heavy, and especially demeaning and unclean, work themselves.

Shocked, the Gandhian reformers rushed to the scenes of these conflicts and tried to persuade the landless that it was their duty to work. Yagnik, of course, sided with the Dublas in this dispute. He reported how striking halis made life difficult for their masters by not taking care of the cattle or removing the manure from the stalls, which were a part of the master's house. He saw this protest as an effective way of forcing the landowners to be more accommodating (Yagnik, vol. v, 1971: 137). Determined not to give in, the landlords set about doing the manual tasks themselves: tilling the land, picking the cotton, loading the harvest on carts, and taking it to the cotton gins. In effect, they did what Gandhi had already called on them to do: to once again become self-working peasants who were not afraid of physical work. To alleviate the economic distress of the Dublas, the social reformers helped them to earn by arranging public works. In some places the dominant landowners resisted these initiatives by turning against the Gandhian activists. They showed neither understanding nor appreciation of these very cautious efforts—as a sign of the changing times—to extend the programme of constructive work to the landless class. The high-caste farmers violently evicted social workers who wanted to come closer to the Dublas by settling down in their neighbourhoods. As time passed, however, the situation became less tense. Not because the agrarian elite saw the light and agreed to the changes, but because the labourers felt obliged to give up their resistance. How and why the tide turned once again in favour of the landlords is the subject of the final section of this chapter. It is remarkable that Sardar Patel thought that he could achieve the liberation of the halis by trusting completely in the free play of social forces. Why did he not insist on a government order or legislation banning bonded labour? There had been a Congress ministry in Bombay Province since 1937 and it would have taken little effort to obtain official endorsement for the legal abolition of halipratha. In his speech on Independence Day he pointed out that bonded labour had no legal basis, but this was no reason for him to call on the authorities to ban the practice and to enforce compliance with the ban. Using local councils with no formal authority—and which could do not much more than persuade the opposing parties to accept a compromise—essentially meant that the whole exercise was doomed to failure from the beginning. It is easy to guess why this disastrous course was chosen in the first place. The political leaders were in the power of the dominant landowners, did not want to antagonize them by introducing radical reforms to the agrarian regime, and were not overly concerned with the lot of the landless masses. Intelligence reports circulating within the colonial bureaucracy concluded that the landowners sabotaged the agreement.

It is reported that the resolution deciding to abolish the 'hali' system, to which reference was made in my letter for the second half of January last, has not been implemented in many of the villages of Bardoli Taluka (Surat District) and that some of the Dhaniamas who are opposed to the settlement are conducting vigourous propaganda against it. The opposition is said to be receiving support in other talukas in the District in which the system obtains. The congress supporters of the settlement are carrying out counter-propaganda and there have been signs of tension at meetings held by the two section (Government of Bombay, S.D. 718, first half of March 1938, pp. 3–4).

A special note in 1940, prepared by the district superintendent of Surat, which elaborated on the kisan movement confirmed that the leadership of the national movement had become unpopular with the landlords of south Gujarat because of their pledge to put an end to the hali system. His report shows that already before national independence was declared, the rural elite did not any longer support the Congress (*Notes Regarding Kisan Movement*, file no. 1019, 6 March 1940).

Have Congress and Gandhian workers succeeded in strengthening the weak bargaining power of the Dublas through initiatives that would promote solidarity, as a first step towards collective action from below? It would appear that such intentions existed. According to Swami Sahajanand, once the Kisan Sabha started to gather more support, Congress politicians toyed with the idea of setting up a union for the landless. In *Khet Mazdoor*—his description of the history, identity, and condition of the agricultural labourers in India[17]—he said that social reformers who claimed to be followers of Gandhi were involved in these efforts and produced pamphlets in English, setting out their aims and strategy. Swami commented that this information would be useless since the target group could not read and certainly not the English language in which these brochures were printed.

It was simply a new means for propaganda and publicity. This was why the report was printed in English, so that the outside world might read it. Not only this, at the time of the Haripura sesssion of the Congress, held in 1938, it was widely reported that a meeting of the *All-India Khet Mazdoor Sammelan* would be held. It was also announced that Sardar Vallabhbhai Patel would be its president. But for whatever reason such a conference was neither held nor did Sardar Vallabhbhai become its president. But this makes it clear who was behind the agricultural labourers' movement and what their motives might be. There is no one who does not know that Sardar Vallabhbhai is perhaps the greatest enemy of the Kisan Sabha (Hauser 1994: 3–4).

The idea of setting up a Gandhian trade union, perhaps along the lines of the Majur Mahajan Sangh which organized the workforce in the textile mills of Ahmedabad,[18] was revived in 1944 by the Congress movement in Gujarat. At a meeting at the end of the year, the GPCC delegates adopted a resolution setting up a committee to investigate the benefits of organizing peasants' unions (Khedut Samaj) whose activities would be based on Gandhian principles. The three members of the committee were prominent figures in the agrarian economy of Gujarat, had been affiliated to the Congress movement for many years, and had an exclusively high-caste identity (two Desais and one Patel). The committee, which reported in January 1945, went on tour through the districts and held consultations. Prior to the tour, the chairman had visited Gandhi in Sevagram to hear his views. His unequivocal answer to the question as to what target group the union would be aiming at was: the landpoor and landless peasants. Was it best to set up a central organization immediately or to wait until a number of local branches were up and running? There was no clear choice: initial steps had to be taken by coordinating action at the top and at grassroots level. The problem that concerned the committee the most was that a union whose members came from the agrarian underclasses would almost inevitably come into conflict with the large landowners. How could the organizers ensure that the emphasis would be on reconciliation of interests and impartial arbitration, rather than militant agitation? Only those who promised to play by these rules would be eligible for membership. But was the level of agricultural production high enough to satisfy the needs of both farmers and landless? The main problem was that there was insufficient work to keep the landless mass employed throughout the year. The union should therefore perhaps devote its attention to other objectives, such as generating alternative employment. In addition, the defects in the lifestyle of the members had to be addressed. One thing was clear from the start—Congress workers should be in over-all charge. The nationalist movement would remain the platform for the union's activities and they should not conflict with Congress policies. Vigilance was called for to prevent the penetration of anti-Congress elements in the new union. The appointment of a full-time organizer in each district and a small core staff at central level was the best and most effective way to tackle the vast amount of work to be done. Deliberating these issues with Gandhi had been difficult. The meeting took place in early 1944, when he had vowed to remain silent and the delegation communicated with him in writing. They asked him four questions, which he answered in telegram style because of the shortage of paper at the time. As was to be expected, Gandhi proved to be more democratic and progressive than the members of the committee. He suggested starting not at the top but in the villages. And the union was only to allow members who were not landowning peasants.

From my point of view genuine Mandal could consist of only one class. It is the class which actually works and which does not own any land. We work only for such class. This may be considered ideal advice. Everything less than this is inferior.[19]

I have provided this information to illustrate the views that continued to dominate the Congress movement on the merits, or not, of collective action, and more specifically of a union made up by agricultural labourers. After the issue was raised and discussed in 1944–5, nothing more was heard of it. The objective and approach, as described above, fitted in with the Gandhian strategy, which excluded the emancipation of the landless both in theory and in practice. That also applied to the Dublas/Halpatis in south Gujarat. This landless community had to wait until fifteen years after Independence for a Gandhian organization to be formed that worked to achieve their advancement. Later in this study, I will return to the activities of this union during the period of my fieldwork in the second half of the twentieth century.

The Eclipse of the Kisan Sabha

How did the Kisan Sabha fare after the wave of agitation that swept across rural south Gujarat in 1937 and 1938? Initially, the movement's good fortune seemed to continue. Yagnik led a march of 1000 demonstrators in Surat on 16 January 1939 to place their grievances before the prime minister and the revenue minister of the Congress Government of Bombay who were in the city. (Home Department [Special], S.D. 340, second half of January 1939, p. 4). A fortnight later he gave a scornful response to Sardar Patel's half-hearted speech about the rights of the halis on Independence Day on 26 January in Bardoli. The Kisan Sabha leader felt encouraged by the growing number of his supporters. More than 6000 had registered themselves as members of the movement in Gujarat (S.D. 440, first half of February 1939; see also Yagnik, vol. v, 1971: 146). Under the chairmanship of Sumant Mehta and with the participation of Dinkar Mehta and other prominent figures, the first conference of the Gujarat branch of the peasant union was held at the beginning of April. The Swami had sent a message, which was read aloud to the crowd, in which he rejected the accusations that the Kisan Sabha had been guilty of inciting violence. What the cultivators did, and which he supported, was defend themselves against attacks by the landlords or their agents, by coming to the meetings armed with sticks. Resolutions were adopted, calling for payment of fair wages to agricultural labourers and recognition of their rights.

The unrest in south Gujarat continued, with the tribal Dhodhia peasants in the talukas of Bulsar and Pardi now asking the activists to join their struggle. Moneylenders and merchants[20] had seized their land. The grass now growing in the fields was sold to Bombay, where cattle breeders had opened up large stalls in the suburbs to provide milk for the city's inhabitants. A dispute arose with the president of the

Congress branch in Pardi taluka, who complained that Yagnik had urged the Dhodhias to hold the meeting without first asking permission from the Congress. He was told in reply that the Kisan Sabha was an independent organization that did not need the approval of anyone else. Yagnik expressed his deep concern about the exploitation of the tribal cultivators:

In the year 1919 I had seen bhils in the famine ridden Dahod. Now 20 years later I saw dhodhias in the same condition with a *langoti* (loin cloth) on the body and a piece of cloth wrapped over it. On inquiry I learnt that most of the farmers' land had been taken away in lieu of their debts and they were reduced to the condition of labourers in this grass growing land. In fact, 60% of the land in Pardi was turned into grass land and therefore many dhodias were suffering in slavery (Yagnik, vol. v, 1971: 159; see also Desai and Desai 1997: 61–2).

Yagnik made agreements for setting up a local branch of the union to support the peasants in their campaign to get the land back. In various incidents thirty-six kisan workers were arrested in Pardi. In a pamphlet, published in leading newspapers, the police were accused of manhandling peasants at the behest of landlords. Minister Morarji Desai denied these allegations in the Bombay Legislative Assembly (*Report of the Committee of Investigations in Conditions in the Mandvi and Pardi Talukas of Surat District*, part III, 1939, pp. 263–79). A note one year later from the district superintendent of police in Surat, however, acknowledged that moneylenders who had seized land from the tribals used to file false cases against their tenants to justify their claims for protection from the police and the judiciary (*Notes Regarding Kisan Movement*, op.cit., p. 167).

Shortly afterwards, in July 1939, the second conference of the Gujarat wing of the Kisan Sabha took place, with Subash Bose as the guest of honour. Yagnik had arranged for Bose to stop off at around ten places on his journey to Ahmedabad. His speech to the supporters of the Congress left-wing in Bulsar town, his first stop, attracted a large crowd.

The real beauty of this trip was that in the big cities of Gujarat, regarded as a fortress of Gandhiji and Sardar, the pro-Subash people, who were regarded as the opposition party, for the first time held dignified meetings along with Socialists and Communists and received the strong backing of the people. Hearing the policy which the top circles of Congress had adopted against Subash Bose certainly produced an echo (Yagnik, vol. v, 1971: 163).

Sardar Patel arranged a meeting in Ahmedabad to express criticism of Bose, who had tried earlier in the year to secure a term as president of the Congress. His diatribe came to an abrupt end when the crowd began to chant 'Shame, shame on Sardar'.

A month later, there were reports of a strike by 500 halis in the village of Mota, near Bardoli. They resisted their employers who wanted them to bring their midday meal to the field and not go home for it. In reaction the Halpatis resolved that their womenfolk should cease doing domestic work for the dhaniamos (Home Department [Special], file S.D. 2867, first half of August 1939). There was every reason to celebrate the kisan day on 1 September in a large public gathering. It was decided that the headquarters of the Gujarat Kisan Sabha should be located in Ahmedabad, from where the activities of the local branches would be supervised and coordinated. The union had already joined forces with Bose and his marginalization within the Congress resulted in further deterioration of the already tense relationship between the Kisan Sabha leadership and the high command of the nationalist movement. Events followed in quick succession. Throughout Gujarat, including in Surat district, marches, meetings, and other forms of agitation brought large crowds of landpoor and landless peasants onto the streets. Thakor Patel, a staff member from Bulsar, wrote a booklet about the campaign, *Kisan Rangit*. The police banned the publication and impounded every copy. In Mandvi, long processions marched on local government offices to make their demands more forcefully and to protest against a ban on public meetings. In Pardi there were clashes between moneylenders and tribal cultivators. While the agricultural labourers asserted themselves with growing fervour, their employers seemed to realize that an escalation of the conflict would be harmful to their interests.

In October 1939 a party of Shahukars was proceeding from Degam to Vapi in tongas (= horse carts). As they arranged to bring foreign (= outside) labour and refused to engage local labour, who demanded more wages, they were waylaid by 22 Naikas who caused simple and grievous injuries. A case under sec.147,325, 34 was sent up against 15 Naikas by the S.D.I.S.D. who was deputed to make the investigation. The Shahukars were brought round and they approached the District Magistrate for the withdrawal of the case stating that as they were their permanent servants it was necessary in the interest of their future relations to withdraw the proceeding against the Naikas (*Notes Regarding Kisan Movement*, op.cit., pp. 169–70).

The agitation of the Dublas had also continued. In March 1940 the dominant landowners pledged that they would cancel the old debts of the halis and would from then on pay them in cash.[21] As with the previous agreement, they did not keep their word. The mood of resistance among the landpoor and landless peasants had not abated, the colonial authorities concluded in early 1940 on the basis of intelligence reports; they expressed their concern about 'the growth of a spirit of lawlessness' (*Notes Regarding Kisan Movement*, op.cit., p. 175). Although the police knew that the sticks the cultivators carried with them were used for agricultural purposes (for example, to remove thorns in the fields) these *paronas* were labelled as arms used by the peasants to attack the forces of law and order.

In early 1940 there were a series of kisan marches in Pardi taluka on which the adivasis shouted slogans such as 'Down with capitalism!', 'Down with landlordism!', 'Down with Gandhism!', 'Down with British imperialism!'. By March of that year the authorities had become sufficiently alarmed to ban the carrying of sticks in processions in Surat district (Hardiman 1987: 213).

But the end was in sight. Ranga and Swami Sahajanand had been arrested on charges of disturbing the peace. The kisan conference in April 1940 was the last one of the Gujarat branch which Yagnik organized and led. While the police looked on, a three-headed monster effigy representing imperialists, large landowners, and moneylenders was set on fire. Yagnik closed the conference with the words: 'Victory is imminent.' At the end of 1940 he was arrested and sentenced to eighteen months in prison. However, the colonial authorities were not convinced that law and order had been restored once and for all. Only a few months earlier the district magistrate of Surat reported that 'the agitation has already resulted in a number of minor clashes and in the growth of a spirit of lawlessness (*Notes Regarding Kisan Movement*, Government of Bombay, file no. 1019, 1940–1).

There was great disappointment among the peasants' activists at the refusal of the Congress to introduce far-reaching reforms in favour of the landpoor and landless classes. The agrarian programme approved at the Faizpur session of the AICC in 1936 did not even include the abolition of the zamindari system. Politicians from the nationalist movement who came to power in several provinces the following year did introduce reforms to the tenancy system but stopped short of a radical redistribution of landownership. The gap between demands and promises increased as the leadership of the All India Kisan Sabha became more radical. This applied in particular to Swami Sahajanand, who had gradually come to the conclusion that the union had grossly under-represented the interests of the landless labourers, the largest agrarian class. In an essay entitled 'Who cares for the poor' he examined the origins of landlessness and social identity of the mass of people who belonged to the landless class. In the introduction, written in prison in 1941, the Swami commented that the Kisan Sabha had many members who fought to promote their own interests without being prepared to give up their brutal treatment of the labourers they put to work in their fields. This observation showed that he was acutely aware of the divisions between the agrarian classes.

During his repeated visits to Gujarat the Swami had become acquainted with the system of bonded labour to which the Dublas were subjected in Surat district and which was strikingly similar to the kamiauti system in Bihar. In his description of the most prominent characteristics of halipratha he noted that such practices of subjugating the landless to the power and whims of the landlords was dying out across the country. Only in Gujarat had this regime of serfdom been preserved, until the Kisan Sabha appeared on the scene:

Beating and assaulting the *halis* is common. And the remarkable thing is that whereas in other provinces the *kamiauti* system and similar forms of bonded labour are dying out of their own accord, the *hali* system is gaining momentum. Now, however, through the agitations of the Gujarat Provincial Kisan Sabha even this system is being rooted out. Once a *dubla* youth in the area of Haripura in Gujarat, narrated to me his story. He explained that he worked like a slave in the home of a Parsi. He had to go there at four in the morning, boil the water and bathe him. The slave had to soap and rub his *malik's* body and wash him. In this process, if the Parsi felt the least irritation from the rough hands of the *dubla*, he would slap him. But the slave had heard speeches of the Kisan Sabha and this gave him courage and one day when his Parsi owner gave him a slap, he returned the slap and since that time he has been free (Hauser 1994: 78–9).

Where Swami Sahajanand saw in the slap the boy gave his master the urge for freedom, Sardar Patel had forbidden the halis to answer violence with violence. It would, however, be mistaken to see these different reactions in terms of a contrast between the supporters and opponents of violence—the distinction was not so black and white. Time after time, the peasants' activists had to deny that they incited their followers to violence. But they did see self-defence as admissible and justified. Since the landlords and their agents committed brutalities of various kinds to try and break the resistance of the sharecroppers and agricultural labourers, it was they and not their victims who were guilty of practising violence. At one of the first protests the Swami organized in Bihar, he called his followers to come armed with sticks—not to be aggressive themselves, but to make it clear that they would not be browbeaten into docility.

For Gandhi, non-violence was a moral principle to which no concessions could be made, even in situations of extreme oppression. But Sardar was more pragmatic and instrumental. The way he addressed the Dublas did not disguise the contempt he felt for their inferior way of life. By interpreting acts of resistance to their masters as a lack of self-restraint, he concluded that they were at the beginning of a long road to a civil code of conduct. Discipline was the first priority. On the systematic violence used by the agrarian elite against the landless proletariat, Sardar maintained a steadfast silence.

Sardar's fight against colonial rule did not weaken his determination to keep the social framework of the agricultural economy intact. Shankardass concluded a report on the performance of the Congress leader in Gujarat at the time of the Bardoli agitation in 1928 with the following observation:

The backward classes were in fact encouraged to preserve the status quo. Curiously, the 'weapon' of nonviolence, supposedly intended to strengthen the weaker sections of society, actually disarmed them and exposed them to greater exploitation by those who could manipulate them for their own ends. Patel had no commitment to nonviolence; he adhered to it and discarded it at his convenience. In the 20s and 30s when Congress was in the process of ascending, Patel considered nonviolence useful in keeping control over widespread movements. In the 40s when Congress was strong and entrenched, he was willing to use violence against rivals and opponents. In Patel's hands nonviolence and other Gandhian methods were tools to be used for wider political goals. Peasants, whether one or many, would not derive any economic benefit from the agitations to compensate the loss of lands or movable property that would result from supporting the agitation (Shankardass 1988: 87).[22]

Underlying the disapproval of violence was also the rejection of militant action because it did not solve the conflict of interests but threw them into sharper relief. The Congress ministry that had come to power in the province of Bombay took the side of the landlords in Surat district by announcing that, given the organized and random violence that was going on, it had no other choice than to take forceful steps to counteract the class hatred preached by the agitators and their followers. This was in fact the same argument that the colonial authorities had always used at times of agrarian revolts to justify sending in armed police to preserve law and order.

While the subaltern agitation in south Gujarat intensified and the membership of the Kisan Sabha grew, there were radical changes in the political configuration. This realignment was preceded by rising irritation among the conservative leadership that held power in the nationalist movement, firstly about the mobilization of the landpoor and landless peasants and then about its remarkable success. It was the same displeasure with which the Congress leaders had responded to the mobilization of urban labour in trade unions that fell outside the reach of Congress politicians. The accusation was that these separate initiatives jeopardized the unity of the nationalist movement and were a cover for a course that continued to give priority to the interests of the industrial entrepreneurs in the cities and to the agrarian elite in the countryside. Against the radicalization of the left-wing agitators, who joined forces in the CSP and the AIKS, there was a Congress rank and file with its origins in the propertied classes and which resisted, in the cities as well as in the countryside, the pressure to adopt a more progressive political agenda. The refusal of the subaltern masses to bow to this pressure from below became even more resolute after 1937 when Congress politicians came to power in several provinces. Six months after the Haripura meeting, the AICC adopted a motion condemning the agrarian agitation as a form of class warfare. It was a direct reference to the activities such as those undertaken by the Kisan Sabha in south Gujarat. Gandhi himself was critical of the radical agitators, writing in April 1938:

My study of separate kisan organizations has led me definitely to the conclusion that they are not working for the interests of kisans but are organized only with a view to capturing the Congress organizations. They can do even this by leading the kisans along the right channels, but I am afraid that they are misleading them (Gandhi in *Harijan*, 23 April 1938).

This hardening of attitudes on both sides led to a confrontation. The Swami was expelled from the AICC and Congress members were forbidden to make speeches at meetings organized by the peasants' union. At the beginning of 1940 there was a break in the CSP when the more moderate wing expressed its support for the official Congress line. As a result of the subsequent expulsion of the communists, the party in Gujarat lost not only Dinkar Mehta, but 90 per cent if its members.[23] That was much higher than the national average, because in the organization as a whole the communists accounted for about half the support base. The CSP had evolved into a typical cadre-based party, with far greater political influence than its limited membership—only 700–800 in Gujarat—would suggest. It was important to the way that the nationalist movement addressed the agrarian issue that the CSP acted as advocate for the Kisan Sabha. As a consequence of the marginalization of the CSP within the Congress, the radical approach of the AIKS also met with increasingly vehement criticism from the nationalist leadership. This was a nationwide phenomenon that was thrown into even greater relief in Gujarat. Here, the Congress machine had for many years been operated and controlled by Sardar Patel. His small administrative staff were all appointed by him personally and he supervised appointments right up to subdistrict level. His opposition to the CSP and the AIKS was a response to the pressure they brought to bear to promote the interests of other agrarian classes than those specified in the nationalist programme. It did not concern him at all that these radical voices were silenced; he had spoken out strongly in favour of such measures for many years. Thanks to his heavy-handed intervention, the left-wing was no longer represented in the GPCC after 1940 (D. Mehta 1975: 155). Members of the Congress who advocated radical action in dealing with the agrarian question were asked to leave the nationalist movement and were thrown out if they refused to do so, as happened to the joint secretary and the president of the Bulsar Taluka Congress Samiti.

… the local Congresswalas have realised the seriousness of the situation and are trying to oust the black sheeps from their ranks. Both Thakorbhai and Burjorji have been warned to resign from the Congress Samiti otherwise disciplinary action will be taken against them. A meeting of the Congress Committee for that purpose was held on 3-3-1940 at Bulsar and the explanation submitted by Thakorbhai was read over and as it was found not to be satisfactory, a resolution for his removal from his his present post as Joint Secretary and the appointment of Mr Nanabhai Govindbhai as his successor was unanimously passed (*Notes Regarding Kisan Movement*, op.cit., p. 173).

While the Congress movement was purging itself of undesirable elements, another political shift was making itself felt. As a British colony, India became involved in the Second World War. This weakened the colonial hold on the country and the nationalists wanted to take advantage of the situation to make demands that would hopefully expedite the transition to Independence. The refusal of the British rulers to accede to these demands led at the end of 1939 to the resignation of the already unpopular Congress ministries. In 1942, confronted with the stubborn refusal on the part of the British rulers to make concessions and to draw up plans for the imminent transfer of power, the nationalist movement launched the 'Quit India' campaign. With its call for 'mass struggle on non-violent lines on the widest possible scale' the campaign soon took on the character of a popular uprising. In Surat district it was once again the dominant Anavil and Patidar farmers who were in the forefront of the action (Hardiman 1988).[24] Gandhi, who this time took a firm stand on the side of what was in effect a political strike, was taken into custody, together with the other Congress leaders. The Communist Party, however, had taken the opposite course. In the 1920s it had fought against much greater oppression than the nationalists were now facing, and its exclusion from political power continued in the years that followed. One of the causes of this was undoubtedly a marked sectarian approach. The CPI failed to take advantage of its growing support base, especially among the working class in the big cities, to achieve concrete political results. After 1934—much to Congress' pleasure—the communists were forced underground. This isolation also had a detrimental effect on their political effectiveness. Through the back door, by joining the ranks of the CPS and the AIKS, they managed to maintain a fragile contact with social dynamics and, from this low-key position on the sidelines, exert a limited influence. After having initially condemned the Second World War as a struggle between the imperial powers, they curried favour with the colonial government by insisting that priority must be given to the anti-fascist war effort. This change of course, which followed the German invasion of the Soviet Union in 1941, gathered little support among the Indian population. On the other hand, the Congress achieved greater popularity with the imprisonment of its leaders. According to Sumit Sarkar, this repositioning of the two movements had the net effect of hampering, rather than favouring, a more progressive political course in the long term (S. Sarkar 1983: 104–5).[25]

This brief and hasty sketch of party political developments is relevant in that it affected the subject of my study. Generally speaking, the agrarian question was no longer considered urgent and, in the new political situation, there was a different view of the significance and desirability of peasant agitation. The purge within the CSP of elements that did not toe the Congress line strictly enough severely weakened the left-wing. Conversely, the AIKS was now dominated only by communists—and confusion reigned. While anti-fascists called on peasants at first to work together with the police to protect their villages against the foreign enemy, later on anti-imperialists prepared their supporters for the advent of a 'kisan-labourers *raj*' after the collapse of British rule.

Both urged the baffled kisans to organise the village defences, not for protecting themselves against the landlords' men and the police, but for either resisting 'the Japanese fascists', or dealing a 'death blow' to the Raj, and they often came into physical conflicts with each other (Gupta 1996: 205–6).

The split among the different factions came to the fore at the third Gujarat Provincial Kisan Conference in Bulsar in June 1942. The new leaders of the Kisan Sabha asked their members to support the 'peoples' war' that had long been under way, and gave it priority over the long-term struggle for free labour and land reform. One by one, the old stalwarts left the organization they had founded. Ranga, who had always remained loyal to the interests he served, those of the dominant landowners, was the first to go. Yagnik, who had been elected President after his release from prison in 1942 and had expressed friendly criticism of the new political course, withdrew with no fuss at the end of 1943. In the case of Swami Sahajanand, the differences of opinion were much more heated—and public. After his release from prison, his charisma and reputation enabled him to transform the AIKS into an organization exclusively for the poor peasant masses, although he was not in favour of a union solely for landless labourers:

... should the *khet mazdoors* have a separate organization? But this inevitably suggests that they should be totally separated from the Kisan Sabha. And as I have already said, this will be a completely wrong approach. But if it is suggested that they be in the Kisan Sabha and also have an organization of their own, this possibility can be discussed (Hauser 1994: 113–14).

But the communist leaders now gave priority to the war effort, for example, by supporting the government's 'grow more food' campaign, and rejected action aimed at increasing antagonism between the different agrarian classes. This strategy left no room for a radical agitator. The definite break came in 1945 when the Swami was called to order for 'irresponsible deeds'. He returned to the CSP and set up a new peasant association, the United Kisan Sabha, which was not given space to develop within the Congress Party. His death in 1950 also meant the end of the final initiative.

The Agrarian Agitation in Retrospect

What did the radical agitation under the late-colonial regime achieve? For the landless class relegated to the bottom of the agrarian order, not very much. Although the mass of landless labourers slowly became more visible, their problems and interests were consistently played down in the nationalist repertoire. Even unions committed to a militant agrarian policy rarely mobilized the landless, and when they did so it was on an ad hoc basis rather than systematically. The political terrain won by the Kisan Sabha towards the end of the 1930s was eroded again in the years that followed. This conclusion might not apply in some other parts of the country, but I believe it was certainly the case in south Gujarat.

When I started my fieldwork in Surat district in the early 1960s, it was hardly conceivable that, shortly before Independence, this area had been the scene of a fierce political struggle for the emancipation of the landless population from bondage. It is tempting to conclude that, after a short period of unrest, it was easy to restore law and order in the region because the Dublas themselves had refused to assert themselves.

'History from below' has to face the problem of the ultimate relative *failure* of mass initiative in colonial India, if the justly abandoned stereotype of the eternally passive peasant is not to be replaced by an opposite romantic stereotype of perennial rural rebelliousness. For an essential fact surely is that the 'subaltern' classes have remained subaltern, often surprisingly dormant despite abject misery and ample provocation, and subordinate to their social 'betters' even when they become politically active (S. Sarkar 1980: 3)[26]

Is Sumit Sarkar right in his despondent conclusion on the persistent passivity at the foot of colonial society? It is just as well that Sarkar speaks of a *relative* failure, because a number of reservations can be made which temper his pessimistic assessment. In the first place, the literature dealing with the slow expansion of the Hindu order in the vast tribal tracts is replete with tales on how the adivasis resisted their subordination to the intruders. One such movement which spread among a subgroup of Halpatis in the Broach district of south Gujarat in 1885 called for emancipation from domination along with the promise, which was to be revived later, that the goddess Mata would make the enemies bullets melt (Dosabhai 1894: 299, 301; Hunter 1892: 413). This kind of revolt has unfortunately been largely glossed over in studies on peasant protest. However, in my opinion it would be wrong to regard such struggles as an expression of tribal revivalism only. Close observers have repeatedly noted that in many cases, political activists did not have to try and convince the landpoor and landless peasants of the need to protest, since the peasants themselves came to seek support in redressing the injustices to which they were subjected, be it a reduction in rent or land tax, to gain freedom or to get higher wages. There is sufficient evidence to show that this was certainly the case in the struggle of the halis and sharecroppers in the Surat district. Secondly, the radical agitators were clearly more preoccupied with exerting pressure on the colonial authorities or the Congress leadership. They did this by organizing campaigns rather than setting up standing organizations. Who responded to the call to take part in these campaigns? What was their economic status and social identity? These are questions that remain largely unanswered. There is even a lack of basic information on the activists themselves, such as their age and gender. Women are mentioned only rarely, but that does not mean that they did not play an active role in the protests.

The records show that the membership of the Kisan Sabha expanded in all provinces but there is little detail of what membership entailed, how it was registered, and who drew up the programme of activities. Instead of relying on formal procedures, communication occurred through informal networks and word-of-mouth contact. There was no administrative apparatus or understanding of fund-raising, which led in practice to the formation of a small core of local-level activists who were operating on a shoestring and working with great zeal but without clear agreements about who was responsible for what. The district superintendent of police in Surat wrote a report in early 1940 on the kisan movement in south Gujarat. For each taluka he provided information on the meetings held, the number of members and other details:

Upto date there are 628 members in the Kisan Sabha from Pardi Mahal. The fee is one anna per member. The leaders also collect money by the sale of song books. The meetings usually begin with the shouting of Kisan slogans and reciting of Kisan songs. It is reported that their financial condition is not very sound. In Bulsar taluka the following 10 villages are affected: 1 Bodlai, 2. Dungri, 3 Bhama-

Pardi, 4 Untdi, 5 Parnara, 6 Khaparwada, 7 Dharasana, 8 Gadaria, 9 Undach, 10 Bulsar. There are 275 members. The movement started with a meeting at Bodlai village on 6-1-39. There were 9 meetings last year and 4 in the current year. The movement does not appear to be flourishing in this taluka ... Bulsar is prominently featured because it is the headquarters of Thakorbhai and Barjorji and Indulal Yagnik and Pangarkar confer with these local leaders and pleaders at this place.... The Kisan leaders had tried to penetrate into Chikhli Mahal. They held a meeting on 23-9-1939 and another one on 13-1-40. It appeared that they are not getting any backing from the Kisans, so far, from this Mahal (*Notes Regarding Kisan Movement*, op.cit., pp. 170–1).

None of the kisan leaders mentioned above came from the landpoor or landless milieu themselves. Yagnik and Mehta were born into high castes and were members of the urban middle class in Gujarat. Both displayed a social engagement at a young age that led them to become disciples of Gandhi. Their radicalization was not inspired by political opportunism but by their disappointment with the consistent refusal of their *guru* and of the nationalist movement to improve the lot of the agrarian underclasses. Swami Sahajanand and Ranga were also members of high castes. They may have had a rural background, but they came from landowning families. Although three of them—this clearly did not apply to Ranga—had a great affinity with poor peasants and the landless, there was a wide gap between them and the subaltern mass whose interests they defended. It was a world of living and working with which these outsiders felt empathy, but which they found difficult to approach and to understand. The activists led a very ambulant existence, continually on the road, and their time was taken up entirely by day-to-day politics and infighting. Factionalism prevented them from developing the intimate confidence and thorough knowledge required to effectively articulate local-level events and interests. The gap could have been bridged by building up cadres from the target groups and equipping them with the authority required to initiate activities at the grassroots. But mobilization of the membership remained strongly top-down.

The rural poor could squeeze their nominees only into the *taluk* or the *thana* and the village committees (also known as the 'primary committees'). But even these were so overwhelmed by the directives of the educated, petty bourgeois District and Sub-Divisional leaders that they enjoyed hardly any opportunity for originating a move or taking a crucial decision. The 'primary committees' in effect functioned as the sounding boards or the means of communication between the leftist leadership and the masses at the grass roots. The leftists were yet to realise the importance of, and the urgency for creating local leadership, or generating local initiative (Gupta 1996: 120).

It was also significant that the decision to initiate or end a campaign was often based not on pressure of local circumstances but on its role in a wider political agenda in which other interests took precedence. What this meant in practice was that the supporters had to do what the leaders prescribed, rather than the latter making decisions based on what their members wanted. The landpoor and landless were therefore encouraged to shout slogans at meetings and during marches that had nothing to do with their own predicament. This was however much less important than the fact that decisions to act or not were taken on the basis of a short or longer-term strategy in which the rank and file had no say at all. The political manoeuvring had little to do with party loyalties and it was not so that more left-wing agitators automatically had greater sympathies with the most deprived class, the landless labourers. The communist dogma that peasants were naturally conservative and that the revolutionary potential of the industrial workers in the cities was much greater meant that, even after the AIKS was taken over by CPI supporters, mobilization of the landless mass did not receive the priority it deserved. The Kisan Sabha was a multi-class union and tended, from the very beginning, to represent mainly the interests of the landowning peasants, and this did not change much later on. There was also the question of what to do with the agricultural labourers once Independence was attained. Should they be given land or remain wage labourers, but then employed in urban industries?

Considering all these obstacles and restrictions it is not surprising that the agrarian agitation was short-lived, very localized and fragmented due to a lack of organization and coordination. In other words, its political impact was neither wide nor lasting. Yagnik's claim in 1940 that victory was imminent was illustrative of the wishful thinking among the leaders of the agrarian movement. Or was it a case of whistling in the dark? Having said this, it should not temper our admiration for the many thousands of activists throughout the country who devoted so much time and energy to the series of campaigns in the years leading up to Independence. They gave voice to the rural underclasses, which showed signs of increasing assertiveness, but which were not mobilized by the nationalist movement. It was Yagnik and his Kisan Sabha activists who were mobilized by the landless Dublas to help them in their struggle against bonded labour. And it was in response to the same pressure that Sardar Patel felt obliged to abolish the halipratha system, even though he did it in a way that was doomed to failure in advance.

Here and there, now and then: is it justified to describe the campaigns of agrarian agitation in the late-colonial era in such terms? I have my doubts and therefore do not agree fully with Sarkar in his statement that, while liberation from colonial domination was in sight, there was no change in the state of subjugation at the foot of the agrarian regime. The incapacity to free themselves from exploitation and subordination was not caused by the lethargy of the landless peasants, nor can it be primarily attributed to the shortcomings of the activists who called on them to resist. If the successes were more modest than the agitators themselves claimed, this is very much due to the resistance of the agrarian elite to change. The class of landlords had long experience in repressing demands from below for improvements in living conditions. But this refusal to grant the rural poor their human right to a dignified existence would have been challenged more fundamentally if the rural elite had not maintained their privileged position in the nationalist movement. Those wishing to represent the interests of landpoor and landless peasants in the 1930s during the second round of agrarian agitation stood no chance against the alliance between the dominant landowners and Congress politicians forged a decade earlier in Bardoli:

… the Congress leaders at the central, provincial and district levels—whether in Drug or Surat or Krishna – and the Congress ministries in all the eight provinces under them—whether it was Dr. Khan Saheb's in the N.W.F. P. or G.B. Pant's in the U.P. or B.G. Kher's in Bombay—were wholly unsympathetic, if not always hostile, towards the interactions between the leftists and the rural poor (Gupta 1996: 124; see also Amin 1988: 104).

Does this observation that little changed in the balance of rural power suggest that the relations of domination and subordination continued as before? Not in my opinion. Certainly, there was little scope for manoeuvre, but to suggest that the situation stayed the same as it always had been ignores the fact that the landlords had lost some of their legitimacy and the landless mass had started to express impatience at their exclusion.

This general conclusion is partly based on my assessment of the condition of the 'Dublas-becoming-Halpatis' in south Gujarat around the middle of the twentieth century. My view of that situation was partly formed during the fieldwork that I carried out in the area at village level a decade later (1961–2), and partly by consulting historical records on the period immediately preceding it. How the class of agricultural labourers has fared in the years immediately before and after Independence, how and why the regime of labour bondage faded away, is the subject of the next chapter.

A Colonial Cover-up

A final section, however, is required to draw attention to reports commissioned by the colonial bureaucracy on practices of labour bondage in different parts of the country shortly before Independence. The Government of India asked the provincial authorities in 1938 to provide information on servitude or serfdom in agriculture. The reports received were meant to be forwarded to the League of Nations for discussion in the Slavery Committee. The issue was also raised in the Legislative Assembly by one of its members, N. M. Joshi, in September 1939 who asked for publication and discussion of the document prepared: Memorandum regarding legislative and other measures adopted to combat slavery and debt-bondage akin to slavery in British India. Bihar, Orissa, and Madras figured prominently in the provincial reports but the hali system of south Gujarat was also highlighted in the official document:

At the time of his wedding a Halpati (lord of the plough) takes a loan from the master of the field which he ploughs. The loan is to be repaid by labour on the field and in actual practice the wage paid to him is so low that he can never hope to clear the debt. The Halpati is wholly dependent for his food on his master, and he has no other prospect than that of having to work always for his master. Since the 1938 session of the Indian Congress held at Haripura in the taluka of Bardoli, the leaders of Congress are working with vigorous effort to end this inhuman system. After holding several meetings at which they explained the demoralising effect of the system, the leaders have succeeded in making the workers and their masters agree to a scheme of settlement for liberating the Halis. The scheme laid down amongst other things, hours of work, daily wages in cash and redemption of old debts. This movement of freeing the bondsmen has been mostly confined to Bardoli and Mandvi Talukas. There has, however, been some opposition to the settlement from land-holders. The Congress leaders are quite alive to the situation and are doing everything to counteract the anti-settlement movement (Home Dept., Judicial Branch no. 19/14/39 dated September 1940, pp. 4–5).

The colonial bureaucracy pontificated what to do with this embarrassing information. Did it really make sense to forward a memorandum on current regimes of agrarian labour in various regions of British India to an international forum which had a strong record on human rights? The authorities were clearly not keen to publish the findings and debate the issue in the Legislative Assembly. No definite promise had been made to do so and to keep it out of the public eye would be advisable:

Such publication will only unnecessarily bring into prominence the existence of an evil which is being eradicated but has not yet been entirely rooted out. The contents may perhaps be used for adverse propaganda in the press or abroad. We have stopped sending out to the countries abroad papers, the contents of which might be twisted and used as enemy propaganda. We have also to enquire form the India Office whether the reports to the League should be continued during war time. For these reasons the memorandum need not be sent to the League for the present. If Mr. Joshi raises this question again in the Assembly we can send him, for personal use, a copy of the memorandum prepared (ibid., s. no.1121, 4 October 1940, p. 22).

The evil of bondage was covered up but still existed in the aftermath of colonial rule.

Notes

1. Nearly half a century later, this village became one of the locations of my fieldwork. See Breman 1985.
2. The information provided here comes from the portraits both activists provided of their lives: Yagnik, *Atmakatha*, and *Oral History Review* with Dinkar Mehta. These documents are deposited in the Nehru Memorial Museum and Library in Delhi.
3. *Atmakatha*, vol. v, p. 36.
4. In addition to those already mentioned, this section is based largely on the following sources: Choudhary, *Peasants' and Workers' Movement in India*; Dhanagare, 'Peasant Organizations and the Left Wing in India'; Kumar (ed.), *Congress and Classes*; Hauser (ed.), *Sahajanand on Agricultural Labour and the Rural Poor*; Gupta, *The Agrarian Drama*.
5. For more on this episode, see the passage entitled 'Defusing the Radical Threat' in my study *The Making and Unmaking of an Industrial Working Class*, pp. 65–9.
6. In his report on the hali system, Sedgwick included notes submitted by the Collector and Deputy. Collector of the Surat district.
7. In the interview, Dinkar Mehta, who had been a member of the Communist Party of India since 1935, was asked whether Sumant Mehta had ever been a

member of the party. He replied: 'No, he was never a member. He was not even a member of the Congress Socialist Party. He was the only one among the old Congressmen who was our staunch supporter. He had more or less abandoned the Congress, though he was looked upon as a Congressman. He used to spin and put on *khaddar*. He also ran an Adivasi ashram, at Sherth in Kalol taluka, about ten miles from here, and we often used to have our study classes and camps there' (interview, 1975, pp. 137–8).

8. S.B. Mehta, 'Halis, the serfs of Gujarat', p. 7.

9. Yagnik added the following information on this local activist in a footnote: 'He is a native of Vyara. He had taken part in several movements of kisans and workers in several parts of Baroda state. Therefore, he was externed from the British area. This order was relaxed by the end of 1937 by the Congress government.' D.M. Pangarkar was appointed as secretary of the Gujarat branch of the Kisan Sabha (Government of Bombay, Home Department (Special) S.D., first half of June 1938, p. 8).

10. As Hardiman reports, the site of the meeting was in fact in Masad, a village inhabited by Kolis and Dublas. Haripura was a Patidar village a small distance away. But Gandhi was so delighted at the name, which literally means 'God's place', that the name of this village was bestowed on the Congress session (Hardiman 1987: 211).

11. In an immediate response to what Sardar called an unprecedented provocation, the AICC adopted—at Sardar's suggestion—the following resolution at the meeting in Haripura: While fully recognizing the rights of the kisans to organize kisan sabhas, the Congress cannot associate itself with any activities which are incompatible with the basic principles of the Congress and will not countenance any of the activities of those Congressmen who as members of the kisan sabhas help in creating an atmosphere hostile to Congress principles and objectives. AICC papers (G6-KW1) 1938, deposited in the Nehru Memorial Museum and Library, New Delhi.

12. *Reports on the Kisan Morchas in Mandvi and Bulsar talukas.*

13. This was the new name for the Dublas, given to them by Gandhi, as we shall see below.

14. Sardar Patel's speech at the Halpati Conference held in Swaraj ashram, Bardoli on 21 April 1938, published in Chopra and Chopra, *The Collected Works of Sardar Vallabhbhai Patel*, vol. viii, 1996, pp. 108–10.

15. See Chapter 3, pp. 91–2.

16. Extracts from Sardar Patel's speech delivered at Bardoli on 26 January 1939, in *The Collected Works of Sardar Vallabhbhai Patel*, vol. viii, 1996, pp. 35–6.

17. Walter Hauser translated and edited the text from Hindi and published it in *Sahajanand on Agricultural Labour and the Rural Poor* (1994). His translation of *Mera Jivan Sangharsh*—which Swami Sahajanand Saraswati wrote and published in 1952—is entitled *Culture, Vernacular Politics and the Peasants*.

18. For more information on the origins, organization, working methods, and results of this industrial trade union. set up by Gandhi in Ahmedabad in 1920, see Breman 2004, part I.
19. The minutes of the meeting with Gandhi are included, together with the report from the committee, in the Congress papers collection deposited in the Nehru Memorial Museum and Library in Delhi.
20. The sources identify them as Baniyas, Anavils, and Rajputs (Gupta 1996: 51).
21. Report of the district superintendent of police, Surat 21 March 1940, Home (Special) Department, file no. 1019 of 1940–1, Maharashtra State Archives, Bombay.
22. Shankardass, *Vallabhbhai Patel.* Gandhi responded matter of factly to this side of Sardar Patel's character by remarking: 'Well, if the cow gives milk, then we should tolerate the kicks' (Dinkar Mehta 1975: 145). It is an accurate observation, but not if it is used selectively to excuse violence on the part of the landlords whilst condemning it in the case of the landless.
23. In 1935 Dinkar Mehta joined the CPI and in 1939 he was appointed secretary of the Gujarat State Committee.
24. Hardiman, 'The Quit India movement in Gujarat', pp. 77–104.
26. S. Sarkar, *Modern India.*
27. S. Sarkar, '"Popular" Movements and "Middle Class" Leadership'.

5

Landlessness after Independence

Planning for Agrarian Reform

As Congress president, Subash Bose had taken the initiative in 1938 to set up a National Planning Committee (NPC) under the chairmanship of Jawaharlal Nehru to consider the main outlines of economic policy after decolonization. A number of working groups started drafting preliminary recommendations for the discussion in the plenary sessions of the NPC held in Bombay at the beginning of May and the end of June 1940. Radhakamal Mukherji, secretary of the sub-committee that had written the paper on land policy, also submitted a memorandum of his own calling for land reallotment as a solution to the problem of land being divided into very small, widely dispersed parcels. On the basis of these reports, a panel of experts and politicians met to discuss the issue on 29 and 30 June 1940.[1] The panel adopted a number of resolutions, which were referred back to the sub-committee to be worked out in more detail. Landlordism was to be abolished and ownership rights transferred to actual cultivators. Landlords, absentee or not, who lost their entitlements would be eligible for compensation. Opinions differed on the proposal to allocate uncultivated land to collectives or cooperatives as a way of encouraging people to act jointly. The backbone of the agricultural system was and should remain the private farm, which was to be an economic holding. That is to say, it should be large enough to be run effectively by the members of an average-sized family and to provide sufficient yield to guarantee their livelihood. The family unit would also have a maximum size: 'a family ... should not occupy a holding of a size that may under normal conditions require permanent outside labour'. By establishing both a maximum and a minimum limit for landownership, these planners for the post-colonial era envisaged an agrarian society of self-cultivating owners. They also called for the state to impose an immediate ban on the various forms of debt-based bonded labour still prevalent in different parts of the country. Bonded labourers should be released from debts that were more than five years old and should be allocated as yet uncultivated land to help them provide

▲ Halpati women standing in front of their huts in the early 1950s.
Source: P. G. Shah (1958).

▼ Heads loaded with baskets of mangoes, these Halpati women walk to
the railway station at a distance of 6 kilometres from Atulgam.
Source: V.H. Joshi (1966).

▲ Halpati men dehusking paddy in the harvested fields of Atulgam.
Source: V.H. Joshi (1966).

▼ Packing mangoes in baskets to be sold to city-based traders.
Source: V.H. Joshi (1966).

◀ Among the Halpatis the *bhagat* (healer/exorcist) took care of health problems which were endemic to a life of poverty and bondage. *Source*: P.G. Shah (1958).

▶ Landlord belonging to the dominant caste of Anavil Brahmans in south Gujarat. *Source*: V.H. Joshi (1966).

▲▼   While the high-caste landlords lived in the village centre, the habitat of the agricultural labourers was invariably on the outskirts of the locality. The difference in the quality of housing reflected the gap between masters and servants on both ends of the caste–class hierarchy.
Source: V.H. Joshi (1966) and P.G. Shah (1958).

▲   Mixed dancing was banned as uncivilized by Gandhian activists. The progressive incorporation in the Hindu way of life led to the disappearance of tribal culture.
Source: P.G. Shah (1958).

▼   Dancing troupes of Halpatis performing *gheriya* at the end of the monsoon. The men dressed up in female costumes and the leader wore a hat and rode on a horse made of cloth and wood.
Source: P.G. Shah (1958).

▲▼ The huts in which the Halpatis used to live were gradually upgraded to 'houses'. The mud walls were raised somewhat higher, the opening was bigger than before, although still without a door, and the thatched roofs were slowly covered with tiles or asbestos sheets.
Source: Collection of Dubla photos, Tribal Research Institute at Gujarat Vidyapeeth, Ahmedabad.

for themselves. It was further recommended that unions be set up for farm labourers to ensure them minimum wages, a fixed working day, and other terms of employment.

What came of all these proposed reforms? Thorner is one of many who have pointed out the numerous shortcomings in the redistribution of landownership, both in the legislation itself and in the way it was implemented.[2] I restrict myself here to a brief review of the substance and impact of the package of measures introduced in Gujarat, based on an evaluative study published by G. Shah.[3] The first reform—the 1939 Bombay Tenancy Act—had already been introduced by the end of colonial rule and applied at first only to Surat district, by way of experiment. There is no doubt that it was meant to defuse the campaign launched by the Kisan Sabha leadership against sharecropping arrangements in the tribal hinterland. The Act protected tenants who had worked the land they rented for at least six years. After the Congress came to power in 1946, it was extended to the whole state. In 1948, it was replaced by the Bombay Tenancy and Agricultural Lands Act, but without further amendment. Tenants who fell under the protection clause were entitled to buy the land they worked at the going market price and could spread the payments out over a period of ten to fifteen years. In 1955, the provision was extended to all tenants, including those who did not fall into the protected category. 1 April 1957 was designated Tillers' Day since, from then on, all farmers would be registered as owners of the land they cultivated. The minister responsible expressed his satisfaction with this measure, which he believed would especially benefit landpoor farmers.

It will bring hope to the landless or the partially landless and provide for reasonable means of their subsistence.... It gives him (the tenant) a dignity and status which he never possessed before. He will be able to breathe his native air in his own ground (G. Shah 2002: 135).

The promise was not fulfilled. As would appear several years later, only half the land worked by tenant farmers had changed owners, and that was usually to the benefit of farmers from the higher castes. Tenants from scheduled castes and tribes had much less chance of actually exercising their right to buy the land they worked on. Even if they were aware of their legal entitlement, their subaltern position ensured that the land was not allocated to them—the chances of success were better if the owners did not live in the village and were just rent seekers. This explains why tribal tenants and sharecroppers in Surat district got back a large part of the land that they or their forebears had lost to distillers and urban moneylenders. Hardiman observes that 'Parsis and urban *shahukars* lost the bulk of their estates to their *adivasi* tenants.'[4] He adds that this remarkable achievement would not have been possible without the radical agrarian agitation that had taken place in the district in the preceding decades (Hardiman 1987: 216). The 1960 Land Ceiling Act introduced a ceiling for agrarian land ownership. If the Act had been enforced to the letter, the dominant farmers could have suffered serious land losses, but this was prevented by the many exemptions and loopholes. The ceiling was lowered in 1974, but this had no effect on the concentration of landownership in the hands of the dominant castes. Instead of losing property, they emerged as winners in the land-reform operation in Gujarat.

The Halpatis benefited in no way at all from the land reforms. The few tenant farmers among them generally lost the land that they had sharecropped on an informal basis. Swami Sahajanand had calculated that half of the landless would become landowners if uncultivated land was allocated to the Halpatis (Hauser 1994: 101). The National Planning Committee had welcomed a proposal to this effect but, once again, the promise was not honoured. Uncultivated land not under private ownership was under the control of the village *panchayat*. Everyone had free access to this common land, which was extremely important to the landless, who used it to graze their cattle, cut grass, gather firewood and, not least, for defecation. In the decades that followed, however, this access would be increasingly restricted as a result of the widespread trend to privatize the land. The transfer of the common land into private hands almost invariably meant that it became the property of the dominant farming castes. According to the agricultural economist M.B. Desai, the social order based on a highly inegalitarian ideology was a major reason for the vulnerability of the rural landless in Gujarat. The supply of labour was also much higher than the demand and getting out from agriculture was next to impossible for agricultural workers (M.B. Desai 1971: 117).

A last chance for the Halpatis to become landowners came with the launch of the Bhoodan (land gift) movement by Acharya Vinobe Bhave. This social reformer, who lived and worked according to Gandhian principles, called on landowners to donate land in excess of their requirements to landpoor farmers, voluntarily and without any compensation. His plan was intended as an alternative to the violent communist agitation in the Telengana district of Hyderabad, which had ended in defeat for the insurgents. During a visit to the area in 1951 it occurred to Bhave that his Gandhian approach stood a better chance of success. The movement was launched in the Gaya district of Bihar, which Bhave wanted to turn into Bhoodan's 'Bardoli'. It only lasted a few years, however, grinding to a halt towards the end of the decade largely due to the unwillingness of landowners to surrender their surplus land. Many of them failed to honour promises made under moral pressure. When and where surplus land was transferred it was generally of inferior quality (Thorner 1976: 70–1; Hardiman 1903: 202–7). The Bhoodan movement was not successful in many parts of the country, but was quite popular in south Gujarat. The existing network of Gandhian institutions in the region, especially in the area around Bardoli, enthusiastically added the movement's aims to their programme of constructive work. I encountered the Gandhian workers repeatedly during my first period of fieldwork in 1962–3. They were very keen to tell me why this objective held such promise in their search for a solution to the agrarian question, but it was clear that they had as yet failed to produce any significant results. As one of the social workers told me, Halpatis in particular were not eligible for the allocation of Bhoodan land because the local agrarian elite thought they lacked the necessary qualities to be owner-cultivators in their own right:

Yet they are treated with so much contempt that Shri Narayan Desai reported in 1956 a conversation among people of the land owning class enquiring whether the Dublas at all deserved to be considered fit for being given the gift of Bhudan land (P.G. Shah 1958: 23).

The report by the Hali Labour Enquiry Commission, which will be discussed in detail below, also mentions this attitude of the high-caste landowners, insisting that the Halpatis did not possess the efficiency and sense of discipline required to work the land on their own account (HLEC Report 1948: 36).

This review of the land reforms in post-colonial India leads me to conclude that they were designed and implemented in such a way that social classes like the Halpatis were systematically denied access to agrarian landownership. The most common argument in defence of this strategy was the lack of cultivable land eligible for redistribution.

Increasing the share of land owned by landpoor farmers was given priority above allocating plots of land to the landless masses. The reasoning was that such an uneconomic holding would be more of a burden than a benefit to them, as it would prevent them from leaving the rural economy. The way in which the reform operation was implemented also points to the great importance of non-economic factors. I refer here in particular the complete lack of willingness at local level to put an end to the subjugation and immense poverty of the agrarian underclass. Sardar Patel had already said at the end of the 1930s that what the Halpatis should do to escape their servitude is to leave the region entirely and look for a better life elsewhere. His opponent Swami Sahajanand made it equally clear that the agricultural economy could not provide sufficient employment for the surplus of labour in the countryside. His solution was for at least half the army of agricultural labourers to go and work in the new industrial factories and workshops that would be set up after Independence—a scenario the National Planning Committee also had in mind. Two working groups were set up to consider the development of an industrial infrastructure in the cities and the kind of labour system this would require. The deliberations resulted in the rough outlines of the kind of lives workers would lead in the emerging urban industrial milieu: a dignified existence that was in sharp contrast to the miserable lot of the agricultural labourer.[5]

The Continuing Practice of Unfree Labour

Nothing came of the proposal drawn up by Sardar Patel in 1938 and approved by Gandhi. The main reason was the refusal of the farmers in south Gujarat to accept the disappearance of the system of bonded labour. The halis responded by going on strike, but their employers would not give in, and became even more resolute when the Halpati women also refused to work. Shocked at the furious response of the farmers, the Gandhian reformers urged the Halpatis to perform their customary duties. However, the labourers became angry at the farmers for not keeping to the agreement, and this led once again to a conflict in the village of Sarbhon when the staff of the ashram supported the striking halis by commissioning them to do public works. The project was abandoned only after angry Patidars expressed their displeasure by beating the Gandhian meddlers (I.I. Desai 1971: 167).

The halis had no other choice than to go back to work under the old regime. The terms of employment and the wages they received were completely unchanged. As a result of the rapid rise in food prices in the Second World War, they opted themselves for payment in kind rather than in cash. Therefore, at the end of the day, they received the traditional grain ration: 2.5 *seer* of millet or 4 seer of paddy. The bosses regularly cheated when measuring the rations and labourers received 10 to 25 per cent less than they were entitled to.[6] Both sides knew that this unfair practice was going on, but that was no reason to put a stop to it. Since expenses that the halis had to pay for in cash also rose, their debt to the master increased even further. The 'Grow More Food Campaign' launched by the colonial government in 1944 took up such a large proportion of agricultural land that it became difficult to grow non-food crops. To take full advantage of the high price of grain, farmers claimed back the *vavla*, the small plot of land which the halis were permitted to work on for their own benefit. Many villages had already abandoned this custom, which provided the halis with an increment on their annual income, and those farmers who still allowed it also put a stop to it (C.H. Shah 1952: 450).[7] A number of daily necessities, including sugar, were so scarce that they were no longer available on the free market. The halis in the villages in which I conducted my fieldwork had to surrender their ration cards to the farmers, and the Anavils I spoke to gave the excuse that the Halpatis' wages were too low for them to afford such luxuries anyway (Breman 1974: 212).

Since the Kisan Sabha activists had disappeared from the scene in the final years of colonial domination, the Gandhian social workers were the only outsiders left to represent the Halpatis' interests. These volunteers usually came from the cities and were members of the higher castes. Their bases of operation were the ashrams opened in the 1920s to uplift the tribal population. These *sevaks* (servants) were driven by a moralism which turned them into missionaries with little empathy for the tribal culture and identity of those they were trying to show the way to a better life. The Kisan Sabha activists had been much more closely involved with the people they tried to help, but they left again once the protest was over to continue their agitation elsewhere. The Gandhian workers on the other hand came with the intention to stay and many devoted their whole lives to their mission. After the fiasco in 1924, when a conflict with the high-caste farmers escalated and resulted in the closure of an evening school for children from the landless community, the ashrams did not extend their programme of constructive work to include the Halpatis until the end of the 1930s, and then only in a modest way, and restricted to the area surrounding Bardoli. A small number of sevaks tried to live among the Halpatis but the dominant farmers refused to tolerate this (Dave 1946: 42). From then on the social workers did not concern themselves with the work regime and concentrated their activities on improving their clients' lifestyle. Indirectly they tried to build up the landless labourers' resilience, and this included plans to build huts for the halis on land that did not belong to the masters. In most subdistricts in south Gujarat it had been standard practice for halis to live on their master's property, which meant that debt was not the only mechanism that deprived the labourers of any freedom of movement. In addition to giving the halis permission to build their huts on their land, the masters also provided the straw for the roofs.

The present arrangement in most cases impairs seriously his independence. Even at the slightest provocation, the *dhaniyama* will threaten to throw out the *hali* on the roadside. Particularly when it comes to organizing the *hali* for improving his bargaining capacity this arrangement acts as a serious handicap, because the fear of being ejected summarily by the farmer when the *hali* does anything that goes against his interest hangs like the Damocles' sword on the latter's head (HLEC Report 1948: 19).

The initiative to permit Halpatis to live in specially designated zones in the village had an additional advantage in that by living in close proximity to each other, they developed a greater sense of group identity. Jugatram Dave submitted to Morarji Desai, who was then revenue minister in the government of Bombay, a plan to set up a cooperative housing society for Halpatis. The government would provide the land and a grant of Rs 500 per house, of which the owner would have to repay Rs 400 in instalments. Two of these colonies were initially set up, but enthusiasm for the project waned after a couple of years following unfavourable reports about the locations on which they had been built.

In the case of the Verad colony the village drain which virtually flows into the 'Halpati vas' gives out obnoxious smell and is highly injurious to health. In Wankaner, a stream is found to be flowing by the halis' dwellings which perhaps because of its bad layout has been a nuisance to the residents of the colony (HLEC Report 1948: 18).

A much greater obstacle to the success of the initiative was the condition that the residents pay back the loan of Rs 400. Who had ever thought that they would be able to do so on a wage that was barely sufficient to meet their basic food requirement?

The social workers had greater success with their call for a ban on the sale of alcohol. A ban was first introduced in 1949 in the subdistricts of Bardoli and Valod, followed a year later by the whole of Surat district. This ban has remained in force to the present day but since, its introduction, the illegal distillation and sale of liquor has been widespread. This has not, however, prevented the abolitionists from claiming that their goal has been achieved. Within a few years of the ban being introduced there were reports of enormous progress being made by those freed from their alcohol addiction and much was made of the contrast between the situation before and after the ban.

In pre-prohibition period, a Dubla hamlet at night was but a battleground, crowded with drunkards. Heavily drunk men and women were found making rows, using abusive language and sometime lying unconscious in a most hideous state. But now the fears of punishment and loss of prestige has considerably disciplined their behaviour. In the same way, the drunken brawls at marriage and such other religious and social occasions caused by excessive drinking are certainly less common. The money spent extravagantly in drinks has also been saved to a great extent (P.G. Shah 1958: 218).

The Dublas were principally agricultural labourers and on account of their long addiction to intoxicating drinks, they could never progress for [sic] beyond the borders of penury, indebtedness, illiteracy, economic backwardness and peaceful social and domestic life, to say nothing of political consciousness. Today, however, thanks to Prohibition, all that is a thing of the past. They now own part of the lands themselves (Editorial in *The Farmer*, January 1954, vol. 5/1: 49).

Propaganda like this also created the impression that the Halpatis were able to earn a tidy sum to supplement their incomes by spinning: 'the *charkha* began to hum in their huts'. The farmers sometimes complained about these extra activities, claiming that they were at the expense of the Halpatis' main task of working the land. At the time of the 'Quit India' movement in 1942, an enthusiastic start was made with admitting Halpati children to the ashram schools, but after a short time interest in this project faded and little more came of educating the landless. They had difficulties providing their basic necessities and fell back into their old lethargy (Dave 1946: 43).

In 1947, the government of Bombay set up a commission to investigate the social and economic situation of the halis in south Gujarat. The researchers—M.L. Dantwala and M.B. Desai[8] of the Agricultural Economics Section at the University School of Economics and Sociology in Bombay—were instructed to draw up recommendations on the basis of their findings: 'suggesting measures necessary for rehabilitating this class of agricultural labourers and for enabling them to live a life consistent with human dignity and self respect'. It was the first time that the Halpatis had been the subject of an empirical study and had been asked, along with district officials, farmers, and social workers, about the nature of their employment, their wages, and their way of life. The commission drew up a questionnaire to obtain basic information on the villages visited (twenty villages in nine talukas), invited ninety-two witnesses to make statements, gave 104 interviews and, with the help of a small staff, collected elementary data on around fifteen hali families in each of the surveyed villages.[9] The same data was collected from farm servants (three in each village) who worked as daily wage earners. The report did not examine the system of labour bondage in detail, restricting itself to the economic and social context in which it operated. Submitted to the authorities in 1948 it was meant for official use only.[10] The researchers calculated that a fifth of the rural population in Surat district were halis, the great majority of whom (90 per cent) were Halpatis as the Dublas were nowadays called. The commission's first recommendation was to abolish the system of halipratha by issuing a ban on the practice. Wages had to be at least one rupee a day and paid in cash, unless the labourer himself preferred to receive a grain ration. If the farmer paid the labourer anything extra, he could no longer deduct this from the daily wage. It would now be seen as what it was—extra pay for extra work. Debts older than three years had to be cancelled and repayments on any remaining debts had to be reduced to a level that would enable the labourer to repay them in a maximum of twenty-four monthly instalments. To make repayment easier, the committee recommended setting up multi-purpose cooperatives to encourage the Halpatis to save, help them pay off their debts, provide credit to build their huts, and keep a register of those unemployed so that they could be given jobs on public works. A telling demonstration of the change of times was that the farmers and their spokesmen who were interviewed also agreed that the hali system belonged to the past. They did however impress upon the committee that any alternative arrangement should at least include the obligation to provide labour power in the busy season, arguing that otherwise agricultural production would suffer. Raising agricultural production, so their claim went, was an important national priority and it was therefore the duty of government to ensure that enough cheap labour would remain available.

To fulfil the need for independent accommodation for the halis after their release from servitude, the government would have to help them build huts on their own land. Apart from making them less dependent on the whim of the landowners, there was an urgent need to improve the quality of their housing.

The huts of the Halis are in an indescribably bad condition. Almost invariably, they are improvised out of inadequate and inferior material, with the consequences that they do not provide adequate protection against rain and the sun. The thatching material decomposes after contacting rain water for some time and water percolates into the hut from many spots. There is no arrangement for proper ventilation. Practically none of the huts inspected by us were divided or partitioned in some sort of apartments to ensure privacy. Only when the inside space has to be shared with domesticated animals that some kind of provisional demarcation is made with a few bamboos attached to the wooden pillars supporting the structure. The inside of the hut, therefore, is in perpetual darkness lit up occasionally by the fire place during the day and by a crude kerosene lamp for sometime at night. The provision of the kitchen inside a hut made of lightly ignitable material, no wonder, leads to frequent fires, reducing the huts to ashes and destroying the small belongings of the Halis. ... For the size of the Hali family the space inside the hut is inadequate. Investigation into this aspect indicated 20 square feet of living space on an average per individual. This space is further reduced when animals share the hut in common with the Hali (HLEC Report 1948: 18).

The researchers specified what the halis' small belongings were. Their average value was 11 rupees and 6 annas per family, hardly more than the hali's monthly income. A little less than half of the families included in the study did not even have the millstone necessary to grind the grain ration that the hali received every day. The commission was unable to list the debts of all the halis because many did not know exactly how much they owed their masters. From the figures gathered from a small number of halis, the average debt per family proved to be 27 rupees and 11 annas, more than twice the value of their material possessions. The main reason for the continued indebtedness was that the hali's annual income was insufficient to cover even the minimal expenses needed to survive. The report concluded the description of the halis' consumption pattern described below by saying that 'the hali's requirements and purchases are few and that he exists at a sub-human standard of living'. The commission's comments on the hali's low productivity in comparison to daily wage workers are interesting. The average length of the working day was eight to nine hours, increasing to twelve to fifteen hours in the busy season. Detailed records submitted by farmers in many villages show that the halis might work day in, day out, for quite a long period and then suddenly, without prior warning, not turn up. The masters blamed this erratic behaviour on their servants' laziness and lack of a sense of responsibility. The commission's opinion was, however, noticeably more nuanced:

> The attendance figures do not mean that the hali was intentionally absent for the rest of the days. It is just possible that for some days there was no work on the farm of the dhaniyama and he was therefore not 'called'. Some absenteeism was due to sickness and fatigue. A part of it may be due to festivals. Halis are forced to remain idle during slack seasons and days of heavy rains. Some of the causes are beyond his control. Sickness and fatigue are the direct outcome of sub-human living standard and the low vitality to which it gives rise (HLEC Report 1948: 22).

Lastly, to improve the level of knowledge among the landless, the report advised introducing compulsory school attendance for children and providing vocational education so that land labourers could train for other forms of work. As part of a wider package of social reforms, high priority should be given to reducing alcohol abuse and addressing other shortcomings in the halis' lifestyle.

On 6 September 1951, the government of Bombay responded officially to accusations in the media that it had not acted on the HLEC's recommendation to abolish the halipratha system. In a press release entitled *No Forced Labour in Surat District*, it said that the accusations were incorrect. Since the agreement reached by home minister Morarji Desai and Labour minister Gulzarilal Nanda with farmers and halis in Bardoli in June 1948, the system of forced labour no longer existed. Not only had it been abolished in the interests of both parties, but agreements had also been made about the level of pay and how to settle disputes. In the light of this agreement, the press release continued, the government saw no reason to enforce the ban by legislation. After all, 'there was no legal sanction to the system and, therefore, the question of its abolition by a special law did not arise at all' (P.G. Shah 1958:

211). Although I was unable to verify the accuracy of this report, which came from the director of publicity, on the basis of other documents I assume that the meeting in 1948 actually took place and that an agreement was reached as described. The argument for not introducing a legal ban, however, does not hold water. It is important to note that getting rid of unfree labour was not seen as a government responsibility but, as in 1938, was once again left to the free play of social forces. These forces were represented, on the one hand, by a class of farmers who had not only consolidated their power base at the local level during the process of independence but had further reinforced it, and on the other hand by a large mass of landless labourers whose labour power was only required in full strength for certain parts of the year. For the remainder of the time there was insufficient work to keep them all employed. During these slack periods, the farmers gave the halis the usual grain allowance on credit, but this was seen as an advance on future work and added to the labourers' debt. The commission concluded pessimistically:

All efforts at improving the economic conditions of the Halis are likely to be frustrated unless hope and desire for a radically different and better life are generated among these people. Without this psychological change, no reform has any chance of success. The Hali and his children take for granted the mould of life into which they are born. Long years of suppression have so devitalised them that they have not even the strength of dreaming of a better life. Custom and tradition have stratified not only their living but also their aspirations. Their tallest prayer is, to be blessed with a *dhaniyamo* who is kind and considerate. No wonder, there are many Halis who in their heart of heart dread the abolition of the Hali system (HLEC Report 1948: 36).

The responsibility for being both willing and able to seek work outside agriculture on the basis of different employment arrangements once again fell to the most vulnerable party.

Introduction of a Minimum Wage

A report from the Congress Agrarian Reforms Committee published in 1951 described the halipratha system in such a way as to suggest that it was still fully intact.[11] According to the report, halis rarely ran away, despite the fact that farmers had no legal power to enforce the employment agreements. Indoctrination in subjugation proved much more effective. The landless were led to believe that desertion was a sin for which God would punish their children. Sons followed their fathers in servitude—after all, they had been brought up thanks to the charity of the master. From generation to generation they remained the prisoners of an agrarian regime from which there was no escape. How could this grave violation of the principles of justice and freedom be brought to an end? The authors of the report did not mince their words in rebuking their own party and its leaders: 'To leave out the problem of agricultural labour in any scheme of agrarian reforms—as has been done so far—is to leave unattended a weeping wound in the agrarian system of the country' (*Report of the Congress Agrarian Reforms Committee*, 1951: 112).

The Congress government of India commissioned an extensive enquiry to obtain a better insight into the situation of land labourers and their terms of employment. The purpose of the enquiry was to gather information on existing employment modalities and pay, and to underline the need for the planned introduction of a minimum wage. The National Planning Committee had already expressed its support for a minimum wage in 1940 to provide protection for the most vulnerable class in the rural economy. The Minimum Wages Act, which came into force in 1948, only established the decision to set a minimum wage, without saying anything about how high it should be. This was left to the state governments, which were instructed to stipulate within three years a minimum wage level for wage labourers in the agricultural sector and to include statutory arrangements for reviewing it every five years. The intention was to introduce the minimum wage in 1950, but the period within which the state governments actually had to take concrete steps was continually postponed. Although the authorities claimed that they still had insufficient facts on the nature of employment, labour relations, and pay in the agricultural sector, the real reason for the delay was a lack of political will. They decided not to be too hasty and to wait for the results of the Agricultural Labour Enquiry.[12] A few years after these reports had been published, there was a second round of fact-gathering, which produced an equally comprehensive collection of empirical data.[13] The aim of this second study was to determine to what extent, if at all, agricultural labourers had benefited from the First Five-Year Plan, which had expired in 1956.

The commission studying the situation of the halis in south Gujarat recommended in 1948 a minimum daily wage of one rupee which was considered to be the minimum required for sheer survival. But one of the two members of the commission, M.B. Desai, did not agree with fixing the rate at this level. In a Minute of Dissent he called for a much lower wage: 12 annas for men and 9 annas for women (three-quarters and a little over half a rupee, respectively). This took account only of the rise in the price of food during the war years, meaning that the halis received no more than they had always been paid—an excessively low wage that condemned them to poverty and indebtedness. In Desai's view, the level of the daily wage should be based on the land labourer's spending patterns. This implied that the limited needs of the landless justified the lowest possible payment for their labour. He also argued that the wage level for land labourers should not exceed what the agricultural sector could afford to pay. Moreover, these wage rates were only recommendations and did not mean that labourers could demand that they actually be paid. This became very clear to me ten years later, during the first round of my fieldwork in 1962–3 in south Gujarat. Farm servants in the two villages I was studying, in the subdistricts of Chikhli and Gandevi, had to make do with 8 annas a day. This placed the daily wage of 12 annas paid to casual labourers in a more favourable light—both categories, however, lived out their lives in abject poverty (Breman 1974).

In 1964 a committee was set up in Gujarat to make proposals for a minimum wage for agricultural labourers and to draw up procedures for enforcing it. The report, published in 1966, urged the authorities to act quickly before the landless masses resorted to radical agitation.[14] The report's authors warned that, given the misery at the bottom of the agrarian system, the chances of violence erupting were far from improbable. The passage quoted below illustrates their sense of urgency:

The implication of a lack of policy for agrarian labour to the political and social stability would be easily appreciated. The developments in Asia and Africa are an eye-opener. The working class in general and the agrarian labour in particular in our country have retained their moorings to our basic philosophy of life and living. They might have grown restless and frustrated now and again, but by and large they have shown great patience in the otherwise discouraging situation around them. This is extremely healthy for the country and for all its citizens. This, however, should not make us complacent. It should be treated as a favourable factor to do something quickly to improve the lot of those on whose faces we read signs of discontent and disparagement. The forces of extremism are waiting to take over the situation once these indications intensify a little. Therefore, before developments suddenly take a turn and overwhelm us we should proceed to do our part of the duty. All concerned with the problem should wholeheartedly and enthusiastically join in this task to change the situation and to move towards a generally acceptable society and socio-economic relations (*MWACA Report* 1966: 78–9).

Although this interpretation saw extremism lying in wait, the minimum wage for agricultural labourers was not introduced until 1972. This was preceded by many years of deliberation and consultation. I have reported extensively on the many loopholes in the legislation and inadequate way in which it has been enforced and complied with in a variety of publications. What concerns me here is that the government did not take the first steps to protect agrarian labour, the largest and most vulnerable working class in India, until a quarter of a century after Independence.

What happened to the halipratha system after it was supposedly abolished in 1948? There were occasional reports suggesting that it was still practised. In its 1960–1 annual report, the Scheduled Areas and Scheduled Tribes Commission noted laconically that, despite the claims of the government of Gujarat to the contrary, the system of bonded labour had not been completely eradicated and was still to be found here and there.[15] The committee preparing the introduction of the minimum wage also recognized, making explicit reference to the agrarian regime in south Gujarat, that unfree labour could not yet be seen as a closed chapter, a memory from the past. It concluded, however, that because farmers were no longer willing to provide land labourers with advances, halipratha had become much less important. The report attributed the obstinacy with which this traditional employment arrangement continued to survive to defects in the behaviour of the Halpatis:

It is good that the system is dying. Whatever is left of it is due to ignorance of the Dubla and his apathy to search for an alternative. Maybe the alternative(s) themselves do not exist. In some measure the inertia and stiffened social sinews and the habit of indolent, indisciplined and disorganized village life to which the *hali* is accustomed inhibits a switch-over either in the same occupation elsewhere or in towns and cities in non-agricultural work (*MWACA Report* 1966: 297).

In short, while farmers no longer had the inclination to employ their labourers in bonded servitude, the landless remained what they had always been: lazy, totally lacking in any desire to improve themselves, and unwilling to go in search of better-paid employment outside the village. I will show later that this image of the landless concealed a much different reality.

After the long delay in introducing the minimum wage, it was finally set at such a low level that agricultural labourers could only meet their most basic needs and still needed to go into debt to survive. Inadequate implementation and enforcement of the law continued to frustrate efforts to bring the landless up above the poverty line to what the mandate of the Hali Labour Enquiry Commission referred to as 'a life consistent with human dignity and self-respect'.

Collective Action

The collapse of the Kisan Sabha after the expulsion of communist activists in 1940 meant the end of radical agrarian agitation in south Gujarat. But this did not happen overnight. In a few districts, Halpatis continued their struggle for the abolition of bonded labour. The name of Dattu Pangarkar, a grassroots cadre active in the movement launched by Yagnik at the end of the 1930s, cropped up again when after Independence a section of tribal peasants organized themselves in the Dakshin Gujarat Adivasi Swayat Raj under CPI(M) leadership. Their presence was mainly in the border area between Surat and Broach district where they campaigned in the 1960s for a separate adivasi state (I.P. Desai 1977: 75). The resistance of tribal farmers in Pardi to confiscation of their land by grass traders attracted greater attention. After his first visit to the area early in 1939, Yagnik returned at the end of the same year to lead a protest meeting attended by 4000 Dhodhias. The unrest continued after he was arrested in May 1940. Later, the tribal farmers took advantage of the 'Quit India' campaign in 1942, not so much to protest against the colonial authorities, but to attack the houses of moneylenders and traders. Their resistance had little effect at first—in 1952 three-quarters of agricultural land in the subdistrict was still in the hands of 100 large landowners. The struggle continued, now with the support of a number of leading figures in the Praja Socialist Party. The Pardi *ghasia* (=grass) satyagraha, which began in 1953, opposed the landowners and their allies: the Congress party and the government. After ten years a solution was in sight but some of the Dhodhias' demands were not to be met until 1967. The land would henceforth be used to grow food crops and, under the land reform laws, landowners had to surrender all land in their possession in excess of the land ceiling to its former owners.[16]

The agitation in the Thane district of Maharashtra, which bordered on south Gujarat, aimed to liberate the tribal Varlis from their plight as bonded land labourers-cum-sharecroppers in servitude to high-caste landowners. The tribals, who had lost not only their land but also their power to dispose of their own labour power as they wished, rebelled against their subjugation. At the end of 1944, aided and abetted by a sympathetic civil servant, they went on strike. The Varlis' resistance caught the attention of the Kisan Sabha activists, who took over the campaign of agitation. The objectives of the struggle, which lasted until 1947, were restoration of tribal landownership and abolition of bonded labour.[17] This campaign falls outside the scope of this study, but it is relevant that its outcome was determined by the decision of the Congress ministers in the government of Bombay to repress the revolt in the proclaimed interest of restoring law and order. The radical activists who insisted on far-reaching reforms were now once again portrayed as rebels who only provoked unrest and caused harm to those they claimed to defend.

Congressmen sought to portray the Communists as opportunistic and themselves as committed, patient advocates of gradual, peaceful reform who only needed more time to bring about positive changes. Where the Communists preached conflict of interest, the Congress preached the virtue of harmony (Calman 1987: 330).[18]

The authorities' decision to adopt harsh measures to end the conflict was partly out of fear that the tribal resistance would spread to neighbouring districts, including Surat (Calman 1987: 331, fn. 6). The communist leaders were banned from the district, and the landowners knew that they had the support of the government in continuing to confiscate the land and exploit the tribal population.

The Congress party, which had come to power after Independence both at the central level and in the separate states, put an end to the pressure that had been placed on the leaders of the nationalist movement for decades to pursue a rural policy in the interests of the landless and landpoor peasants. The ban on membership of the Communist Party introduced in 1948 applied also to the Kisan Sabha, and the offices of this militant organization were closed down throughout the country. Its leaders and members were accused of subversive activities and placed in detention. One of them was Dinkar Mehta who was arrested in 1948 and imprisoned until the middle of 1951. These measures, which were intended to put a stop to the threat from left-wing agitators for good, meant that the agrarian question was removed from the agenda without the introduction, in Gujarat at least, of radical changes in the relations between landowners and the landless.

The extent to which radical social transformation was perceived as a threat in this period is clear from a passage in the report of the Hali Labour Enquiry Commission, which candidly admits that left-wing activists had succeeded in making Halpatis aware of their subjugation. This admission was however accompanied by a warning that escalation of the unrest would have a disruptive effect on society and the economy:

... the workers of the Kisan Sabha, a Communist dominated organization, are active among the Halis of Olpad, Chikhli and Bulsar talukas. They have succeeded in enlightening the Halis of these places who were hitherto unconscious of their conditions and rights and privileges. A few unpleasant aspects of their activities should, however, be noted with regret. In their zeal to improve the lots of the Halis, they are unmindful of the economic conditions in the district in particular and the country in general. With their record in the Thana district, grave apprehensions will be felt about their method of approach and the end in view. If things proceed along the lines pursued today in which poisonous propaganda is being dinned into the ears of the Halis without putting the entire question in its proper perspective before them, the conclusion is irresistible that a violent class conflict leading to considerable destruction might be in store. If this were unfortunately to happen it will embitter the relationship between the farmers and the Halis and will be calamitous for the progress of agriculture in the district. It is highly improper to further political motives under the pretext of fighting for the emancipation of the working class. An effort should, therefore, be made to properly appreciate the achievements through constructive efforts by selfless workers in Bardoli and Valod whose life mission is the service of the down-trodden in the true Gandhian way (HLEC Report 1948: 25).

The tribals had recently been renamed adivasis[19] and these groups, including the Halpatis, would henceforth be under the protection of the Gandhian reformers. No other individuals or groups, politically or non-politically motivated, wishing to defend the interests of the landless and landpoor were admitted to the exclusive domain of the sevaks. Between 1942 and 1945 these social workers were not very active, as many had been arrested at the start of the 'Quit India' campaign. As dedicated Congress supporters they had obeyed the call to resist the colonial authorities.[20] In this period, their patriotism had priority above their efforts to elevate the deprived social classes in south Gujarat.

As early as 1942, an association Halpati Mahajan was set up with the aim of developing members of the landless community (I.I. Desai 1971: 170). The Hali Labour Enquiry Commission mentioned the association in its report without providing any details. Most likely it was a network through which the social reformers at the ashrams in and around Bardoli maintained contact with each other. In 1946, the participants registered the network as a formal organization and agreed to base their activities on the Gandhian principles of 'truth, non-violence and arbitration'. The name 'Mahajan' was a direct reference to the union Gandhi had set up in Ahmedabad in 1920 for textile workers, not only to achieve improvements in their material conditions but to imbue discipline into an underclass which were said to lack the character traits to develop on its own initiative.[21] The social workers were not accountable to the Halpatis but had to lead them on the long road to a better future by showing them how to be respectable members of society. The members had no say at all in what the programme of constructive work entailed or the way in which the organization was set up. From the beginning, the driving principle was 'for them, but not by them'.

In 1949, following up on an earlier pilot scheme, the Bombay State Social Welfare Department awarded a grant for the setting up of ten cooperative housing societies, each of which built ten huts for the price of Rs 400 per hut. Rs 100 of this was a donation and the rest had to be repaid by the beneficiaries in ten annual instalments. At the same time, the first two ashram schools were opened, complete with hostels to accommodate their pupils. The funds provided by the government enabled the ashrams to support themselves, allowing them to pay their sevaks a salary and covering the overhead costs of supervision.[22] In 1961 the Halpati Seva Sangh was set up, with the Gandhian veteran Jugatram Dave as its president and Arvind Desai, the son of a family of landlords, as its general secretary. The organization, which was located in Bardoli, initially restricted its activities to Surat district but, from 1967 on, operated throughout south Gujarat. The HSS explicitly avoided presenting itself as a trade union, calling itself an agency for welfare work and acting as an intermediary between the government and the target group.

The custom of Halpatis living in huts on their masters' land gradually died out. They were housed in colonies under the authority of the village panchayat, with the intention of reducing their dependence and increasing their sense of community. It was also in line with the custom of members of the same caste to live in close proximity to each other. The areas in which the landless lived, which were usually a cluster of huts on the edge of the village, had few public facilities, such as a passable access road or a well for fresh water. As noted previously, the first colonies were built on land that was unfit for residential use. This practice changed little over time and, in most villages, the landless continued to live on the most inferior land. The huts, too, were in such a dilapidated state that they were largely unfit to live in, as I observed myself on many occasions during my fieldwork. In most cases, the residents did not have a small plot of land around the hut, which they desperately needed to house their cattle, grow vegetables, etc. Nevertheless, in comparison with the conditions in which the halis had previously been forced to live, in the shadow of their masters and continually under his surveillance, their transfer to the new colonies was undeniably an improvement. The government realized that the housing programme was of great importance to the liberation of the Halpatis, as can be seen from a statement by the minister of social welfare to the Bombay Assembly in 1948:

Effective steps are being taken by the Government to free the members of the Dubla community in Surat District from serfdom. This could be achieved by providing them with houses and therefore the Government of Bombay has made a provision of seven lakhs in the second plan (P.G. Shah, 1959: 57).[23]

The funds made available were no more than a drop in the ocean. Only a small number of houses could be built with the little money that was budgeted and the source from which I took the above quotation also observed that 'the policy has lacked continuity and consistency'. Furthermore, no account was taken of the fact that the landless labourers were completely unable to pay back the loans they had received to buy their houses, even though they were interest-free.

The education programme made even less progress. The level of illiteracy among the Halpatis was so high that it was not easy to persuade parents to allow their children to attend school and nothing at all came of the ambitious plans for adult education. Strikingly, it was the tribal groups who owned their own land, such as Dhodhias, Chodhris, and Gamits, who were more likely to show an interest in sending their children to an ashram school. Consequently, the Halpatis soon fell behind. Even at boarding schools, which had been explicitly intended for them, the majority of the children came from other tribal groups. The Gandhian social workers had little insight into the obstacles that prevented the children of the landless from attending school, such as the absence of both parents during the day, the economic need for children to fend for themselves from an early age by taking on paid work and, more generally, the tendency not to invest in the future because priority had to be given to surviving from day to day. Facilities that were introduced much later—such as allowances for clothing, books and other expenses, or the provision of a school meal in the middle of the day—which would have increased the incentive to send children to school, received little attention in the middle of the last century. The HSS had some success in organizing vocational training courses for carpenters, bricklayers, drivers, etc. But the majority of Halpatis were not eligible, firstly because they had not completed a primary education and therefore did not meet the admission requirements and secondly, because they could not afford not to work for the period required to attend the course.

Within the programme of constructive work, the Gandhian sevaks saw their core task as encouraging the Halpatis to improve the way they lived. Their aim was to eradicate vices that stood in the way of their development. On top of the list was alcohol, which they had to stop drinking immediately. The instruction to desist from eating meat was easier to comply with since this was a luxury that the landless labourers could rarely afford. They had to be taught rules for hygiene not only to prevent disease but also to teach them to live according to Hindu customs. The children learned these rules and customs at school, and through them their parents could be persuaded of the need to adapt their conduct and language to what was considered decent. The Halpatis were encouraged to sing devotional and edifying songs in small groups, and were given musical instruments with which to accompany themselves. To help reduce the costs of weddings, the social workers arranged festive gatherings a few times a year at which several couples could be joined in matrimony according to Hindu custom.

The frank statement that the HSS was a social welfare organization and not a trade union made it clear that its primary objective was not to represent its members' economic interests. The leadership claimed that it had urged the government to introduce a minimum wage and to increase it periodically, but in practice little came of either. Whenever the Halpatis were in dispute with the landlords and went on strike, or threatened to, the social workers were eager to offer their services. Yet they rarely sided wholeheartedly with the landless or took the lead in the protests. They scaled down their role to one of mediating between the two parties, seeking a compromise and the restoration of 'good' relations. The authorities, too, often called on the Gandhian missionaries to cajole the landless into subservience and obedience. During my fieldwork in 1962–3, I found myself listening to Morarji Desai, who was guest of honour at a meeting of the HSS held in a village near Bardoli (Breman 1974: 228). He called on his audience to break their ties of dependence to which they had consented for too long in the conviction that they were unable to stand on their own feet. It was the start of a new era and they should mobilize themselves—also literally, by seeking work outside agriculture and beyond the village. They should not tolerate bad treatment, but they should not respond by being impatient and rebellious. Instead of seeking confrontation they should listen to those who offered good counsel and who could find a solution through consultation. In his autobiography Morarji Desai indicated that, during his childhood in a family of landowners in a village in south Gujarat, he had not considered the halipratha system a problem. It was only later when, as a civil servant working for the colonial authorities, he encountered landlords who used violent means to force runaway servants to return to the village, that he realized that there was no legal basis for this form of bonded labour:

I had not considered Halpati pratha as bad during my childhood but I started thinking about it after I graduated and I felt that this unjust tradition must stop. When I joined the civil service and was working as a Deputy Collector in Thane district many Halpatis used to come there to work in the saltpans. Their maliks who were called dhaniyama use to come there to take them away. Already at that time I made it clear to them that they had no legal authority over these people and I always denied their demands. But I started working against this custom only after I joined Congress in 1930. And after Independence I helped wherever need arose to bring an end to this tradition (M. Desai 1972: 13–14).[24]

The Gandhian social workers lacked any thorough—or even elementary—knowledge of the landless milieu in which they operated. Their own background and education rarely prepared them for the work they did. The one qualification which they had was their complete dedication to Gandhian principles and to conducting themselves as good

Hindus. This was often reinforced by their high-caste identity and their duty to set a good example by leading as pure a life as possible and encouraging those among whom they worked to do the same. It took a long time for potential HSS staff members to emerge from the underclass itself and even then they tended to remain at the grassroots level of the organization. The resentment this caused, fuelled from above by doubts about their capacities and experience and from below by suspicions of discrimination, led to increasing friction as time passed.[25]

The HSS adhered strictly to the Gandhian doctrine, both in its aims and in the methods it applied in pursuing them, but also acted as a loyal instrument for Congress. The landless mass in south Gujarat became an important vote bank for the party that determined the course of Indian politics in the decades following Independence and, during elections, the social workers were unpaid campaign workers for the Congress candidates. They called on the Halpatis to vote for the party that pledged to put an end to their deprivation. The fact that the large majority of the landless heeded this call for many years had less to do with obedience to the Gandhian workers than with an accurate assessment of the political situation. The Anavil Brahmans and Kanbi Patidars, who had benefited greatly from the support they had received from the nationalist movement, were less enamoured of a Congress party which, after 1947, pursued a policy that focused more on the cities than the countryside and which, in word at least, aimed to improve the lot of the lower castes and classes. That objective—or rather the announcement of the intention to pursue it—provoked the displeasure of the dominant landowners. They wanted to maintain and increase the advantageous economic position and greater social status they had acquired or consolidated in the first half of the twentieth century. Although, as I pointed out in later studies[26], Congress policy did tend to further their interests, this privileged treatment did not prevent them from supporting parties more to the right of the political spectrum. At first, this was Swatantra Party and Jan Sangh, and more recently of course, the Bharatiya Janata Party. The desertion of the agrarian elite from the Congress party falls outside the scope of this chapter, which covers the period up to the end of the 1950s.

It is important, however, for a clear understanding of the situation around this time, that the high-caste farmers had lost their political control of the landless labourers. The latter supported the Congress not so much in the conviction that the party would keep its promises to improve their lot but because the high-caste farmers were increasingly hostile in their criticism of Congress politics. The party's election victories after 1947 were largely due to the support of the agrarian underclass. Yet the Congress did not use its mandate to improve the quality of their lives. The promise to guarantee a minimum wage which would release them from poverty was not fulfilled, the housing policy was not implemented until many years later and then only in diluted form, the generation of employment outside agriculture got no further than good intentions, the schooling of children from landless families received insufficient priority, and nothing came of good and affordable public healthcare. Only in one area did the landless benefit considerably, a change that had far-reaching consequences for Indian society: the introduction of universal franchise. A great mass of people who had been largely invisible and had no voice had the opportunity after decolonization to express their views and bring them to the attention of their political leaders. As already observed, those leaders responded to that mandate with carelessness and deceit. This does not change the fact, however, that the introduction of democracy, without restrictions founded on wealth or schooling, had a profound emancipatory impact. If, as is often the case, I have difficulty in finding concrete evidence of this sea change, I need only think of the frustration and powerless rage which it invoked among the high-caste landowners. Since 1947, the vested interests have had resounding success in capitalizing on the added value they claim for themselves. Yet the vote of every 'Dubla', a term that is now loaded with contempt, counts for just as much as that of an Anavil or Patidar. The democratic system in India is far from perfect, but as far as the dominant farmers in the villages of my study are concerned, the worst mistake made by those who formed the new state after Independence was to recognize the principle of universal equality.

Unbinding Labour

In a monograph on the landless mass in the Indian countryside which he wrote in prison towards the end of his career as a political activist, Swami Sahajanand observed that the system of bonded labour was gradually losing its significance. However, he said that south Gujarat was an exception to this trend, since—until the Kisan Sabha appeared and put a stop to it for good—the practice seemed to have become even more widespread (Hauser 1994: 78). This is an overly optimistic assessment of the impact of the militant agitation of the late colonial era on the disintegration of the halipratha system. There has been no lack of well-informed observers in the area of my study in west India to testify to the disintegration of the master-servant relationship over the course of time. Yet very few of them attributed this one-sidedly to political activism. They saw the process as driven more by internal than external factors.

Among those I consider qualified to make a reasoned judgment is Daniel Thorner, who portrayed the development of the underclass in the agricultural economy of South Asia in the 1950s and 1960s. In the volume of essays that he published together with his wife Alice under the title *Land and Labour in India* he expressed sharp criticism of the land reform legislation and observed that there had a been a radical change in the rural labour regime after Independence which had received too little attention: the virtual disappearance of forced or unfree labour:

There may be a few pockets or enclaves of India where some bonded labour persists, but these are small. By and large the force of hired labourers in Indian agriculture is now made up of free men. One could not say this a generation ago. If we go back to the turn of the century, it is probable that the bulk of the agricultural labourers were unfree men, men who were in debt bondage or some other form of servitude. No one to my knowledge has yet traced the transition in Indian agriculture from a force of hired labourers who predominantly were unfree to men (and women) who today are free. This is a change of immense significance, and is likely to have wide ramifications and repercussions in the next few decades (Thorner and Thorner 1961: 8).

In a subsequent essay,[27] Thorner made an inventory of employment modalities in agriculture, dividing them into free and unfree labour arrangements. Workers falling in the latter category were not free to negotiate the terms of their employment. They could not refuse to work for the master on his terms, and were not allowed to offer their labour to another employer without his permission. Along with the kamias in Bihar and others, Thorner included the halis in south Gujarat among those working under such a 'beck and call' relationship. The labourer had to work for the master whenever he was needed, but the latter was not obliged to support the labourer throughout the year. Thorner then described the nature of the halipratha system by referring to the report of the Hali Labour Enquiry Committee.[28] He added that in the middle of 1948, after receiving this report, the government had overseen an agreed settlement between halis and their employers. The agreement did not however change the fact that 'agitation for the complete eradication of the *hali* system has continued' (ibid.: 35). Thorner did not mention who had instigated the continued agitation or where it was directed. He seemed to suggest—a plausible assumption—that despite the settlement, the system survived here and there, noting that halis continued to be a source of guaranteed labour for their masters at a wage below the market price even in the peak season. In a more historical analysis, Thorner summarizes his view of the development of the labour system by observing that, at the start of the twentieth century, the great mass of land labourers were at best 'half free':[29] 'In status and practice they are today almost fully free, but still of course subject to the usual bargaining disadvantages of blinding poverty' (ibid.: 64).

In his introductory article to *Land and Labour in India* Thorner had made a clear link between unfree labour and the absence of a capitalist mode of production in the nineteenth century. The problem he was concerned with was that unfree labour had disappeared while, in his view, the agrarian economy was not yet sufficiently capitalist in nature. He observed that few producers in this primary sector of the economy were inclined to run their farms along pure capitalist lines (ibid.: 12). I now return to the historian Prakash, whose argument I discussed in Chapter 2. Prakash rejects the freedom/lack of freedom dichotomy, interpreting the bond between master and servant in the past in terms of domination and subjugation. To reduce this to an employment arrangement based on bonded labour, as with the kamia in Bihar and the hali in Gujarat, according to Prakash, is a colonial construction that does little justice to the non-economic aspects of the relationship. In my own explanation of the workings of the halipratha system, I emphasized the central importance of patronage in encouraging the master to employ servants on the basis of bonded servitude. In my view, the subsequent disintegration of halipratha is clearly the result of the gradual introduction of a capitalist mode of production. I have discussed the arguments for this interpretation in detail in Chapters 2 and 3. But this does not mean that the work regime that replaced halipratha did not contain elements reminiscent of the former system of bonded labour. The reservations regarding the freedom/lack of freedom dichotomy put forward by Prakash refer to one end of the spectrum. My concerns relate to the other end, to the claim that after the disappearance of the halipratha system, the halis were free to hire out their labour at the highest possible price. Although this freedom was restricted, I do not see this as detracting from the capitalist character of the agrarian economy.

Thorner uses the concept of capitalism with great caution and equally refuses to label the 'ancien regime' in India as feudal. Like many other authors, he rejected the notion that the country's development can be seen in such evolutionary terms. In his view, the feudal-capitalist dichotomy did not do justice to the unique nature of Indian economy and society in the past or the present. He did not, however, go to the other extreme and claim that the situation was so unique that no general pattern of social and economic change could be identified. The fact that he occasionally expressed reservations about his conclusion that labour in the agricultural sector was free does not mean that he contradicted himself. After travelling through the countryside in 1967, Thorner wrote a series of essays under the heading 'Capitalist Stirrings in Rural India' in which he mentioned the survival of bonded labour in Bihar (Thorner 1980: 232).[30] In a subsequent article a year later he observed that 'in every major region of India today there is a boom in capitalist agriculture'. He described the employment system that accompanied this development, and the exceptions to it, as follows:

... the various forms of bondage and unfree labour services, which were formerly rampant in many parts of India, have now virtually disappeared, except in States still notorious for this, as parts of Bihar and adjacent areas (ibid.: 246).[31]

Among the changes in the patterns of employment I observed in the early 1960s was an increase in the percentage of casual labourers who were paid a daily wage. However, farmers continued to employ labourers on a permanent basis, as *kaim major*. This arrangement was similar to the contract entered into with the halis. It was usually based on a loan by the farmer to the labourer to enable the latter to get married or to cover some other expense that he could not afford himself. The obligation to work to pay off the loan did not mean that the farmer was obliged for his part to provide continual employment. On days when there was no work the Halpati was free to seek work elsewhere. If there was none to be found he would try to persuade his boss to give him an advance in money or grain, which would be added to the debt. The farmer could only be assured that the labourer would be available to him when he was needed if he was prepared to provide this credit. He would therefore adopt the strategy of keeping the level of the loan to a minimum, since both parties knew that repayment—other than by working—was as good as impossible.

Thorner was concerned on the one hand with the transition to capitalism and on the other, the obstinacy with which the old forces of production survived, so that the agricultural system could not develop the dynamism it needed to advance:

This complex of legal, economic and social relations uniquely typical of the Indian countryside served to produce an effect which I should like to call that of a built-in 'depressor.' Through the operation of this multi-faceted 'depressor,' Indian agriculture continued to be characterized by low capital intensity and antiquated methods (Thorner 1976: 16).[32]

When Thorner returned to the country in the mid-1960s after an absence of five years, he concluded that his earlier pessimism about the stagnation in the primary sector of the economy had perhaps been premature. I have already referred to the impressions he noted during short field visits in which he observed a clear breakthrough in the impasse and acceleration in the transition to capitalism. Thorner identified one of the components of the 'depressor' as the primary aim of all landowning classes in the agrarian structure to improve their social status by avoiding physical labour as much as possible rather than maximizing their income by introducing more efficient methods of production. In my view, however, this attitude of prioritizing leisure cannot be taken to signify the absence of the qualities required for the emergence of capitalism.

The dominant landowners in south Gujarat transformed themselves into capitalist farmers without forfeiting a lifestyle in which they substituted their own labour power for that of labourers, their wives, and even their children. Among the Anavil Brahmans, the lower Bhathelas followed the example of their more illustrious fellow caste members, the Desais, by employing landless adults and children not only to work on the land but also to perform all kind of chores in and around the house. When their wealth began to increase after they began to grow money crops, the Kanbi Patidars responded in a similar fashion, satisfying their social aspirations by no longer working their fields themselves. In this way, self-employed cultivators adopted the behaviour of supervisory farmers. The fact that they employed landless labourers therefore confirmed rather than denied their capitalist mentality. Other than in the past, however, the halis were no longer an expression of their masters' aspirations for power and prestige—the landowners did not use the revenue from their land to invest in the upkeep of landless clients. The rationale behind the behaviour of the high-caste landowners can be seen in their preference for crops that were less labour-intensive. In the late colonial era, the Anavil Brahmans had already started planting mango orchards, which enabled them to fulfil their aspirations as landed gentry, but on the basis of a capitalist mode of production (Breman 1974). The Kanbi Patidars achieved the same aim a decade after Independence by switching to sugarcane. They set up sugar cooperatives which took over supervision of the work in the fields and which employed a large army of seasonal migrants to bring in the harvest (Breman 1978 and 1985).[33]

The farmers saved on labour costs by paying the landless—both farm servants and casual labourers—a wage that was insufficient for them to meet their basic needs. Thorner's observation that labour had essentially become free also applied to south Gujarat in the early 1960s. I concluded this from my own research and it was confirmed by the findings of other empirical studies conducted in the same area in that period. The sociologist I.P. Desai, who had conducted a study of the socio-economic situation in his home village near Navsari, wrote that the Halpatis had been freed from bondage but remained so poor that they suffered from severe hunger (I.P. Desai 1964: 126, 140).[34] My own findings confirmed this observation in the villages of my fieldwork. The 'blinding poverty' noted by Thorner persisted because the dominant farmers refused to provide the landless with work and pay wages that would permit them a decent standard of living. To make up this permanent shortfall in meeting their basic needs the landless had no other choice than to try and obtain credit from their employers, with their labour as security. Given the excessively low level of their wages, for most of them it was impossible to avoid going into debt.

The dominant farmers became extremely wary of providing loans, small or large. Although they had little choice other than to give in to the persistent pressure to provide credit, they tried to keep the scale and frequency of the advances to a minimum. After all, the chances of repayment were minimal. As a result, relations between the two sides were continually strained and could easily erupt into serious conflict. The landowners used the loans as an instrument to remind their employees of their duty to work. For their part the labourers tended to see the credit that they acquired with such difficulty as a normal supplement to a wage that did not provide enough for them to live. They therefore felt no obligation to repay it. In the eyes of each party the other refused to act reasonably and, consequently, there was a complete lack of trust on both sides. It is unlikely that relations were better in the old situation, but now the landless no longer displayed the obedience and humility expected of a hali. Poverty clearly perpetuated the dependence of the Halpatis but they steadfastly refused to subordinate themselves to the high-caste farmers or recognize their claim to dominance. Bonded labour came to an end not because of government intervention but because employers and employees, for different reasons, wanted it that way. Freedom did not come overnight and was by no means complete, with one side fighting to achieve it and the other granting it only with great reluctance in a process that unfolded slowly throughout the first half of the twentieth century. Just as the emergence of unfree labour cannot be interpreted in purely economic terms, its disappearance must also be related to social and political factors. The disintegration of the halipratha system was an expression of the resistance of the landless underclass to the ideology and practice of inequality.

In the middle of the last century, rural south Gujarat suffered from a large surplus of labour. Apart from earning a wage that was insufficient to survive, the landless also only had work for part of the year. Periodic lack of employment in agriculture and in the village added to their misery. The HLEC Report described this situation as follows:

... the agricultural worker in the Surat district gets work for 210 days on average in the year. It must be noted that even the Hali remains unemployed during the rest of the period of 155 days. For, whereas he is bound to work for the Dhaniyama on the same wage whenever he has any work, the Dhaniyama is not bound to keep him employed throughout the year. When he has no work to give, the Hali has to shift for himself (HLEC Report 1948: 28).

Work became even scarcer for the landless when the landowners started taking on migrant workers during the peak season. In the villages where I conducted my fieldwork, this occurred during the mango and sugarcane harvest. It was a good reason for the Halpatis themselves to seek work further afield and they tried to do so in greater numbers in the second half of the twentieth century. This became easier as the villages became less isolated from the outside world, a process accelerated by new roads and the possibility of transport by bus, truck, and bicycle. For the landless underclass, escape from the village also meant escape from the grip of the landowners. The resulting migration was not only dictated by a necessary search for work elsewhere, but also testified to a growing aversion to agricultural work which reached right down to the base of the rural economy.

Escape from the village and from the farm—this became the ambition of younger generations of Halpatis. It did not mean, however, that the scenario foreseen by politicians and policymakers at the time of Independence had been fulfilled. The surplus of landless labour may have been expelled from agriculture, but it was not absorbed into the urban industrial economy. The industrialization process did not move forward as intended. In my research in south Gujarat up to the end of the twentieth century, the departure of increasing numbers of Halpatis from the village was a recurring theme, but so was their return. They failed to find a lasting foothold in the towns and cities and sooner or later were driven back to their home villages. Their lives became a cycle of departure and return and the work they found outside in the informal sector of the economy did not release them from poverty. Instead, it added new dimensions to their deprivation and their continual circulatory migration in search of work produced new mechanisms of loss of freedom, which I have described elsewhere as neo-bondage (Breman 1994, part II; 1996). These developments fall outside the scope of this historical introduction, which extends to the middle of the twentieth century.

My account would appear to end on a pessimistic note. Rightly so— in many respects—but with one important reservation: the landless in south Gujarat are no longer subjected to a regime in which they are only visible or have any significance as the servants of their former masters. They want to extricate themselves from the captivity of agricultural employment. The extension of the labour market has encouraged them to permanently seek better employment and has kept alive a belief in a better future. I endorse Thorner's comment when he drew up the balance of the situation in the countryside in the middle of the 1960s from the perspective of the agrarian underclass and expressed his scepticism about the efforts of the Congress to ensure that economic progress mainly benefited the dominant landowners, identified in the new jargon of developmentalism as 'progressive farmers'. The policy of privileging the already privileged inevitably led to growing inequality.

This did not, however, prevent him from noting the other side of the process:

I do not mean that the poor are getting absolutely poorer. I would be the last to deny, or try to minimize, the hardships of life of the bottom of one third of the rural population—India's millions of small cultivators and rural labourers who do not earn enough to eat regularly three square meals a day. My contention, nonetheless, is that even they have been affected by the prosperity of their neighbours, and by the changed conditions of life generally since 1967. Their actual level of living may still be miserable, but the level to which they aspire has risen (Thorner 1967).[35]

Thorner's conclusion confirms my own findings when I returned in the middle of the 1980s to the villages in south Gujarat where I had conducted my original fieldwork. I summed up my findings with the observation that the situation was no longer as hopeless as in the early 1960s (Breman 1993: 327) The question that now arises is whether there is still reason now, at the beginning of the twenty-first century, for the same cautious optimism I expressed then.

Notes

1. The minutes of the meetings of the National Planning Committee, together with the Interim Report of the Sub-Committee on Land Policy and R. Mukherji's Note on Land Policy, are included in the collection of AICC papers deposited in the Nehru Memorial Museum and Library in New Delhi under file no. G-23 (KW-5).
2. Thorner and Thorner, *Land and Labour in India*, chapter I and 61–4; Thorner, *The Agrarian Prospects in India*; Thorner, *The Shaping of Modern India*.
3. 'Caste and land reforms in Gujarat', in Shah and Sah, *Land Reforms in India*, pp. 127–43.
4. For a detailed study of this issue see Baks, *Afschaffing van pacht*.
5. For more information on the ideas underlying the deliberations of these panels of experts and politicians, see my essay 'The Study of Industrial Labour in Post-colonial India'.
6. HLEC Report 1948: 12.
7. C.H. Shah, *Effects of World War II on Agriculture in India*.
8. M.B. Desai was a professor at the M.S. University of Baroda, to which I was affiliated during my fieldwork in 1962–3. Together with I.P. Desai, at the time a professor at the same university and, like his colleague, from south Gujarat, he monitored the progress of my work and commented on my findings.
9. Among the witnesses interviewed was a deputation of halis from the village in Chikhli taluka where I later conducted fieldwork.

10. Thorner refers to the report 'which has not to date been publicly released' (Thorner 1961: 35). Since Thorner gives no details on the content of the report, my assumption is that he himself did not see it. I managed to get hold of the report when Professor Desai conveyed to me in one of our regular meetings that a copy was kept in the collection of the Department of Agricultural Economics in the University of Bombay.
11. *Report of the Congress Agrarian Reforms Committee*, New Delhi, 1951.
12. *Agricultural Labour Enquiry, 1950–51.*
13. *Agricultural Labour Enquiry, 1956–57.*
14. *Report of the Minimum Wages Advisory Committee for Employment* in *Agriculture.*
15. *Report of the Scheduled Areas and Scheduled Tribes Commission 1960–61.*
16. The history of the peasant resistance to the loss of their land in south Gujarat, and in particular of the Pardi satyagraha after Independence, is described by Hakumat Desai and Kiran Desai, *The Pardi Annakhed Satyagraha*. For an abridged version of this tribal protest which went on for decades before and after Independence, see also I. Desai, 'Land Reforms through People's Movements', pp. 319–48.
17. Parulekar, *Revolt of the Varlis*; Parulekar, *Revolt of the Warlis*.
18. Calman, 'Congress Confronts Communism'.
19. Hardiman discusses the introduction of this term to Gujarat in the 1940s by social worker A.V. Thakkar, explaining its meaning: *adi*= 'beginning' or 'of earliest times' and *vasi*= 'resident of'. He points out that the term refers to the origins of these communities, but fails to include the Dublas/Halpatis. What was true of the Dhodhias, Chodhris, Gamits, and Konkanas—that before the colonial period they 'had remained free, or at least relatively free, from the control of outside states' (Hardiman 1987: 15)—did not apply to them. However, as one of the largest Scheduled Tribes in south Gujarat, the Dublas/Halpatis are, nevertheless, counted among the adivasis. In a later publication Hardiman draws attention to the objections of Hindu nationalists against the use of the term 'adivasi' (Hardiman 2003: 153).
20. Hardiman, 'The Quit India Movement in Gujarat', pp. 97–101.
21. See Breman 2004, pp. 42–5, 100–4.
22. Privileges provided by the Bombay State Government for Backward Classes, Government of Bombay, 1955.
23. P.G. Shah, 'A Serf Tribe'.
24. M. Desai, *Marum Jivan Vrutant.*
25. This is discussed in detail in an essay on the HSS which I based on data gathered during the early 1970s. See Breman, 'Mobilisation of Landless Labourers'.
26. Breman, *Of Peasants, Migrants and Paupers*; Breman, Part II and III in, *Wage Hunters and Gatherers.*
27. 'Employer-labour Relationships in Agriculture', originally published in the

Indian Journal of Agricultural Economics, vol. xii (April–June), 1957, pp. 84–96.

28. This report was not publicly released and Thorner bases his short description of the halipratha system on that given by M.B. Desai, one of the two members of the enquiry commission, in another publication 'Rural Labour' in M.B. Desai, *Rural Economy of Gujarat*, chapter VI, Bombay: 1948.

29. Originally published in *The Encyclopedia Americana*, vol. 15, 1960, pp. 12–19.

30. During the same visit Thorner recorded the unforgettable words of a farm labourer, as told to him by a capitalist landowner in Tanjore, Madras. On meeting the wife of his master, who was wearing earrings, the labourer said: 'Madame, your ears are adorned with my blood' (Thorner 1980: 236). The articles appeared in the daily newspaper *The Statesman* in Calcutta and Delhi from 1–4 November 1967 and are included in the collection of essays compiled by Alice Thorner after her husband's death, D. Thorner, *The Shaping of Modern India*.

31. D. Thorner, 'The Emergence of Capitalist Agriculture in India', presented as a paper at the Conference of European Scholars on South Asia, Cambridge 1968, and included in Thorner 1980, pp. 238–53.

32. D. Thorner, *The Agrarian Prospect*. The original edition in 1956 was based on a series of five lectures that Thorner gave at the Delhi School of Economics in 1955. When the volume was republished in 1976, it contained an introduction in which he adjusted his earlier opinion in the light of his new findings.

33. Breman, 'Seasonal Migration and Co-operative Capitalism'.

34. I.P. Desai, *The Pattern of Migration and Occupation in a South Gujarat Village*.

35. This quotation comes from one of the articles published in the newspaper *The Statesman*, 1–4 November 1967 and republished as 'Capitalist Stirrings in Rural India: Tour Note', in Thorner 1980: 233).

Bibliography

Agricultural Labour Enquiry, *Report on Intensive Survey of Agricultural Labour* 1950– 51, vol. i (All India) and vol. v (West India), Delhi, 1955.

Agricultural Labour in India, *Report on the Second Enquiry*, 1956–57, vol. i (All India) and vol. v (West India), Delhi, 1960.

All India Congress Committee Papers, G6-KW, deposited in the Manuscript Section of the Nehru Memorial Museum and Library, New Delhi.

Amin, S., 'Agrarian Bases of Nationalist Agitations in India: A Historiographical Survey', in D.A. Low, *The Indian National Congress Committee: Centenary Hindsights*, New Delhi: Oxford University Press, 1988.

Baines, J.A., *Ethnography, Castes and Tribes*, Strassburg: Karls Trubner, 1912.

Baks, C., 'Afschaffing van pacht; een onderzoek naar de gevolgen van de afschaffing van pacht in twee dorpen van Zuid-Gujarat' (An Investigation into the Consequences of the Abolition of Tenancy in Two Villages of South Gujarat), PhD thesis, University of Amsterdam, 1969.

Baks, C., J.C. Breman, and A.T.J. Nooij, 'Slavery as a System of Production in Tribal Society', *Bijdragen tot de Taal-, Land-en Volkenkunde*, vol. 122 (1), 1966, pp. 90–109.

Baks, C. and S.D. Pillai (eds), *Winners and Losers: Styles of Development and Change in an Indian region*, Bombay: Popular Prakashan, 1979.

Banaji, D.R., *Slavery in British India*, PhD thesis, University of Bombay, 1933, revised and enlarged 2nd edn, Bombay: D.B. Taraporevala Sons & Co., 1933.

Baroda Economic Development Committee, 1918–19, Report, Bombay, 1920.

Baroda Enquiry Commission, vol. I, Correspondence, Bombay, 1873–5.

Bellasis, A.F., *Report on the Southern Districts of the Surat Collectorate, selections from the Records of the Bombay Government*, New Series 2, Bombay, 1854.

Beyts, N., *Revenue Survey and Settlement of the Jalalpur taluka of the Surat Collectorate*, Bombay, 1868.

———, *Survey and Settlement Report of the Bulsar taluka of the Surat Collectorate*, Bombay, 1870.

Bhatt, A., 'Caste and Political Mobilization in a Gujarat district', in Kothari, *Caste in Indian Politics*, 1970, pp. 299–339.

Bhattacharya, N., 'Labouring Histories: Agrarian Labour and Colonialism', NLI Research Studies Series no. 49, New Delhi, 2004.

Bhattacharya, S., ' Swaraj and the Kamgar: the Indian National Congress and the Bombay Working Class' in Sisson and Wolpert (eds), *Congress and Indian Nationalism*, 1988, pp. 223–49.

Breman, J., *Patronage and Exploitation: Changing Agrarian Relations in South Gujarat, India*, Berkeley: California University Press, 1974(a).

————, 'Mobilisation of Landless Labourers; Halpatis of South Gujarat', *Economic and Political Weekly*, vol. ix (12), 23 March 1974(b), pp. 489–96.

————, 'Seasonal Migration and Co-operative Capitalism: The Crushing of Cane and of Labour by the Sugar Factories of Bardoli, South Gujarat', *Journal of Peasant Studies*, vol. vii, 1978–9, pp. 41–70, 168–209.

————, *Of Peasants, Migrants and Paupers: Rural Labour Circulation and Capitalist Production in West India*, Delhi/Oxford: Oxford and Clarendon Press, 1985.

————, 'The Shattered Image: Construction and Deconstruction of the Village in Colonial Asia', *Comparative Asian Studies*, no. 2, Dordrecht: Foris Publications, 1988.

————, *Beyond Patronage and Exploitation: Changing Agrarian Relations in South Gujarat, India*, New Delhi: Oxford University Press, 1993.

————, *Wage Hunters and Gatherers: Search for Work in the Rural and Urban Economy of South Gujarat*, New Delhi: Oxford University Press, 1994.

————, *Footloose Labour: Working in India's Informal Economy*, Cambridge: Cambridge University Press, 1996.

————, *The Making and Unmaking of an Indian Industrial Working Class: Sliding Down the Labour Hierarchy in Ahmedabad*, New Delhi: Oxford University Press, 2004.

Breman, J., A.N. Das, and R. Agarwal (photographs), *Down and Out: Labouring Under Global Capitalism*, Delhi: Oxford University Press, 2000.

Broomfield, R.S. and R.M. Maxwell, *Report of the Special Enquiry into the Second Revision Settlement of the Bardoli and Chorasi talukas*, Bombay, 1929.

Bukhari, J., in *National Front*, 6 March 1938, pp. 8–11.

Calman, L.J., 'Congress Confronts Communism', *Modern Asian Studies*, vol. 21 (2), 1987, pp. 329–48.

Campbell, J., 'Notes on the Spirit Basis of Belief and Custom', in *Indian Antiquary*, Bombay 1885.

Census of the Baroda Territories, 1881, vol. v, report, Bombay, 1883.

Census of India 1901, vol. ix, Bombay, part I, Report, Bombay, 1902.

Census of India 1901, vol. xviii, Baroda, part I, Report, Bombay, 1902.

Census of India 1921, vol. viii, Bombay, part I, General Report, Bombay, 1922.

Census of India 1921, vol. xvii, Baroda State, part I, Report, Bombay, 1921.

Census of India 1931, vol. xix, Baroda, part I, Report, Bombay, 1932.

Census of India 1941, vol. xvii, Report, Baroda 1941.

Chandravarkar, R., *The Origins of Industrial Capitalism in India; Business Strategies and the Working Classes in Bombay, 1900–1940*, Cambridge University Press South Asian Studies (51), Cambridge, 1994.

Chaplin, W., *A Report Exhibiting a View of the Fiscal and Judicial System of Administration under the Authority of the Commissioner in Deccan*, Bombay, 1824.

Charlesworth, N., *Peasants and Imperial Rule; Agriculture and Agrarian Society in the Bombay Presidency, 1850–1935*, Cambridge South Asian Studies, Cambridge, 1985.

Choksey, R.D., *Economic Life in the Bombay Gujarat (1800–1939)*, Bombay: Asia Publishing House, 1968.

Chopra, N. (ed.), *The Collected Works of Sardar Vallabhbhai Patel*, vol. ii, 1926–1929, Delhi: Konark Publishers, 1991.

Chopra, P.N. and P. Chopra (eds), *The Collected Works of Sardar Vallabhbhai Patel*, vol. vii (1 July 1937–31 December 1938), vol. viii (1 January 1939–31 March 1939), Delhi: Konark Publishers, 1996.

Choudhary, S., *Peasants' and Workers' Movement in India*, 1905–29, New Delhi: People's Publishing House, 1971.

Cole, V.S., *Papers Relating to the Revision Settlement of Mandvi taluka*, Bombay, 1904.

Correspondence Regarding the Concealment by the Hereditary officers and others of the Revenue Records of the Former Government and the Remedial Measures Program. Selections from the Bombay Government Records, New Series no. 29.

Correspondence and Abstracts of Regulations and Proceedings, 1831–2, Report from the Select Committee of the Affairs of the East India Company: Minutes of Evidence, Appendix and Evidence: 1834. Slavery in India, Correspondence, 1841, Report from the Indian Law Commissioners Relating to Slavery in the East Indies. For a summary of these reports, see D.R. Banaji, 1933.

Dave, J., *Halpati mukti* (halipratha ane muktidani hilachal), Ahmedabad: Navjivan, 1946.

Desai, H. and K. Desai, *The Pardi Annakhed Satyagraha: Adivasi Assertion for Rights*, Surat: Centre for Social Studies, 1997.

Desai, I.I., *Raniparajma Jagruti*, Swatantra Itihas Samiti, no. 3, Surat, 1971.

Desai, I.P., *The Pattern of Migration and Occupation in a South Gujarat Village*, Poona 1964.

———, 'The Slogan of a Separate State by Tribals of South Gujarat', Indian Council of Social Science Research, ICSSR Research Abstracts 4, Delhi: 1971, pp. 7–20.

———, 'The Vedchhi movement', in I.P. Desai and B. Choudhry (eds), *History of Rural Development in Modern India*, vol. II, New Delhi: Impex India, 1977.

Desai, K., 'Land Reforms through People's Movements', in Shah and Sah, *Performance and Challenges*, pp. 319–48.

Desai, M., 'Face to Face with the Pauper', *Young India*, 31 March 1927.

———, *The Story of Bardoli*, Ahmedabad: Navjivan, 1929.

———, *Marun jivan vrutant (My life history)*, Ahmedabad: Navjivan Trust, 1972.

Desai, M.B., *Rural Economy of Gujarat*, Oxford: Oxford University Press, 1948.

———, *Tenancy Abolition and the Emerging Pattern in Gujarat*, Baroda: Department of Agricultural Economics, M.S. University of Baroda, 1971.

Dhanagare, D.N., 'Peasant Organizations and the Left Wing in India, 1925–47', in *Peasant Movements in India, 1920–1950*, New Delhi: Oxford University Press, 1983, pp. 119–54.

Dosabhai, E., *A History of Gujarat from the Earliest Period to the Present Time*, Ahmedabad: 1894.

Dutt, K., *Sardar Patel in the Bardoli Movement*, Meerut: Anu Books, 1986.

Enthoven, R.E., *Tribes and Castes of the Bombay Presidency*, 3 vols, Bombay: Government Central Press, 1920–2.

Epstein, S.J.M., *The Earthy Soil: Bombay Peasants and the Indian Nationalist Movement, 1919–1947*, New Delhi: Oxford University Press, 1988.

Fernandez, T.R., *Settlement Report on Bardoli taluk, Surat district*, Selections from the Records of the Bombay Government, no. 359, New Series, Bombay, 1895.

Forrest, G.W., *Selections from the Minutes and Other Official Writings of the Honourable Mountstuart Elphinstone*, London: Richard Bentley and Son, 1884.

——— (ed.), *Selections from the Letters, Dispatches and Other State Papers preserved in the Bombay Secretariat*, Home Series I, Bombay, 1887.

Gandhi, M.K., *Harijan*, 23 April 1938.

———, *Young India*, 16 June 1927.

———, *Navjivan*, 15 June 1924.

———, *Letters to Sardar Vallabhbhai Patel*, translated from the Gujarati original and edited by Valji G. Desai and Sudarshan V. Desai, Ahmedabad: Navjivan, 1957.

Gazetteer of the Bombay Presidency, vol. ii, Gujarat: Surat and Broach, Bombay, 1877.

Gazetteer of the Bombay Presidency, vol. ix, Gujarat population: Hindus, Bombay, 1901.

Gazetteer of the Baroda State, vol. i, Report, Baroda, 1923.

Gazetteer of India, Gujarat State, Surat District, Ahmedabad, 1962.

Gooptu, N., *The Politics of the Urban Poor in Early Twentieth Century India*, Cambridge Studies in Indian History and Society 8, Cambridge, 2001.

Government of Bombay, Home (Special) Department, S.D. 718, first half of March 1938, Maharashtra State Archives.

Government of Bombay, Home (Special) Department, S.D., first half of June 1938.

Government of Bombay, Home (Special) Department, S.D. 115, first half of January 1939.

Government of Bombay, Home (Special) Department, S.D. 340, second half of January 1939.

Government of Bombay, Home (Special) Department, S.D. 440, first half of February 1939.

Government of Bombay, Home (Special) Department, S.D. 2867, first half of August 1939.

Government of Bombay, Home (Special) Department, file no. 1019, 6 March 1940, Maharashtra State Archives.

Guha, R., *A Rule of Property for Bengal: An Essay of the Idea of Permanent Settlement*, third edn, Durham: Duke University Press, 1996.

Gupta, A.K., *The Agrarian Drama; The Leftists and the Rural Poor in India, 1934–1951*, Delhi: Manohar, 1996.

Hardiman, D., *Peasant Nationalists of Gujarat: Kheda District 1917–1934*, New Delhi: Oxford University Press, 1981.

———, *The Coming of the Devi: Adivasi Assertion in Western India*, New Delhi: Oxford Univeristy Press, 1987.

———, 'The Quit India Movement in Gujarat', in G. Pandey (ed.), *The Indian Nation in 1942: Writings on the Quit India Movement*, Calcutta: K.B. Bagchi and Co., 1988, pp. 77–104.

———, *Gandhi in His Time and Ours*, Delhi: Permanent Black, 2003.

Hauser, W., *Sahajanand on Agricultural Labourer and the Rural Poor*, Delhi: Manohar, 1994.

———, *Culture, Vernacular Politics and the Peasants*, Delhi: Manohar, 2006.

Hove, *Tours for Scientific and Economic Research made in Guzerat, Kattiawar and the Conkans in 1787–8, Selections from the Records of the Bombay Government*, New Series 16, Bombay.

Hunter, W., *Bombay 1885–1890: A Study in Indian Administration*, London/ Bombay: H. Frowde, 1892.

Jayakar, M.S., *Settlement Report on Bardoli Taluk, Surat District*. Selections from the Records of the Bombay Government, no. 647, Bombay, 1925.

Joshi, V.H., *Economic Development and Social Change in a South Gujarat Village*, Maharaja Sayajirao University of Baroda Press, Baroda, 1966.

Keatinge, G., *Agricultural Progress in Western India*, London: Longmans, 1921.

Khanapurkar, D.P., 'The Aborigines of South Gujarat', PhD thesis, University of Bombay, 2 vols, 1944.

Kishore, J., 'The Village Labourer in Western India', *Hindustan Review*, 1924: 425 ff.

Kosambi, D.D., *An Introduction to the Study of Indian History*, Bombay: Popular Prakashan, 1956.

Kothari, R. (ed.), *Caste in Indian Politics*, New Delhi: Orient Longman, 1970.

Kumar, K. (ed.), *Congress and Classes: Nationalism, Workers and Peasants*, Delhi: Manohar, 1988.

Low, D.A., *The Congress and the Raj: Facets of the Indian Struggle, 1917–47*, London: Arnold-Heinemann, 1977.

———, (ed.), *The Indian National Congress: Centenary Hindsights*, New Delhi: Oxford University Press, 1988.

Lumsden, W.J., Collector of Surat, letter of 9 April 1823, Bombay Revenue Proceedings, Range 368, vol. xxxviii, 4816.

———, Collector of Surat, letter of 9 August, 1825 to David Greenhill, Acting Secretary to the Government of Bombay, consultation 108 of 1825, Judicial Department, 1826, vol. 25–126, Bombay Record Department.

Maconochie, E., *Revised Survey and Settlement Report on Chikhli taluk, Surat district*, 1897. Selections from Records of the Bombay Government, New Series 381, New Series. Bombay 1897.

Majmudar, M.R., 'Social Life and Manners in Pre-British Gujarat', M.A. thesis, School of Economics and Sociology, University of Bombay, 1929.

Malkani, N.R., 'The Agricultural Condition of Bardoli', in *Young India*, vol. 8, 1926, no. 29, pp. 263–5; no. 30, pp. 266–7; no. 32, pp. 286–7; no. 33, pp. 290–1 and no. 34, pp. 302–3.

Mehta, B.H., 'Social and Economic conditions of the Chodhras, an Aboriginal Tribe of Gujarat', PhD thesis, University of Bombay, 1933.

Mehta, D., Oral history interview with Shri Dinkar Mehta, Ahmedabad, 27 July 1975 by Dr Hari Dev Sharma for the Nehru Memorial Museum and Library.

Mehta, J.M:, *A Study of the Rural Economy of Gujarat*, Baroda, 1930.

Mehta, S., 'Marriage and Family Life in Gujarat', PhD thesis, University of Bombay 1930, Bombay 1934.

Mehta, S.B., 'Halis, the Serfs of Gujarat', *National Front*, 13 March 1938.

——, 'Kaliparaj ke Raniparaj', *Yugdharma* 3, 1923–4.

——, *Atmakatha (Autobiography)*. Bhogilal Gandhi (ed.) Ahmedabad: Mahakavishri Nanalal Smarak Trust, distributed by Gurjar Granth Ratna, Ahmedabad, n.d.

Mehta, Shirin, *The Peasantry and Nationalism; A Study of the Bardoli Satyagraha*, Delhi: Manohar, 1984.

Memorandum regarding legislative and other measures adopted to combat slavery and debt-bondage akin to slavery in British India, Home Department, Judicial Branch no. 19/14/39, dated September 1940, s. no. 1121, 4 October 1940.

Minutes of the meetings of the National Planning Committee, together with the interim *Report of the Sub-Committee on Land Policy* and R. Mukherji's *Note on Land Policy*. Deposited in the collection of AICC papers at the Manuscript Section in the Nehru Memorial Museum and Library, file number G-23 (KW-5).

Misra, S.C., *The Rise of Muslim Power in Gujarat*, Bombay: Asia Publishing House, 1963.

Mohapatra, P., 'Regulated Informality; Legal Constructions of Labour Relations in Colonial India', in S. Bhattacharya and J. Lucassen (eds), *Workers in the Informal Sector: Studies in Labour History, 1800–2000*, Delhi: Macmillan India–SEPHIS, 2005, pp. 65–95.

Morison's Report, letter from the Collector of Surat, dated 13 November 1812.

Mukhtyar, G.C., *Life and Labour in a South Gujarat Village*, Bombay: Longman Green and Co., 1930.

Mundle, S., *Backwardness and Bondage: Agrarian Relations in a South Bihar District*, New Delhi: Indian Institute of Public Administration, 1979.

Naik, T.B., 'Social Status in Gujarat', *Eastern Anthropologist*, vol. x, 1957, pp. 173–82.

Nieboer, J.H., *Slavery as an Industrial System*, The Hague: M. Nijhoff, 1910.

Notes Regarding Kisan Movement, report by district superintendent of police, Surat, 21 March 1940. Government of Bombay, Home (Special) Department, file no. 1019 of 1940–1, Maharashtra State Archives, Bombay.

Pandey, G. (ed.), *The Indian Nation in 1942: Writings on the Quit India Movement*, Calcutta: K.B. Bagchi and Co., 1988.

Papers relating to a summary settlement of alienated revenues in the Bombay Presidency. Revenue Department, Bombay, 1858.

Parikh, N.D., 'Bardolina Kheduta', in *Young India*, vol. 7–8, August–October, 1926.

Parliamentary Papers on Slavery in India, published by the Order of the House of Commons, London, 1828.

Parry, J., J. Breman, and K. Kapadia (eds), *The World of Industrial Labourers in India*, New Delhi: Sage Publications, 2002.

Parulekar, G., *Revolt of the Warlis*, All India Kisan Sabha Golden Jubilee Series, 1936–86, no. 1, New Delhi, 1986.

Parulekar, S.V., *Revolt of the Varlis*, Bombay, 1947.

Patel, G.D., 'The Land Revenue Settlements and the British rule in India', PhD Thesis, Gujarat University, Ahmedabad, 1969.

Patel, N., 'A Passage from India', *Transaction*, April 1972, 25 ff.

Patel, S.J., *Agricultural Labourers in Modern India and Pakistan*, Bombay, Current Book House, 1952.

Pedder, W.G., *Papers Relating to the Settlement of Hereditary District Officers' Watans in the Deccan and Gujarat, Reported in 1865, Selections from the Records of the Bombay Presidency*, no. 174, New Series, Bombay, 1865/1895.

Peyt, M., Bombay Presidency, Miscellaneous Official Publications, Minute, 15 October, Bombay, 1830.

Prakash, G., '*Bonded Histories; Genealogies of Labour Servitude in Colonial India*', Cambridge South Asian Studies 44, Cambridge, 1990.

———, *The World of the Rural Labourer in India*, New Delhi: Oxford University Press, 1992.

Prescott, C., *Survey and Settlement Report Chikhli Taluka*, Bombay, 1865.

Privileges provided by the Bombay State Government for Backward Classes, Government of Bombay, 1955.

Rabitoy, N., 'System versus Expediency: The Reality of Land Revenue Administration in the Bombay Presidency', *Modern Asian Studies*, vol. 9, 1975, pp. 529–46.

Report from the Select Committee of the House of Lords appointed to inquire into the present state of the affairs of the East India Committee together with the Minutes of Evidence and Appendix, London, 1830.

Report of the Bardoli Enquiry Committee, 1926.

Report of the Committee of Investigations in Conditions in the Mandvi and Pardi Talukas of Surat District, Government of Bombay, Home Department (Special), file 800 (53.3), part III, 1939, Maharashtra State Archives.

Report of the Congress Agrarian Reforms Committee, Delhi, 1951.

Report of the Hali Labour Enquiry Committee (RHLEC) by M.L. Dantwala and M.B. Desai, (unpublished), Bombay, 1948.

Report of the Minimum Wages Advisory Committee for Employment in Agriculture, Government of Gujarat, Ahmedabad, 1966.

Report of the Royal Commission on Agriculture, vol. ii, part 2, evidence taken in the Bombay Presidency, London, 1926.

Report of the Scheduled Areas and Scheduled Tribes Commission, 1960–61, Government of India, Delhi, 1961.

Report of the Select Committee of the House of Commons, (Public) 1832, with Appendix.

Reports on the Kisan Morchas in Mandvi and Bulsar talukas, Government of Bombay, Home (Special) Department, file no. 1019 of 1940–1, Maharashtra State Archives, Bombay.

Revised Survey and Settlement Report of the Mahuva taluka, Bombay, 1916.

Revision Settlement Report of the Palsana taluka of the Navsari district, 1910-11, Baroda, 1911.

Revision Survey Settlement Report of the Jalalpur taluka of the Surat collectorate, Selections from the Records of the Bombay Government, no. 350, New Series, Bombay, 1900.

Risley, H., *The People of India*, Bombay, 1915.

Robb, P. (ed.), *Dalit Movements and the Meanings of Labour in India*, New Delhi: Oxford University Press, 1993.

Robertson, E.P., *Glossary of Gujaratee Revenue and Official Terms*, Bombay, 1865.

Rogers, A., *The Land Revenue of Bombay: A History of its Administrative Rise and Progress*, 1892, 2 vols., Delhi: reprinted by B.R. Publishing Corporation, 1985.

Sarkar, S., ' "Popular" Movements and "Middle Class" Leadership: Perspectives and Problems of a "History from Below" ', S.G. Deuskar Memorial Lecture on Indian History, 1980, Calcutta, 1983.

———, *Modern India*, Delhi: Macmillan India, 1983.

Sarkar, T., 'Bondage in the Colonial Context', in U. Patnaik and M. Dingwaney (eds), *Chains of Servitude, Bondage and Slavery in India*, Madras: Sangam Books, 1985.

Second Revision Survey Settlement of Kalyan taluka of Thana district, Bombay, 1927.

Settlement Report of the Vyara taluka of the Navsari division, 1906–7, Baroda, 1907.

Shah, C.H., 'Effects of World War II on Agriculture in India' (with Special Reference to Gujarat), PhD thesis, University of Bombay, 1952.

Shah, G. and D.C. Sah, *Land Reforms in India*, vol. 8, *Performance and Challenges in Gujarat and Maharashtra*, New Delhi: Sage Publications, 2002.

Shah, G., 'Traditional Society and Political Mobilization: The experience of Bardoli Satyagraha (1920–1928)', *Contributions to Indian Sociology* (NS), no. 8, 1974, pp. 89–107.

Shah, P. G., 'A Serf Tribe', *Journal of the Gujarat Research Society*, vol. 21, no.1/81, January, 1959, pp. 42–58.

———, *The Dublas of Gujarat*, Delhi: Bharatiya Adimjati Sevak Sangh, 1958.

Shankardass, R.D., 'Provincial Consolidation: 1928', in *Vallabhbhai Patel: Power and Organization in Indian Politics*, New Delhi: Orient Longman, 1988, pp. 60–91.

Shukla, J.B., *Life and Labour in a Gujarat Taluka*, Calcutta: Longmans, Galla and Co., 1937.

Sisson, R. and S. Wolpert (eds), *Congress and Indian Nationalism: The Pre-Independence Phase*, Berkeley: University of California Press, 1988.

Solanky, A.N., 'The Dhodias of South Gujarat', M.A. thesis, Department of Sociology, University of Bombay, 1955.

Tagore, S., 'Gandhism and the labour-peasant problem', in U.K. Sharma (ed.), *Labour Movement in India, Pre-independence Period*, vol. I, Delhi, 2006, pp. 329–42.

The Farmer, 'Editorial', January 1954, vol. v, no. 1.

Thorner, D., 'Employer Labour Relationships in Agriculture', *Indian Journal of Agricultural Economics*, vol. xii (April-June), 1957.

———, *The Agrarian Prospects in India: Five Lectures on Land Reform Delivered in 1955 at the Delhi School of Economics*, Bombay: Asia Publishing, 1976 (second edn).

———, *The Shaping of Modern India, part II: The Changing Countryside of Independent India*, Bombay: Allied Publishers, 1980.

Thorner, D. and A. Thorner, *Land and Labour in India*, Bombay-London: Asia Publishing House, 1962.

Toothi, N.A., *Vaishnavas of Gujarat*, Calcutta: Longmans, 1935.

Wallace, R. *The Guicowar and his Relations with the British Government*, Bombay, 1863.

Yagnik, I., 'Lavet Makes a Little History', in *National Front*, 19 June 1938a, p. 12.

———, 'Agrarian Unrest in South Gujarat', *National Front*, 24 July 1938b.

———, 'The Raniparaj are Stirring', in *National Front*, 25 December 1938c.

———, *Gandhi as I Know Him* (revised and enlarged edition), Delhi: Zaehner, RC, 1943 .

———, *Atmakatha* (Autobiography), translated from Gujarati, vol. III, (Mehmedabad 1956) and vol. v (Ahmedabad 1971). The English translation of the manuscript is deposited in the Nehru Memorial Museum and Library, New Delhi.

Index

Baniyas 30, 31, 42, 91, 98, 163n20
Bardoli, agrarian satyagraha in 75–7,
  99, 104, 125, 138, 150
  economic growth in 90
  satyagraha, and position of Dublas
    111
  victory in 108
Bardoli Enquiry Committee 91, 99,
  104
Barodlise India, motto of 77
Bengal, recognition of zamindars as
  landowners 18
  zamindars of 23
bhandela halis 41
Bhathelas 8, 25, 191
  Anavils and 38
  desais 39
Bhave, Acharya Vinoba 167
  launch of Bhoodan movement by
    166
Bhoodan movement 166–7
Bihar, debt bondage in 56
Bohras 42–3, 61
Bombay, agglomeration of 61
Bombay government, housing
  programmes for landless 182–3
Bombay State Social Welfare
  Department 182
Bombay Tenancy Act 1939 127, 165
Bombay Tenancy and Agricultural
  Land Act 1948 165
bondage 37, 44–5, 70
  causes of 46, 62
  as colonial phenomenon 62, 63
  forms of 190
  of *halis* 52
  and patronage 35–43
  relationship 68
bonded labour, debt and 164
  continuation of 178
  end of 193
  in Gujarat 168
  status of 41

struggle for abolition of 179
system of 35–71, 187
Vallabhbhai Patel on 142
Bose, Subash 128, 146
  at Kisan Sabha conference 146
  as President of Indian National
    Congress 164
Brahmanism 4
British administration, ban on distilling
  liquor by tribals 31
  dismantling the system of tax faming
    by 22
  on labour bondage 160–1
  on lawlessness in Gujarat 148
  and revenue collection in south
    Gujarat 12
  on runaway *halis* 56–7
British control, over south Gujarat 10
Broomfield, R.S. 100, 113, 116
Burjorji 152

capitalism, concept of 190
  transition to 191
capitalist agriculture, boom in 190
  and mode of production 62
  and change in relationship between
    master and servant 113–15
caste(s), awareness 101
  cultivation, in villages 25
  interaction between 25
casual labour 66
census of 1881 6
Chaplin, William 45
Cherumars, as slaves in Malabar Coast
  45
chhuta halis 41
Chikhlis 28
Chodra tribals 4, 85, 112
Chodris, landowning by 183
civil disobedience campaigns/
  movements, in Bardoli 77, 81–90
collective action 179–87
colonial era, dawn of 12–20

among tribals in south Gujarat 84–6

Dhaniamo 50, 53, 67, 141
Dhodhia tribals 4, 28, 29–30, 85, 112
  landowning by 183
  protests by 179
  struggle by 145–6
domination, doctrine of 53
dominant castes, assertiveness by 41
Dublas, agitation by 147–8
  as agricultural labourers 1, 171
  alcohol addiction of 105, 106, 171
  animistic practice by 52–3
  as bonded servants 1, 3, 36, 41, 125, 105–6
  clans among 54
  condition of 89–90
  debt and bondage of 91–2
  as 'depressed class' 59
  deprivation of 65
  domestic work by girls 64–5
  exploitation and oppression of 104, 136
  as halis 40, 42, 49, 50
  as Halpatis 159–60, 172
  kinship among 54
  mobilization of 133, 158
  poverty among 5, 70
  as semi-Hindus 6
  relations with landowners 101, 137
  role of 87–8
  servitude of 9, 35
  as shifting cultivators 1
  as slaves 43
  and status in Hinduism 52
economic development 60
  pre-colonial 3
education programme, for Halpatis 183–4
Elphinstone, Governor 15, 19
European employers, contract with labourers 57
exploitation, of halis/ labourers 36

falias 31
famine, of 1899-1900 49
food security, bondage and 48
free labour/ labourers 44, 46, 58
  British authorities' support for 68
Frontier character, closure of 28–33

Gaekwad, of Baroda 10, 23
Gamit, Panabhai 97
Gamit tribals 4, 112
  landowning by 183
Gandhi, Kasturba 84
Gandhi, Mahatma 50, 74, 76, 77, 83, 86, 87, 88, 89, 90, 96, 116, 118
  and agrarian elite of Bardoli 105
  constructive programme of 118
  on discrimination 102
  and non-violence 150
  popularity of, in tribal villages 112
  return to India 80
  social upliftment mission of 107, 112
  speech at Swaraj ashram 89
  strategy of 144–5
  visit to Bardoli 81
Gandhian activists/ reformers 82–4, 170
  and adivasis 181
  commissioning public works to halis 168
  and halipaths' interests 169
  and Kisan Sabha agitators 134–5
  and the landless 185
  landowners' resistance against 141, 143
  on schooling for children of landless 184
Gandhian institutions, and Bhoodan movement in Gujarat 167
Gandhian movement, of tribal uplift 133
Gandhian solution 133–8
Gangetic Doab 2